THE PROCEEDINGS OF THE TWENTIETH WORLD CONGRESS OF PHILOSOPHY

A Twelve Volume Series

Philosophy Documentation Center

TITLES IN THE SERIES

THE PROCEEDINGS OF THE TWENTIETH WORLD CONGRESS OF PHILOSOPHY

VOLUME 11
Social & Political Philosophy

EDITOR
David M. Rasmussen, Boston College

Philosophy Documentation Center
2001

THE PROCEEDINGS OF THE TWENTIETH WORLD CONGRESS OF PHILOSOPHY

Publisher

Philosophy Documentation Center
Bowling Green State University
Bowling Green, OH 43403-0189 USA

Phone: 800-444-2419

ISBN   1-889680-15-X
Library of Congress Catalog Card Number: 99-066878
© 2001 Philosophy Documentation Center

CONTENTS

SERIES INTRODUCTION

Jaakko Hintikka
Robert Cummings Neville
Ernest Sosa
Alan M. Olson
Stephen Dawson

One enduring legacy of the twentieth century will be the slow, certain transformation of the world from insular civilizations to interactive societies enmeshed in global systems of electronic communication, economics, and politics. Financial news from Thailand or Brazil is often more important globally than political events in the old centers of power. Some bemoan the uncertainty and flux of all this. However, the mutual definition of the world's societies presents an extraordinary opportunity to humanize a situation that all too quickly could degenerate into a Weberian 'iron cage' of truly global proportions. What contribution can the world's great philosophical traditions make toward humanity's common task of civilizing the rise of globalization? Here the ancient concept of *paideia* walks upon the stage of the Twenty First Century.

The Twentieth World Congress of Philosophy (held August, 1998 in Boston, USA) took as its theme *Paideia: Philosophy Educating Humanity*. With over thirty-five hundred participants, it was surely the largest gathering of serious philosophers in history. (Gigantism is one of the marks of global interaction!) Yet, the Twentieth World Congress was not simply large, but *inclusive*. Philosophers representing all of the world's cultures assembled that hot August week in Boston. Not only were the most important representatives of the various major and minor Western schools of philosophy present, but distinguished leaders of thought from south and east Asian cultures were heard, as were the philosophers of the Islamic world, of the African, and of traditional cultures such as the Native American and the Oceanic.

However, one would be incorrect to confuse the inclusiveness of the Congress with sheer diversity. In America, 'inclusiveness' and 'diversity' are politically-correct catchwords that enjoy a certain cachet. In fact, diversity often issues forth as a series of social problems that are simply exasperated by a heavy-handed emphasis on inclusion. No, philosophers from around the world did not assemble for the sake of diversity; rather, these philosophers met in order to engage in the serious business of conversation and dialogue. Sometimes these conversations had the character of consciousness-raising. Western thinkers were sometimes surprised to discover that there are other kinds of philosophy. Thinkers from the so-called second and third worlds were sometimes surprised to discover that others were interested in the philosophy of their heritage. Beyond consciousness-raising, however, the Congress witnessed numerous instances of genuine engagement and learning across cultures.

Although these inter-cultural philosophic engagements were sometimes tentative, never again will it be possible to represent any one philosophical tradition as philosophy *tout court*. Never again will it be possible to say that some "other" culture's philosophy is not really philosophy in the proper sense. Never again will it be possible to assert the truth of one's own position without promising to defend it in a philosophical public that includes the heirs of all the world's philosophic cultures.

The situation in philosophy now mirrors the emerging geopolitical reality at the turn of the Twenty First century: each philosophic culture defines itself in part by how it stands with regard to the other cultures, and the arguments made in one require attention in the others. Put differently, philosophy now is an indelibly inter-cultural activity. To be sure, the forms and genres in which we write philosophy do not yet reflect much of the changed situation. They mainly follow the stylistic trajectories of the separate philosophic cultures, sometimes with appended attention to cultural interactions. But there is now an underlying awareness—brought into sharp focus during the Congress—of the multiple dimensions of rationality that constitute public argument in a public increasingly comprised of many cultural traditions.

John Silber, Chancellor of Boston University, opened the Congress with a fiery defense of philosophy as rational inquiry, arguing that various forms of irrationalism be eschewed. Of course, the forms of rationality put forward were far more various and daring than anyone could have enumerated at the beginning of the Congress. The nature of reason and philosophic inquiry was itself one of the chief concerns of the Congress. In fact, the Congress theme of *paideia*, upon reflection, is even better than "rationality" as an organizing principle: not only did the participants *learn* from one another about reason, but they *learned* in part how inter-cultural reasoning will have to take place in order to civilize a public of many intellectual heritages.

At one extraordinary session honoring distinguished senior philosophers who were asked to speak about what we have learned in philosophy in the Twentieth Century, three analytic philosophers said they had come to appreciate the worldwide reach of philosophy; another said nothing about the topic, presumably because that is not a philosophic question for his kind of analysis; another philosopher reminded the others that they all assumed that analytic philosophy is all there is and noted the importance of Heidegger for global philosophy; and finally a Muslim philosopher pointed out that none of the speakers recognized the philosophic traditions of all the other world cultures and yet it is *precisely* those other philosophic traditions that are growing and burgeoning in educational institutions around the world. The last speaker was cheered. While one might be tempted to regard that session as a sad instance of Western cultural blindness, a much more productive perspective would be to see it as a transition to a much more encompassing and (dare we say it) inclusive vision of philosophy. Western thinkers have grown accustomed to thinking that the philosophy of the Twentieth Century belonged exclusively to them. Now they realize that their comfortable expectations no longer hold.

The papers published in these volumes are a showcase of the vigor and health of philosophy around the world at the end of the Twentieth Century. We have organized the essays into twelve volumes which, taken together, bring some measure of coherence and focus to the work of the Congress as a whole. These volumes—and the more than 1,000 contributed papers which are posted at the World Congress website (www.bu.edu/wcp)—amply display the vigorous chaos of the encounter between hitherto unengaged philosophic approaches. Simply put, philosophic life is spreading beyond the cultivated gardens of the West.

The Executive Board of the American Organizing Committee and the Editorial Board of *The Paideia Project: Proceedings of the Twentieth World Congress of Philosophy* is pleased to present what we believe is the definitive picture of our discipline at the end of the Twentieth Century. For any large-scale project of this kind, there are numerous debts of gratitude owed by the end. First and foremost, we thank Chancellor John Silber and the administration of Boston University for providing the necessary support for organizing the Twentieth World Congress as well as publishing the Proceedings. Special thanks go to Drs. Kevin L. Stoehr and Mark D. Gedney, who supervised the day-to-day organization of the Congress. We thank our managing editor, Stephen Dawson, and his editorial staff: Helena Gourko, Brian MacDonald, Georgia Maheras, Mark Mann, Angela Turek, and Amos Yong. Our thanks as well go to the editors for each of the twelve volumes. We feel confident that the high standards of excellence established by Mark and Kevin in the organization of the Congress will be upheld in the publication of the Proceedings. Appreciation is also due to George Leaman and Lori Fells of the Philosophy Documentation Center. Both George and Lori bring a rich background in academic publishing to our project. Special thanks go to Lori for designing the layout for the Proceedings. But most of all, we salute our colleagues, the contributing scholars, who have made it possible to bring the publication of the Proceedings of the Twentieth World Congress of Philosophy to fruition.

VOLUME INTRODUCTION

David M. Rasmussen

GLOBAL JUSTICE

In a response to John Rawls's 1993 article entitled, "The Law of Peoples," Karl-Otto Apel argues that the concept of "overlapping consensus" is not sufficient for a basis or foundation for global justice. Apel makes the claim that when Rawls transfers the problem of justification from a general moral conception of justice to overlapping consensus the "weight of justification" is transferred to a "freestanding" conception of justice. To the extent that it does this, Rawls's theory fails to show why a freestanding conception of justice ought to be acceptable. In order to do so, Apel believes that, since citizens' reason must be addressed, the weight of justification for a freestanding view must be based on a philosophical consensus theory. This would not mean that the need of a factual consensus would be dispensed with. Rather, it would mean that a freestanding view would be grounded philosophically "by a conception of an *ideal consensus* that serves as a *regulative principle* for searching and also for *questioning* an overlapping consensus."

One consequence of following this reconstruction would be that it would strengthen the distinction between the right and the good because the priority of right would be justified independent from all forms of the good hence accommodating and strengthening the conception of "freestanding" based on the autonomous conception of justice. When one turns to "The Law of Peoples" this would mean that the principle of "legitimacy," which is at the basis of a freestanding conception of justice as Otto sees it, would be fundamental to any "extension" from liberal to non-liberal peoples. If one would base the notion of a "freestanding" on the basis of ideal consensus one would avoid what from Otto's point of view is the flaw in Rawls's theory of extention, i.e., the "legitimation of hierarchical societies without the attribution of consent."

In "Intercultural Diologue and Human Rights: A Latin American Reading of Rawls's 'Law of Peoples'" Antonio Perez-Estevez argues that even though Rawls's "The Law of Peoples" attempts to overcome ethnocentricism, it fails from a Latinamerican point of view. Perez-Estavez lists several reasons for this. It is assumed by Rawls that liberal-democratic nations present the best model for the development of a society of nations which defend human rights. As a consequence, liberal democratic societies are given priority over hierarchically organized societies. They determine when hierarchically organized societies will be acceptable. Human rights, when reduced to a minimum under the liberal paradigm, are only those appropriate to liberal societies. Concretely, this is to be seen by the way Rawls applies his original position to other hierarchical societies as a model for achieving human rights. As a consequence of this, there is no room for real dialogue in the Rawlsian position. Perez-Estevez argues that the condition for the possibility of opening such a dialogue should be the realization of the limitedness of each culture, the impartiality of each culture's claim to truth, and the willingness to profit from the expressions of the other. Only when this happens will we discover human rights acceptable to all.

William L. McBride approaches the issue of global justice from a somewhat different perspective. In "Consumers and Cultural Hegemony within a Cosmopolitan Order—Why Not?" he separates cosmopolitanism from consumerism, arguing that the advance of the former need not bring with it the latter. McBride argues that consumerist culture generally does not allow for the realization of diverse conceptions of the good. Rather, globalization under the aegis of a consumerist culture enforces standardization rather than diversity. For McBride, this leads to the further claim that diversity does not flourish under a "liberal philosophical consensus." Instead, given the individualist ontology of philosophers like Rawls, the notion of the public good is more or less off the agenda. As a consequence, the power of critique which might be available for the critique of the consumerist hegemony implicit in globalization is diminished. In the end, McBride argues for a kind of globalization where particular civil societies are strengthened, and the reductionism of human values characteristic of consumerist culture is avoided.

The question for Jonathan L. Gorman in "Justice and Toleration: A Western Perspective on Philosophy and Social Justice" is whether "there are independent standards of justice by which we measure our activities," or whether "justice itself is to be understood in realistic terms varying with locality or historical period." This is a concrete problem brought into focus by the enduring conflict in Northern Ireland. Gorman cites Bryce Gallie who claims that justice is an "essentially contested concept." Following from this reference to the history of Northern Ireland, Gorman gives us a philosophical account of such a claim. Such an account would first deny a first person singular position that identifies reality and truth with a certain form of consistency. When one moves to a "we" perspective, it is acknowledged that the views of others are not necessarily consistent with one's own. When one turns to the question of justice in Northern Ireland, Gorman argues, it will be necessary to create institutions that will "tolerate inconsistent views of the world." Hence, there is a close relationship between justice and toleration in the sense that the political world created in Northern Ireland will be one in which "people believe inconsistent things about their identity, their citizenship, and the grounds and object of their allegiance."

RULE OF LAW

In "Rhetoric and the Rule of Law" Neil MacCormick argues that there is a certain incomenserability between the claim that the propositions of law are arguable, and the claim that the rule of law assumes certainty. MacCormick's strategy is to weave a synthesis between these two seemingly contradictory propositions. MacCormick first attempts to persuade us regarding the seeming validity of both propositions. But the problem remains, "how is it possible to believe in both?" In the end, MacCormick will show us that it is not only possible, but also necessary to believe in both simply because the Rule of Law in a free society is the guarantee of the indeterminacy of law. In a free society the Rule of Law means that whenever, in cases pertaining to law, there is an operative fact there must be a normative consequence. This is to claim that the guarantee of a free society is that action be governed by rules. But those very rules are subject to contestation, or alternative interpretation. Hence, MacCormick's point is that the very notion of "Rule of Law" has within it the phenomenon of argumentation.

Olúfẹ́mi Táíwò, in his essay "On the Limits of Law at Century's End," argues that society governed by the Rule of Law is the norm, however, there are instances where the law has "definite limits." The emergence of the phenomena of Truth Commissions and Truth and Reconciliation Commissions supports this thesis. With specific reference to the Truth and Reconciliation Commission (TRC) in South Africa, Táíwò offers four arguments for showing that "law may not serve . . . the purpose of healing and reconciliation." First, there is the problem of constitutional law. Under the "apartheid constitution" defendants could have claimed that they were merely following the law. Second, the "motivating force of the law" is "punishment and retribution." The function of the TRC was and is "national unity and reconciliation." Third, Táíwò argues that "legal processes" are not necessarily the best means of "truth-finding." Finally, law has no memory, in the sense that it cannot make the victims of apartheid speak. The TRC invented a process whereby the victims could be represented through the voice of another as well as, when possible, speaking for themselves. Although, the TRC may have its critics, Táíwò argues that the choice of this model of truth discovery, rather than choosing the model of legal retribution, reflects what kind of society South Africa will become.

Law is approached in a somewhat different way in Rex Martin's "Rawls on Constitutional Consensus and the Problem of Stability." When Rawls made the transition from *Theory of Justice* to *Political Liberalism* he changed the basic account of political stability. As Martin points out, one of the most significant features of the new theory is the claim that the public political culture of contemporary democratic theory provides the "deep background for the entire theory." Justification of the theory must occur in reference to that culture. In relationship to "freestanding" justification, Martin's fundamental question regards what kind of support Rawls can generate for the two principles of justice. In Martin's view, Rawls could generate support for the two principles by generating a second stage for constitutional consensus, the essentially new idea to appear with the publication of *Political Liberalism* (*PL*). Constitutional consensus begins to emerge from a *modus vivendi* when one begins to get agreement on certain "rights" and "practices" within a liberal culture. Martin argues that there would be a second stage of constitutional consensus, historically understood, in which the two principles of justice could be justified. Finally, Martin's historical reading of Rawls, constructs a link between constitutional consensus and public reason. "In sum, two of Rawls's leading *new* ideas in *PL* (constitutional essentials and public reason) are not only linked to each other but, more importantly, are also linked to the idea of constitutional consensus as their grounding principle. And this consensus is itself a historically developing thing."

DEMOCRACY AND PUBLIC LIFE

Gabriel Vargas Lozano, in "Liberal Democracy and Radical Democracy: The Two Faces of Janus," argues that we are in the paradoxical situation of seeing in certain parts of the world where there is "no strong democratic tradition" the emergence of interest in democracy while in other parts of the world where democracy has existed certain disillusion has developed. It is Lozano's position that a "liberal democracy" committed to a "market economy" is in "crisis." To meet this crisis, Lozano argues for the realization of a radical democracy. Radical democracy would go beyond the defense of political rights to the defense of social rights; it would include an economy of distributive justice; it would represent the various ethnic groups within the Mexican and Latin American societies; and it would combine social justice with political justice.

Peter A. French, in "The Meaning of Democracy: A Western Perspective," argues that contemporary discussions of democracy tend to blur the distinction between the communitarian and the liberal approaches to democracy. In actuality, French holds that "there is very little in common between the Athenian/communitarian democratic ideal and the conception of the liberal democrat that has dominated the political scene in the West for the past three or four centuries." The communitarian story, traced back to Athens, features a "shared conception of the good," public participation is central and moral development of the citizen is associated with the practice of democracy. French associates the liberal democratic paradigm with individualism, personal self-interest, and contractualism. French argues that liberal democracy is based on rational choice, while communitarianism is based on "public will." Having associated the communitarian tradition with a pre-modern history, one expects that the current dilemmas of democracy will be contained within the parameters of liberal democracy.

In "Reconciling Public Reason and Religious Values," James P. Sterba argues against those who would claim that Rawls's idea of public reason is too restrictive with regard to religious considerations. This is, of course, a problematic issue inasmuch as Rawls originally ruled out a role for religious considerations in public debate given his distinction between the comprehensive and the political. As Sterba points out, Rawls has changed his position on this issue, particularly with reference to the abolition movement of the 1830s and the civil rights movement of the 1960s. Wolterstorff has objected to this earlier claim by Rawls, raising the following question: "Is it equitable to ask of everyone that, in deciding and discussing political issues, they refrain from using their comprehensive perspectives?" In order to make this claim Wolterstorff appeals to the ideal of fairness. Sterba argues "by putting his justification for rule by a religious majority in terms of fairness, Wolterstorff must think that he is providing a moral justification that everyone in liberal democratic society regard as sufficient to justify that rule." Inadvertently, argues Sterba, Wolterstorff satisfies Rawls's ideal of public reason. Hence, Sterba concludes, "Once Rawls's ideal of public reason is correctly interpreted, critics of that ideal, like Walterstorff, can be seen to be endorsing that very ideal, while possibly disagreeing with Rawls concerning its political consequences."

In "Philosophy in American Public Life: De Facto and De Jure," Jorge J. E. Gracia poses two questions: "Does philosophy have a place in contemporary American public life?" and "Should philosophy have a place in American public life?" His answer to both questions is negative.

On Community and Social Reality

In "Communitarianism and Western Thought," Sirkku Kristiina Hellsten distinguishes between descriptive and prescriptive communitarianism. The former, associated with MacIntyre, Sandel, Taylor, and Walzer, "criticizes modern liberalism for its universalism and atomism." The latter, associated with Amitai Etzioni and his group, attempts first to "redefine theoretically the moral meaning of a democratic regime and, second, to provide some guidelines on how to realize them in practice." Hellsten associates prescriptive communitarianism with the attempt to work out a certain "normative agenda" for modern society. In a peculiar way, Hellsten finds that prescriptive communitarianism in the West supports liberal values. "The communitarian stress on communal duties, family values, and community care is in general an attempt to promote the originally modern liberal values of tolerance, individual autonomy, and individual rights." She concludes the essay by suggesting that, "when we talk about the normative agenda of communitarianism in the West, we should always start by taking the descriptive criticism of modern liberalism seriously."

In "Sociality, Unity, and Objectivity" Margaret Gilbert addresses the questions, "insofar as social groups are plural subjects, what kind of unity do they have? In what sense, if any, is that unity objective?" In order to answer those questions, Gilbert explores the nature of "joint commitments." Joint commitment includes "*joint* acceptance of a goal." "People *jointly accept a particular goal* . . . when they are jointly committed to accept that goal as a body." She argues—against John Searle—that joint commitment is not simply a matter of being "all in the mind." Rather, "plural subjectivity involves an important kind of unity that is *more than subjectively real.*" Insofar as social groups are plural subjects, they may be reasonably deemed "objective units."

Raimo Tuomela, in his essay "Collective Acceptance and Social Reality," presents a specific collective acceptance account of sociality and the social world. In addition to performative and reflexive accounts of social phenomena, he adds another feature, namely, "collective availability" or '*forgroupness*' of collective social items. Tuomela develops the collective acceptance thesis which assumes we can distinguish between "sentences whose obtaining of 'truth' is essentially up to the members of the group . . . and sentences whose truth is at least in part up to nature . . . to the way the world is, and this is in part dependent on the casual processes occurring in the world 'outside them'." In answer to the question "Is the social world real?" one must answer, according to Toumela, that at least that "part of the social world is dependent on group acceptance," which means "part of the social world must be conceptualized as inhabitants conceptualize it."

Wolfgang Balzer, in "Freedom and Equality in the Comparison of Political Systems," presents a theoretical model for the analysis of freedom and equality which will enable the comparison of political systems. Whereas more traditional analyses juxtapose freedom and equality, this model sees them as complimentary.

ETHICS AND POLITICS

In "Love, Honor, and Resentment," Daniel O. Dahlstrom considers that the "possibility of resentment springing from the performance or non-performance of an action serves as a means for further determining or specifying the moral correctness of an action." Using Thomas Nagel's conformist or consensus-driven ethics as a point of departure, Dalstrom shows that a conformist ethics, when it attempts to "justify an actions that amounts to helping a neighbor in need when it appears to be in fact against the agent's best interests," considers not only the "impersonal" point of view, but also whether "the neighbor would have reason to resent the agent if the latter did not lend a hand." Hence, the move is made from impartiality and universality to resentment. Dahlstrom goes on to show how an ethics of honor—in some way the consequence of resentment—contributes to ethical thinking.

In "A Western Perspective on the Problem of Violence," Robert L. Holmes presents us with a "constellation" of perspectives that currently prevail in the modern world. In his view, violence is justified by "an instinctive desire for security." The quest for security "has led to the organized and institutionalized violence of warfare." Violence can be further justified through the distinction between good and bad violence. Whether one supports a "just war theory," or simply the function of the police in ordinary society, good violence is said to protect bad violence. A further justification for violence has been its biological function. Hannah Arendt has called this "organic thinking." Holmes concludes, "it is clear that most of those who deplore violence do not oppose all violence." Secondly, the "manipulation of fear and force backed by violence in the end seems to most people to be justified." Finally the author believes that those who work for peace and justice must face the "philosophy of violence that has deep roots in widely accepted ways of thinking."

In "Politics and Anti-Politics," Newton Garver sets forth a typology of politics. The first type owes its origins to Carl Schmitt, whose distinction between friends and enemies and the exercise of power has associated politics with partisanship. In this view, Clausewitz's statement that "war is a confirmation of politics by another means" illustrates the essentially ideological nature of politics. Garver calls this zero-sum politics to which he contrasts integrative politics which features "respect and civility towards one's adversaries and recognition of the legitimacy of the interests of all parties." Here, dialogue is the essence of politics. A third alternative is anti-politics. "The central thought behind anti-politics is that government needs to be limited." Anti-politics or alternative politics through actions and organizations provide alternative resources. Garver allies this notion with Pettit's reflections on freedom as anti-power. The author concludes with a suggestion that integrative politics and anti-politics offer refreshing alternatives to the zero-sum political game.

In "Aestheticism or Aesthetic Approach in Arendt and Heidegger on Politics," Michael Halberstram evaluates Hannah Arendt's political philosophy in relationship to the Romantic tradition of German philosophy that promotes the "ideal of the aesthetic state." This issue comes down to whether or nor Arendt is able to distance herself sufficiently from Martin Heidegger's aestheticization of politics present in his "Origin of the Work of Art" and other works. In order to do this Halberstam makes a distinction between an aesthetic approach and aestheticism. Halberstam concludes: "Where Heidegger relies on the modern narrowing of the aesthetic to the realm of art and then seeks to impose its criteria on the realm of politics, Arendt harkens back to a broader conception of the aesthetic as the realm of taste." In Halberstam's view, Arendt, by linking aesthetics with judgment, is able to associate aesthetics and politics on a level that is truly intersubjective, an area to which Heidegger remains closed.

PAIDEA: EDUCATION FOR HUMANITY

In "Educating for Practical Reasoning" Thomas Magnell makes the case for types of practical reasoning following from Aristotle's categorization of reasoning into the theoretical, the productive, and the practical. Practical reasoning can be distinguished by context, systematically closed, and systematically open reasoning. The former is associated with a specific practice, while the latter is associated with moral decision-making. The latter, it is argued, must proceed by precept. This is given, of course, through education. Hence, education in the arts and the sciences is the vehicle by which practical reasoning is developed.

In "Paideia as the Subjective Condition for a Sagacious Implementation of Human Rights," Ioanna Kuçuradi begins by asking "What kind of education could be called paideia?" The answer focuses first on "capacity." The student must have the capacity to know where to look and to develop ethical potentialities in order to make "right evaluations." In order to do this it is necessary to involve "the possibility of abolishing social injustices and of implementing human rights in general." Human rights are composed of "basic rights, i.e., rights possessed by human beings because they are human, and rights to develop human potentialities or limited rights. Social injustice appears as a question related to the connection between those two kinds of rights." The "principle of social justice" can be constructed as a "demand" that the state "must afford uninterruptedly the equal protection of the indirectly protected rights for all citizens." Kuçuradi concludes that "the implementation of human rights depends on our capacity to make right evaluations." This requires *paideia*.

In "Paideia et Physis dan la Conception Grecque Antique," Pierre Aubenque examines the relationship of education and nature as it occurs first in Plato and later in Aristotle. For Plato, education has to do with the dual nature of the human being and the ability to form nature by education. Hence, the Allegory of the Cave becomes an example of the attempt to educate. In Aristotle, it is the discovery of the teleology of nature that provides the basis for the insight into education. The author concludes that education is not simply the realization of the abstract idea of humanity, but it is humanity itself in the plurality of its manifestations. Hence, education is a way of legitimating cultural difference.

Is a Political Conception of "Overlapping Consensus" an Adequate Basis for Global Justice?

Karl-Otto Apel

This paper considers how the problem of justice is to be globalized in the political theory of John Rawls. I discuss first the conception of "overlapping consensus" as an innovation in Rawls's *Political Liberalism* and point out the recurrence of the problem of a philosophical foundation in his pragmatico-political interpretation. I suggest an intensification of Rawls's notion of the "priority of the right to the good" as a philosophical correction to his political self-interpretation, and then finally carry through on a theory of globalization of the problem of justice as extended from his "The Law of Peoples."

I. The Conception of "Overlapping Consensus" as an Innovation in the Context of Rawls's *Political Liberalism*

The essential point is this: as a practical matter no general moral conception can provide the basis for a public conception of justice in a modern democratic society: The social and historical conditions of such a society . . . profoundly affect the requirements of a workable conception of political justice: such a conception must allow for a diversity of doctrines and a plurality of conflicting and indeed incommensurable conceptions of the good affirmed by the members of existing democratic societies.[1]

This passage is supplemented by the following one, which introduces the conception of an "overlapping consensus" which constitutes the characteristic innovation of Rawls's book *Political Liberalism*:

> Justice as Fairness is a *political conception* partly because it starts out from a particular political tradition. We hope that it is supported at least by a, as I would like to call it, 'overlapping consensus', that is a consensus that includes all the controversial philosophical and religious doctrines which presumably will persist and find adherents in a more or less just constitutional democratic society.[2]

From these passages at least this much becomes immediately clear. The new contention of Rawls's—after and in contradistinction to the *Theory of Justice* of 1971—namely, the claim that his conception of justice is not *metaphysical*, in fact not even a "general moral conception," is meant as a response to the *challenge of the fact of pluralism* of controversial philosophical (i.e., metaphysical) or religious views or doctrines that make up the background for a possible acceptance of a conception of justice in a modern democratic society.

Later, in his discussion with J. Habermas of 1995,[3] Rawls makes it clear that he considers even Habermas's *discourse-theoretical* and *proceduralistic* conception of justice a "comprehensive doctrine," which for this reason could not hope for an "overlapping consensus" in a pluralistic society. He now points out his own conception very rigidly in the following words:

> The central idea is that political liberalism moves within the category of the political and leaves philosophy as it is. It leaves untouched all kinds of doctrines, religious, metaphysical and moral, with their long traditions of development and interpretations. Political philosophy proceeds apart from all such doctrines, and presents itself in its own terms as freestanding. Hence; it cannot argue its case by invoking any comprehensive doctrines, or by criticizing or rejecting them . . . .[4]

A bit later, Rawls offers a reformulation and elucidation of his conception of the relationship between the "freestanding" political theory of justice and the "comprehensive doctrines." This elucidation is especially interesting because it seems to suggest a sophisticated answer to the question as to how the "freestanding" political conception of justice may be grounded independently of the presupposition of a comprehensive philosophical doctrine. Rawls's answer reads as such:

> It [sc. the political conception of justice] can be formulated independently of any particular comprehensive doctrine, religious, philosophical, or moral. While we suppose that it may be derived from, or supported by, or otherwise related to one or more comprehensive doctrines (indeed we hope it can be thus related to many such doctrines), it is not presented as depending upon, or as presupposing, any such view.[5]

I understand that this answer corresponds to the Rawlsian method of "contructivism," which in his later writings was interpreted as a method of "avoidance" in respect of *foundational* questions of philosophy. It wants to avoid or bypass *philosophical foundations*, which according to Rawls must belong to "comprehensive doctrines," by *hypothetical constructions* that try to provide a common platform for many or even for all citizens of a pluralistic society "notwithstanding the background of their different, or even incommensurable, world views." Thus the *political* conception of justice, on Rawls's account, could be accepted by all citizens not on the *basis* of their different comprehensive views but nevertheless in more or less accordance with them, and this means: on the basis of an "overlapping consensus."

Now, in the face of all these features of the reformulation of Rawls's theory of justice in *Political Liberalism*, it is very self-suggestive to conceive of the conception of the "overlapping consensus" as being something like a device for a *pragmatico-political compromise*. That is to say, it is a methodical suggestion that dispenses with a *moral-philosophical foundation of justice* in favor of delivering or surrendering itself to the contingent circumstances of a constellation of comprehensive views in a particular situation of a pluralistic society. I suggest that there are many strong reasons for such an interpretation of Rawls's new conception.

II. THE INSUFFICIENCY OF THE PRAGMATICO-POLITICAL INTERPRETATION OF RAWLS'S INNOVATION AND THE RECURRENCE OF THE PROBLEM OF A PHILOSOPHICAL FOUNDATION

For example, the fact that he now—along with the *communitarians*—shares the opinion that all possible *foundations* of morality necessarily may be traced back to *comprehensive* and *culture-dependent metaphysical or religious doctrines*; and, furthermore, the undeniable fact that, in our day, we must cope somehow with the problem of ensuring *common justice*, and hence just institutions and laws, in and for a *pluralistic*, or even a *multicultural* society. Thus far, a purely *pragmatico-political* solution of the problem would not even be so contemptible as it has been considered by some critics. For, reaching a purely political solution of the problem constitutes, after all, a task that is posed by an *ethics of responsibility*. Finally, I would like to mention that *any consensus-theory* (of a possible redemption of normative validity-claims) must deliver itself, to a certain extent, to the contingent circumstances of a historical situation, if it only aims at reaching a *factual* consensus (agreement) in space and time without being orientated, at the same time, toward the possibility of questioning any factual consensus in light of the "regulative principle" (Kant) of an *ideal* (and thus far *ultimate*) *consensus*. (I shall come back to this point later.)

My last remark shows that, from a *philosophical* point of view, we could and should be dissatisfied with the *purely pragmatico-political* interpretation of Rawls's conception of the "overlapping consensus" (or with a similar interpretation of his "freestanding" conception of *political justice* as a whole). As a matter of fact, Rawls himself does not confirm our attempted *pragmatico-political* interpretation. He rather refuses it as "political in the wrong way,"[6] because it does not take into account the demand that the "overlapping consensus" must be a "reasonable" one, reached among "reasonable" comprehensive doctrines on the basis of the *right reasons*. In his reply to Habermas, Rawls in fact even seems to answer any objection against a merely factual consensus by a distinction between "two different ideas of consensus." He says:

> One idea of consensus comes from *everyday politics* where the task of the politician is to find agreement . . . . This idea of consensus is the idea of an overlap that is already present or latent and could be articulated by the politician's skill in bringing together existing interests the politician knows intimately.[7]

This idea of consensus obviously corresponds to the *purely pragmatico-political interpretation* I suggested. But Rawls continues:

> The very different idea of consensus in political liberalism—the idea I call a *reasonable overlapping consensus*—is that the political conception of justice is worked out first as a free-standing view that can be justified *pro tanto* without looking to, or trying to fit, or even knowing what are, the existing comprehensive doctrines (PL 39f.). It tries to put no obstacles in the path of all reasonable doctrines endorsing a political conception by eliminating from this conception any idea which goes beyond the *political* and which not all *reasonable* doctrines could reasonably be expected to endorse. (To do that violates the *idea of mutuality*.) When the political conception meets these conditions and is also complete, we hope, the reasonable comprehensive doctrines affirmed by reasonable citizens in society can support it, and that in fact it will have the capacity to shape those doctrines toward itself. (PL IV: 6–7)[8]

This clarification is very informative; but, in the context of our problem, it obviously shifts again the *weight of justification* from the "overlapping consensus" to the "freestanding" *conception of justice*. This conception, according to Rawls, must be "worked out first" and, "justified pro tanto," which obviously means that it can be traced back to the theory of justice of

1971 or a reformulation of it. The conception of the "overlapping consensus" seems indeed—as Rawls suggests in many places[9]—to be only a *second stage* of the whole theory of "justice as fairness," a stage that presupposes already the elaboration of the "freestanding" conception of justice on a *first stage* of the whole theory but becomes itself necessary as an answer to the question as to how the "stability" of the well ordered democratic society can be ensured.

Yet I think that this interpretation is not completely satisfactory, neither hermeneutically nor as an answer to the problem we have to cope with. For it does not explain why the "freestanding" conception of justice *ought to be acceptable* from the perspective of all reasonable "comprehensive views" as being somehow related to them, to the effect that in case it cannot be accepted by the citizens on the basis of their reasonable comprehensive views, this would be a good reason for *changing* the "freestanding" conception of justice.[10]

Rawls himself declares that:

> the kind of stability required of justice as fairness is based; then, on its being a liberal political view, one that aims at being acceptable to citizens as reasonable and rational; as well as free and equal, and so addressed to their public reason . . . . [J]ustice as fairness is not reasonable in the first place unless in a suitable way it can win its support by addressing each citizen's reason, as explained within its own framework.[11]

Thus everything seems to come down to the need for an adequate *philosophical consensus-theory*, one that is primarily based not on *pragmatico-political* reasons but on a *principled demand of public reason* to be realized under the conditions of mutual acknowledgment of all citizens as being equally free and reasonable. This would not mean that the *political* need for reaching a *factual* consensus again and again, in order to ensure the "stability" of a democratic order and its reproduction, could be dispensed with. But it would mean that the normative conditions of reaching a *reasonable* consensus, and hence also of possibly questioning each *factual* consensus, must be grounded *philosophically*, say by a conception of an *ideal consensus* that can serve as a *regulative principle* for *searching* and also for *questioning* an "overlapping consensus."

By this contention, we have already questioned the *rigid* claim of Rawls's new political conception of justice: the claim that it leaves not only *religion* or *metaphysics*, but moreover, *moral philosophy* "as it is." Indeed Rawls himself, in the paper of 1985, says the following about the "political conception of justice": "It is of course also a *moral* conception, but such one that was worked out for a *particular area of subjects*, namely for political, social, and economical institutions."[12]

One could think that, on this account, the restriction to the "political" in *Political Liberalism* would be rather harmless, seen from an epistemological point of view. For it seems not to eliminate the problems of a moral-philosophical foundation of justice, as it is suggested by Rawls in other places, according to the method of "avoidance." Rather, now it seems to suggest only an *applicative restriction* of the principles of moral philosophy (i.e., of a philosophy of the "right" or *justice*) to the *political* problems of justice. But again this interpretation is expressly denied by Rawls in the same context.[13] Instead, he suggests the possibility that his conception of "justice as fairness," which was originally conceived in view of "the basic structure of a modern democratic constitutional state," might be "extended" to a general political conception for different forms of societies with different historical and social conditions or even to a general moral conception (or at least to an important part of it).[14] I shall come back to this suggestion.

III. THE "PRIORITY OF THE RIGHT TO THE GOOD": A PHILOSOPHICAL CORRECTION OF RAWLS'S POLITICAL SELF-INTERPRETATION

From a philosophical point of view, I would like to take the decisive hint for the solution of our problem from Rawls's original *Theory of Justice*, namely from his distinction between the "right" and the "good" and his claiming a priority of the "right."[15] However, in *Political Liberalism* Rawls seems to weaken this claim, since he now suggests that ultimately the "truth" of a *moral foundation* of justice must be a matter of a "comprehensive doctrine" of the good, whereas the "political" conception of the "right" and its possible acceptance by all citizens can at best be "reasonable," i.e., based on the presupposition that—for reasons of *tolerance* and *reciprocal recognition of autonomy*—a well ordered society is not entitled to impose a philosophical truth-claim on its citizens.[16] This last verdict seems to me to be indeed a necessary implication of "political liberalism," but does this mean that a philosophical justification of just this verdict—i.e., of the neutrality of the democratic constitutional state with regard to philosophical theories—is not possible or not necessary?[17] I think that this assessment of the situation rests on a confusion with regard to different levels of reflection. It is true, of course, that the citizens of a democracy, who want to follow a reasonable procedure of reaching an "overlapping" consensus based on mutual acknowledgment of free and equal persons, have to *bracket* the *truth*-claims of their comprehensive background doctrines, as long as they want to be *"reasonable."* But this does not mean that *the philosophical theory of justice*, which is based on these and similar insights and therefore has to defend the *priority* of the "right" to the "good" of the "comprehensive doctrines," could or should dispense with a *truth-claim* (or, respectively, a truth-analogical *rightness-claim*). To the contrary, it can and should advance and defend its own *truth-claim* (or, respectively, *rightness-claim*) as a *criterium* for distinguishing between *reasonable* and *unreasonable* truth-claims of comprehensive doctrines: religious or metaphysical.

Thus it should understand its own *rightness*-claim not as an *abstractive minimal part* of the contents of all reasonable comprehensive doctrines of the *good*, but as an *autonomous* concern of *justice* and therefore as a *public constraint on all goodness-claims of comprehensive doctrines* held by the citizens as private persons. On this account, the difference between the *right* and the *good* would not be explained by a *more or less of moral comprehensiveness*, but by a distinction between different leading interests or *perspectives* of practical-reason.[18] The *plurality* of the comprehensive doctrines of the *good* then corresponds to the given plurality of ways toward the good life or happiness chosen by individual persons in more or less accordance with sociocultural forms of life and their traditions. The *unitary* liability of *justice* or the *right*, on the other hand, corresponds from the outset, to an *intersubjectively valid universalization principle of moral norms.*

In this sense then the moral and politically applicable principle of justice would indeed be "freestanding," i.e., independent from all doctrines of the good, although it, at the same time, would presuppose the *complementary* dimension of the different views and ways of the good life in a modern, pluralistic society.[19]

If this is an adequate interpretation of the priority of the *right* to the *good*, then our last question that has to be addressed is what can count as Rawls's own *foundation* of the "freestanding" conception of justice as fairness.

IV. RORTY'S HISTORICISTIC AND CULTURE-CENTRIC INTERPRETATION OF RAWLS'S *POLITICAL LIBERALISM* AND RAWLS'S INSINUATION THAT IT MAY BE SHOWN TO BE "UNIVERSALISTIC" THROUGH ITS GLOBALIZED EXTENSION AS A "LAW OF PEOPLES"

At a first reading of *A Theory of Justice* of 1971, one could think that Rawls, by the constructive fiction of the "original position," wanted to base the choice of the principles of justice of a just society on the instrumental rationality of the economical decision theory. But Rawls soon made it clear that he only supposed this rationality as *one* of a person's capacities that has to be taken into account besides his "reasonableness" or "sense of justice."[20] In the name of this latter capacity he "framed" the rational choice of the parties "in the original situation," by restrictive conditions, as the "veil of ignorance" with regard to one's place in the society to be chosen in order to ensure the *equality* and thus the *fairness* of the original choice. But how did Rawls explicate and justify his own presuppositions of "fairness" and of the "sense of justice"?

As we have seen already in the preceding, Rawls denies that a "general moral conception" can provide the basis for a "public conception of justice in a modern democratic society." Instead, he starts out from some central intuitive ideas of political justice that are implied in the tradition of Western democracy. He then tries to unite these ideas into a coherent conception through the method of establishing a "reflective equilibrium" between them. In his discussion with Habermas he points out that "justice as fairness is *substantive* and not *procedural*," in the sense "that it springs from and belongs to the tradition of liberal thought and the larger community of political culture of *democratic societies*." Therefore, Rawls concedes, his conception "fails then to be properly formal and truly universal, and thus to be part of the quasi-transcendental presuppositions (as Habermas sometimes says) established by the theory of communicative action."[21] Such a "general conception," Rawls supposes, would belong to the *metaphysical* and hence *culture-dependent* comprehensive doctrines. However, one could object, is not Rawls's starting out from the tradition of Western democracy a *fortiori* culture-dependent?

It is well known that Richard Rorty has interpreted Rawls's position in *Political Liberalism* along the lines of an extreme form of *historicism* and affirmative *culture-centrism*. In his notorious paper, "The Priority of Democracy to Philosophy," Rorty claims that the cultural tradition of Western democracy is indeed the "contingent" but nevertheless solely possible basis of consent for all discussions about questions of political justice. Therefore, he suggests, "Rawls did not need 'Socratism', i.e., the idea that anybody who is willing to listen to reason—to hear all the arguments—can be brought around to the truth," because "the human self has a center (a divine spark, or a truth-tracking faculty called 'reason') and . . . argumentation will, given time and patience, penetrate to this center . . . we are free to see the self centerless, as a historical contingency all the way through."[22]

Therefore, according to Rorty, Westerners have to think "of enemies of liberal democracy like Nietzsche or Loyola as, to use Rawls's word, 'mad' . . . . They are not crazy [Rorty adds] because they have mistaken the historical nature of human beings. They are crazy because the limits of sanity are set by what *we* can take seriously. This, in turn, is determined by our up-bringing, our historical situation."[23]

Rawls, to be sure, did not accept this interpretation, which, in my opinion, is politically disastrous because it makes it so easy for *fundamentalists* and *nationalists* of all stripes to defend their *culture-centrism* or *ethno-centrism* against the idea of *liberal democracy* and *human rights*. But Rawls suggested the following way out of his dilemma: *The political conception* of justice is

> not political in a false sense (i.e., surrendering itself to the contingencies of a situation) but it is appropriately adapted to the public political culture its own principles shape and support. And although such a conception does not hold for all societies at all times and places, it is therefore not yet historistic or relativistic; rather it is universalistic insofar as it is possible to extend it appropriately toward a reasonable conception of justice for the relations between all nations.[24]

By the last sentences Rawls obviously alludes to his contribution to the *Oxford Amnesty Lectures on Human Rights* of 1993 under the title "The Law of Peoples."[25] Here, in my opinion, an adequate vantage point is reached indeed for a philosophical discussion of the problems of *global justice*. For, in our time, there is not only *the fact of pluralism and multiculturalism with regard to particular societies*, but, above all, there is the same problem as that of *global justice*. If I am right, then this problem belongs to the task of a *second order globalization* through which we have to provide a philosophically reflected response to the challenge of that *globalization* that has taken place, in advance of our reflection, as an irreversible fact of *technology, ecology*, and, recently, *economy*.[26] Now, what about Rawls's step into that dimension, which may be found in "The Law of Peoples?"

V. Rawls's Globalization of His "Theory of Justice" in "The Law of Peoples"

I have to say in advance that, from the point of view of those problems we have discussed, I find the Rawlsian way of globalizing the problem of justice rather disappointing. I would trace the reason for this fact back to his method or strategy of *extending* the scope of his theory of justice to the global problems. For lack of time, I have to simplify my critical commentary.

First, I will summarize those viewpoints and arguments in Rawls's approach that I find promising. Thus, e.g., the following remarks of Rawls's seem to me to express a great progress of insight beyond the usual naiveté of the Western equation of problems of justice with those of a domestic theory of democracy. Rawls justly states: "Every society must have a conception of how it is related to other societies and of how it is to conduct itself toward them . . . . [I]t must formulate certain ideals and principles for guiding its policies toward other peoples."[27]

Therefore Rawls now sees his task in showing, how the topic of his original conception, the case, as he says, "of a hypothetically closed and self-sufficient liberal democratic society [. . .] can be extended in a convincing way as to cover a society's relation with other societies to yield a *reasonable law of peoples* . . ."; Rawls now realizes that otherwise "a liberal conception of political justice would appear to be historicist . . . ."[28] He also recognizes that, together with the global extension of the ideas of justice, he would have to extend these ideas "to future generations," which would raise "the problem of just savings."[29] I myself would be inclined to supplement this remark with regard to the interests of *the poor* in the *Third World*, which also could not be taken into account by the search for an "overlapping consensus" that would be restricted to "the case of a hypothetically closed and self-sufficient liberal democratic society."

But Rawls obviously does not want to subsume this problem under the *normal* or *ideal* case of extending the conception of justice to the "law of peoples." Instead, he mentions these kinds of problems under the head of the "second step" of his "*nonideal theory*," where he would have to deal with the *case of "unfavorable conditions*," e.g., with the problem of "how the poorer and less technologically advanced societies of the world can attain historical and social conditions that allow them to establish just and workable institutions . . . ."[30]

Here for me the question arises: How Rawls can know *how to proceed* in his extension of his theory of justice, in order to project not only an "ideal theory" of the "law of peoples," but also a "nonideal theory," where he also can derive duties and obligations of the "wealthier societies" with regard to the other ones, in order to help them to reach the "conditions that make a well-ordered society possible"?[31]

It has to be noticed, in this context, that here again—as in the case of the domestic application of the principle of "overlapping consensus"—Rawls's problem is not primarily one of reaching a *pragmatico-political* solution dependent on contingent circumstances. Such a solution has even to be reached in the case of "outlaw societies" or of "tyrants" and "dictators," and that would even be a duty imposed on us by an ethics of responsibility, as I have pointed out. But Rawls expressly excludes these problems from his *ideal* extension project. By contrast, he is prepared to provide for the possibility—nay even necessity—of a coexistence between "liberal-democratic" and "non-liberal-democratic," namely "hierarchical societies," and this concession even makes up the point of the "ideal" part of his extension project. But this project as a whole, even including the step from the "ideal" to the "nonideal theory," should obviously be understood as one that exposes itself to the possibility and necessity of a "reasonable overlapping consensus" of, I would say, all the affected: human beings. What then should be the unitary principle or yardstick for this conception of justice?

Rawls's answer to the question concerning the foundation of his *globalized* theory is similar but, in my opinion, more informative than that given to Habermas in the case of the unextended conception of political justice. It reads:

> . . . a constructivist view . . . do[es] not begin from universal first principles having authority in all cases. A constructivist liberal doctrine is universal in its reach once it is extended to give principles for all politically relevant subjects, including a law of peoples for the most comprehensive subject, the political society of peoples. Its authority rests on the principles and conceptions of practical reason, but always on these as suitably adjusted to apply to different subjects as they arise in sequence . . . .[32]

In contradistinction to traditional comprehensive (say, metaphysical) theories of reason,

> constructivism assumes . . . that there are other forms of unity than that defined by completely general first principles forming a consistent scheme. Unity may also be given by an appropriate sequence of cases and by supposing that the parties in an original position . . . are to proceed through the sequence with the understanding that the principles for the subject of each later agreement are to be subordinate to those of subjects of all earlier agreements, or else coordinated with and adjusted to them by certain priority rules.[33]

The main example for the procedure characterized so far is Rawls's justification of the necessary admission of "non-liberal-democratic" but "well ordered hierarchical" societies in the case of an extension of the original conception of political justice to the conception of the "law peoples." For his main argument is that the subordination of the new agreement to the earlier one can be realized by a certain *argument by analogy.* The new theory can only be *liberal*, according to Rawls, by applying the principle of liberalism that underlies the "overlapping consensus" within a democratic society to "the society of political societies." "As before, the parties [in the original position] are representatives, but now they are representatives of peoples whose basic institutions satisfy the principles of justice selected at the first level"; thus it turns out, according to

Rawls "that liberal and hierarchical societies can agree on the same law of peoples."[34]

Now, my question is this: Can the fact that the admission of the "hierarchical societies" would include a considerable reduction of the "human rights"—according to Rawls in particular a cancellation of the right of "free speech"[35] (I would comment that this would imply all the rights of equal participation in the public sphere of politics which Rawls expressly claimed for his conception against Habermas's doubts[36])—be plausibly justified by the *argument by analogy* I mentioned (i.e., the transfer of the liberal attitude from the level of *citizens* to the level of *states*)?

My answer is that in principle, this procedure cannot be justified. For that would imply that the "internal sovereignty of a government" in subjecting its citizens to a religious or secular form of totalitarianism could not be criticized at all by *appeal to human rights*. To be sure, this is not the contention of Rawls's theory. Rather he follows a right intuition in formulating certain incisive conditions for the possible toleration of "hierarchical" regimes. As far as I can see, the crucial criterion in this context is the demand that the "system of law" in question "meet the essentials of legitimacy *in the eyes of its own people!*"[37]

This is indeed a plausible criterion, but why is it plausible? Obviously the criterion does not follow from that strategy of extension that is based on the argument of analogy or liberal transfer from the level of persons to the level of societies; it rather leads us back to the level of persons. But the new criterion is also incompatible with the "overlapping consensus" to be reached in the context of a "liberal democracy" of the Western tradition, to which Rawls's original conception of the *Theory of Justice* was oriented. For this would have made impossible that kind of "liberal extension" to a global theory of the "law of peoples" Rawls has in mind. Thus it cannot be "subordinated" at all to the principles of the earlier cases of the sequence of Rawls's extension of his political theory of justice. The way out of this dilemma, in my opinion, can only be provided by a *reflective philosophical* recourse behind all *political*—and thus *historical*—concretizations of the problem of *justice as fairness*: a recourse to the *moral* presuppositions of that *primordial discourse* through which philosophy has to discuss these problems.

Here we find a unitary point of departure for a "general theory of justice" (and of "human rights"). For the principle that could ultimately support Rawls's intuitive criterion of "legitimacy" for *liberal-democratic* and for *non-liberal-democratic* societies could be based on the postulated, acknowledged a priori in any practical discourse, that the proposed solutions of a theory of justice ideally should fulfill the condition that they would be *acceptable for all affected persons* (i.e., for the citizens of constitutional states and, before and beyond, even for all persons outside the limits of well-ordered constitutional states, as e.g., for the inhabitants of the so called "Third World"). There should be no factual agreements at the expense of non-represented but affected persons.

This would of course be only a "regulative principle" in the Kantian sense, and it would be grounded by a *reflection* that is not yet *political* but *philosophical.* But it would be a general foundation for *any political consensus theory* that would try to avoid the risk of being "political in the false sense." For it formulates a principle by appeal to which one cannot only strive for, but also, at any time, criticize a factual, and hence context-dependent, "overlapping consensus."

Rawls would presumably suspect at this point, that my approach must be based on *metaphysics,* i.e., on some "comprehensive doctrine." And, in fact, I am even a worse fellow than Habermas, since I resort to a *transcendental-pragmatic foundation of discourse ethics* without any quasi-empirical recourse to *sociology* or *linguistics.*[38] But I think it is a fatal error of our time to confuse the radical method of *transcendental reflection on the validity conditions of argumentation* with *metaphysics,* even with the metaphysics of Kant.[39] By contrast, I consider it to be the only reliable way of avoiding any metaphysics, i.e., any "comprehensive," culture-dependent doctrine.

Of course, I cannot go into that in this paper. I should only point out that my proposal of a discourse-ethical foundation of the theory of justice does by no means depreciate the main arguments of Rawls's original *theory of justice.* For these arguments may have their place as *proposals* within a *practical discourse,* whose procedural principles have already been justified by self-reflective discourse ethics.

Karl-Otto Apel, Fachbereich Philosophie und Geschichtswissenschaften, Institut für Philosophie, Johan Wolfgang Goethe-Universität, Frankfurt am Main, D-60054 Germany

NOTES

1. See J. Rawls, "Justice as Fairness: Political not Metaphysical," *Philosophy and Public Affairs* 14:3 (1985): 225.

2. Quotation from J. Rawls, *Die Idee des politischen Liberalismus* (Frankfurt: Suhrkamp, 1992), 258 (English trans. from the German by K.-O. Apel).

3. See J. Rawls, "Reply to Habermas," *The Journal of Philosophy* 92:3 (1995): 132–80.

4. Ibid., 134.

5. Ibid., 134f.

6. Cf. J. Rawls, *Political Liberalism* (New York: Columbia University Press, 1993), 39f., 142.

7. Rawls, "Reply to Habermas," op. cit., 145.

8. Ibid., 145; Rawls's references in the text are to *Political Liberalism*.

9. Cf. Rawls, *Political Liberalism*, op. cit., xx, 38f., 64ff., 133f., 140–44.

10. Ibid., 65f.

11. Ibid., 143.

12. Quotation from Rawls, *Die Idee des politischen Liberalismus*, 257 (English trans. from German by K.-O. Apel).

13. Ibid.

14. Ibid.

15. Cf. J. Rawls, *A Theory of Justice* (Cambridge, Mass.: Harvard University Press, 1971), § 6; and "The Priority of Right and Ideas of the Good," *Philosophy and Public Affairs* 17 (1988): 251–76.

16. Cf. Rawls, "Justice as Fairness."

17. This, in my opinion, is the false conclusion that lies at the ground of R. Rorty's paper "The Priority of Democracy to Philosophy," *Objectivity, Relativism and Truth* (Cambridge and New York: Cambridge University Press, 1991), 175–96.

18. Cf. J. Habermas, "Vom pragmatischen, ethischen und moralischen Gebrauch der praktischen Vernunft," *Erläuterungen zur Diskursethik* (Frankfurt: Suhrkamp, 1992), 100–18.

19. Cf. K.-O. Apel, "Plurality of the Good? The Problem of Affirmative Tolerance in a Multicultural Society from an Ethical Point of View," *Ratio Juris* 10 (1997): 199–212; idem, "The Problem of Justice in a Multicultural Society: The Response of Discourse Ethics," *Ethics in Question*, ed. R. Kearney (forthcoming).

20. Cf. Rawls, *Political Liberalism*, op. cit., 48–54.

21. Cf. Rawls, "Reply to Habermas," op. cit., 179.

22. See Rorty, "The Priority of Democracy to Philosophy," op. cit., 188.

23. Ibid., 187–88.

24. Quotation from Rawls: *Die Idee des politischen Liberalismus*, op. cit., 358 (English trans. from the German by K.-O. Apel).

25. J. Rawls, "The Law of Peoples," *On Human Rights: The Oxford Amnesty Lectures 1993*, ed. S. Shute and S. Hurley (New York: Basic Books, 1993), 41–81.

26. Cf. K.-O. Apel, "Globalization and the Need for Universal Ethics" (forthcoming).

27. Rawls, "The Laws of Peoples," 44.

28. Ibid.

29. Ibid.

30. Ibid., 52–53; cf. also 74ff.

31. Ibid., 76.

32. Ibid., 46.

33. Ibid., 46–47.

34. Ibid., 48.

35. Ibid., 62.

36. Cf. Rawls, "Reply to Habermas," op. cit., 151ff.

37. Rawls, "The Law of Peoples," op. cit., 79; my emphasis.

38. Cf. K.-O. Apel, "Normative Grounding 'Critical Theory' through Recourse to the Lifeworld? A Transcendental-Pragmatic Attempt to Think with Habermas against Habermas," *Philosophical Interventions in the Unfinished Project of Enlightenment*, ed. A. Honneth, et al., (Cambridge, Mass.: The MIT Press, 1992), 125–70.

39. Cf. K.-O. Apel, "Diskursethik als Verantwortungsethik—eine postmetaphysische Transformation der Ethik Kants," *Kant in der Diskussion der Moderne*, ed. G. Schönrich and Y. Kato (Frankfurt: Suhrkamp, 1996), 326–59.

INTERCULTURAL DIALOGUE AND HUMAN RIGHTS: A LATIN AMERICAN READING OF RAWLS'S "THE LAW OF PEOPLES"

Antonio Perez-Estevez

In "The Law of Peoples," John Rawls proposes a model for multi-culural dialogue based upon agreement. In liberal societies, we find agreement on issues such as human rights. However, I argue here that this proposal overcomes neither Eurocentrism nor Western-centrism, as liberal nations would decide which nations are "well organized hierarchical societies." This second circle of nations would be merely *invited* peoples, who would not be allowed to contribute new proposals but only to accept the proposals of the liberal nations. I propose a model for attaining human rights through truly universal dialogue in which the representatives of all peoples are able to speak, make proposals, and accept the proposals of others on an equal basis.

I. RAISING THE ISSUE

Human rights, especially those belonging to the first generation, as expressed in the Universal Declaration of Human Rights of 10 December 1948, are the end product of a long historical process within Western culture and whose previous stages are the English Revolution of 1648, the Declaration of American Independence of 1776, and the Declaration of the Rights of Man and Citizen of August, 1789. These documents, at the same time, harken back to earlier sociopolitical thought: the supreme value of reason as basis for any sociopolitical relation (such as we discover at the Greek *polis*, as it is presented by the great thinkers Plato and Aristotle); the intrinsic value of human person (by virtue of being created by the Christian God and capable—because of his freedom—either of salvation or of condemnation, as those concepts were understood by the main thinkers in the Middle Ages); the human individual, considered as a juridical subject and capable of making contracts and assuming rights and duties and, therefore, serving as the foundation for any sociopolitical organization (as he was thought by the liberal tradition embodied by Hobbes, Locke, and the Encyclopedists). The concrete praxis of these theoretical principles in democratic societies and nations where individuals are the cause and end of sociopolitical order is found in Great Britain, Switzerland, Holland, the United States, France, Sweeden, Norwegen, Canada, and many other nations throughout the five continents.

The origin and the content of human rights, as presented by the Declaration of 1948, belong to a concrete cultural and political tradition, that is, the Western, liberal, individualistic, and democratic tradition. But the Declaration of Human Rights intends to be *universal*; that is, valid for all kind of cultures and nations, at any place and any time—valid not only in a theoretical, logical, and metaphysical sense, but also in a cultural and political sense. The rights established by the Universal Declaration of the Rights of Men intend to be juridical and political rights, concrete and real rights for any human individual at any culture and at any nation.[1] Jürgen Habermas, for instance, in his commentary on Kant's *Die ewige Friede*, argues that human rights can and must be the minimal juridical rights for any citizen inside the cosmopolis we must build up in order to ensure worldy peace.[2] Domestic and international law must be extended in order to create a *iuscosmopolitanum*, a worldy Law, according to which citizens of all states become subjects of right and all states become obliged to satisfy them.

Which political and juridical foundation can justify the transit from the Western, particular, to the universal? How can we find the political and juridical basis that justifies the transit from Western human rights to human rights so that human rights can be accepted and respected by any type of sociopolitical organization existing inside the different cultures, nations, and peoples?

Past and present history tells us that, in practice, human rights continue to be understood in an equivocal way. One reason is that freedom and equality (as established by the Universal Declaration of Human Rights) are understood in different ways according to the different cultural traditions and different types of nations and states in which such understanding is embedded.

This juridical political foundation for the universality of human rights cannnot be the rationalist, religious-metaphysical, personalist, liberal-individualistic, Western tradition. This Western tradition, originally religious and metaphysical, has steadily lost its religious and metaphysical character in modernity.

Other cultural traditions, different from the Western, can hardly justify human rights by means of a tradition of religious and metaphysical values they do not share. That is why we are concerned to find a pragmatic foundation (i.e., a multinational and multicultural agreement or contract) that could justify the *universality of human rights* so that they could be considered as *juridical rights for all human beings* and, therefore, accepted and respected by all nations and peoples. One of these efforts is the one recently presented by John Rawls in his "The Law of Peoples."

II. THE LAW OF PEOPLES AND HUMAN RIGHTS ACCORDING TO RAWLS

John Rawls raises the problem of the universal, juridical, and political validity of human rights in a lecture, "The Law of Peoples," delivered at Oxford in 1993. Rawls argues that his theory of justice, such as it is explained in his previous writings, is not sufficient to establish a non-ethnocentric foundation that justifies the universal validity of human rights.[3] Its insufficiency is due to the fact that his theory of *justice as fairness* is only a political understanding of justice rooted in the intuitive and basic ideas of public culture of democracy; so, it could not be extended outside this democratic culture. His theory of *justice as fairness* has the following three features: 1) it applies to basic political, economic, and social institutions; in the case of domestic society, to its basic structure, in the present case, to the law and practices of the society of political peoples; 2) it is independent of any particular comprehensive religious, philosophical, or moral doctrine, and though it may be derived from or related to several such doctrines, it is not worked out in that way; 3) its content is expressed in terms of certain fundamental ideas seen as implicit in the public political culture of a liberal society.[4] It is, consequently, illogical to apply such theory of justice outside of its sociopolitical context in order to build up a foundation for the universal validity of human rights.

In "The Law of Peoples," Rawls tries to find a foundation—one different from his theory of *justice as fairness*—that can justify the universal validity of human rights as a part of the Law of Peoples without falling into metaphysics and ethnocentrism. He uses the Law of Peoples, that is, the theory of international justice, in order to establish universal norms so that these norms can govern the reciprocal conduct of many states and nations and can promote the construction of a Society of Nations. Rawls begins from the same principles of political liberal justice, as presented in *The Theory of Justice*, and tries to apply these principles to nonliberal states and nations. From a constructivist point of view, Rawls's "The Law of Peoples" attempts to answer the question: Which kind of agreement or understanding among nations should be attained so that rights so fundamental as the right of any human being to life, to security, to personal property, to free conscience and religion, to freedom of going and coming (e.g., to emigrate), can be accepted by a great number of states, including those without a liberal democratic tradition?

Rawls carefully describes a hypothetical original position that promotes agreement on minimal and fundamental principles acceptable and accepted by all. This hypothetical original position will have to satisfy the requirements of *The Theory of Justice,* realizing that, in this case, the individuals must be representatives of nations and/or peoples. The essential conditions of this original position are:

> First, the original position represents the parties (or citizens) fairly, or reasonably; second, it represents them as rational; and third, it represents them as deciding between available principles by appropriate reasons. We check that these conditions are satisfied by observing that citizens are indeed represented fairly or reasonably, in virtue of the symmetry and equality of their representatives' situation in the original position. Next, citizens are represented as rational in virtue of the aim of their representatives to do the best they can for their essential interests as persons. Finally, they are represented as deciding by appropriate reasons.[5]

Rawls distinguishes two different stages in this process of getting an agreement in order to work out a Society of Nations that governs international politics between all its members. The first stage begins with the agreement and understanding among these nations holding the liberal-democratic tradition. The principles of justice between free and democratic nations will include certain familiar principles long recognized as belonging to the Law of the Peoples—among them, peoples are to honor human rights.

Once these liberal-democratic nations attain a minimal agreement, the second stage begins in order to extend and apply these principles to states and nations without a liberal-democratic tradition, so that these nations too can share in the original position. Rawls speaks of well-ordered, hierarchical societies. These well-ordered, hierarchical societies are those that do not accept the political fact of pluralism and are organized according to a comprehensive metaphysical or religious doctrine. But they will have to satisfy three requirements: 1) They must be peaceful and gain their legitimate aims through diplomacy, trade, and other ways of peace. Their religious doctrine is not expansionist. 2) They need to have a reasonably well-organized legal system. This requires that their government has the power to impose moral duties and obligations on all persons within its territory, that its system of law is guided by a common conception of justice, and that there exists a reasonable belief of the part of judges and other officials who administer the legal order that the law is indeed guided by a common conception of justice. 3) They admit a measure of liberty of conscience and freedom of thought, even if these freedoms are not in general equal for all members of society. 4) They admit the right of emigration.[6]

The conception of the common good of justice secures for all persons at least certain minimal rights to means of subsistence and security—the right to life—to liberty, to property, as well as to formal equality as expressed by the rules of natural justice (similar cases should be treated in like manner). The nations or societies that satisfy these requirements must be considered well-ordered, hierarchical societies with the right to belong to the Society of Nations and, so, with the right to share the hypothetical original position in order to attain an agreement or a contract with the liberal-democratic states to a minimum of human rights, such as: the right to life and to personal security, the right to personal property, the right to the requirements of a legal rule, the right to a certain amount of liberty of conscience and association, and finally the right of emigration.[7]

III. INTERCULTURAL DIALOGUE AND HUMAN RIGHTS

A. Critique of Rawls's Constructivist Conception

Rawls thinks that his procedure avoids any ethnocentrism and, at the same time, states a juridical foundation for the universal validity of human rights. With such purpose, human rights have been reduced to a minimum considered *politically neutral.*

From a Latinamerican point of view, I think that ethnocentrism or Eurocentrism has not been overcome; on the contrary, Rawls's theory of "The Law of the Peoples" is an obvious sample of ethnocentrism and Eurocentrism:

1. He begins from the prejudice (not explicit, but implicit), that Western-liberal-democratic society is the best sociopolitical organization human beings have developed today and, therefore, must be the only model of society and the only criterion to be followed in order to create a Society of Nations for the defense of human rights.

2. As a consequence of the previous paragraph, in the Club of the Society of Nations only the following societies or nations must be accepted: in the first stage, the liberal-democratic nations, all with the same right; in the second stage, the well-ordered, hierarchical societies, that is, those other societies or nations that, besides the liberal-democratic nations, are the most similar to the liberal-democratic ones. Universality is thus reduced to the Western-liberal-democratic nations and to those societies that are the most similar to the Western-liberal-democratic ones.

3. No word is said on which organism is going to decide if and when a people or nation satisfies the requirements of a well-ordered, hierarchical society, and can be accepted at the Club of the Society of Nations. But, judging by the context, we can state that liberal-democratic nations will decide which nation or people satisfies the requirements of a well-ordered, hierarchical society. Well-ordered, hierarchical societies, thus, will always be the invited and the accepted second-circle, while liberal-democratic nations will always be the inviting and accepting first circle.

4. Human rights have been reduced to a minimum, and are considered fundamental and neutral; therefore, they are acceptable to all nations and cultures. These few human rights, nevertheless, maintain their Western character by dint of origin and historical development. Western human rights intend to be the *only* human rights. The confusion between the *Western* and the *human* continues to exist in Rawls's way of understanding human rights.

5. Rawls's "The Law of the Peoples" is not open to the possibility of widening the minimum of human rights with new human rights arising from non-Western societies and non-Western cultures. Rawls's minimal human rights are understood as a grant of liberal-democratic societies to well-ordered hierarchical societies. Rawls's theory on human rights is a new effort to apply and to widen Western values in concentrical circles to other societies and cultures in order to make them similar to Western societies.

6. It is the old Western way of acting: our truth—in this case, practical and political truth—is the greatest truth. Therefore, we have to coerce other societies and cultures to accept it, not by violence and war but by more subtle means, such as barring them from the new Society of Nations and from the sociopolitical benefits deriving from that Society.

7. It does not seem that the rights and duties of the well organized, hierarchical societies satisfy all the requisites of the hypothetical original position, especially the requirement of absolute equalilty among the participants of the original positions, such as described by Rawls.[8] The well organized, hierarchical societies seem to be accepted to share these

concrete Western human rights, but they do not seem to be able to make proposals on new human rights others than the few agreed on by the liberal democracies.

B. Intercultural Dialogue as Means to Attain Legitimacy and Universality for Human Rights

Rawls's proposal, with his hypothesis of an original position and the two stages or circles of nations accepting human rights, does not imply the possibililty of a true and real dialogue among the representative persons coming from different peoples, from different cultures and different sociopolitical organizations in order to attain an agreement on which human rights must be acceptable to all of them. Human rights may come from any culture and from any society.[9] Such dialogue must be an universalist true dialogue.

Universalist dialogue means that the authentic, representative persons who enter into dialogue need to come from a broad spectrum of peoples, cultures, and sociopolitical organizations across the world. *True dialogue* means that all representatives would have the same real right to talk and propose possible human rights and the same right to mutually listen. To talk and to listen are the two essential moments of any dialogue. Talking is the moment of the "I"; listening is the moment of "You," of the "Other." Each person entering into dialogue has to be ready, from the very beginning, to satisfy both moments; that is, each person entering into dialogue needs the original disposal to take the double position of talking and listening, of the "I" and of the "Other," or "You." Even at the moment of talking, of "I," each participant must be open to listening, to being "You." Listening must always be present even when "I" talk; if "I" talk without the original disposal of listening, of being "You," then "I" am not ready to enter into dialogue and *I* will fall into the temptation of controlling and dominating *you.*

I want to point out the right—or better the duty—to mutually listen, which is completely forgotten by Rawls. For Rawls, the liberal-democratic nations that belong to the first rank circle of the Society of Nations have only the right to talk and to propose human rights that must be accepted by the well-ordered hierarchical societies, but not the duty to listen and to accept others' human rights. The non-liberal, democratic nations, on the contrary, have only the duty to listen and to accept others' human rights, but not the right to talk and to make proposals. The duty to listen implies the disposal to open oneself to the other's world and to the other's values, that is, to otherness. The disposal to listen means to be open to the other's cultural world and to the other's personal world. And to be open to the other's world implies on the part of the persons entering into dialogue: 1) a deep conviction by each participant that each culture is a partial and imperfect expression or manifestation of humanity and, therefore, no participant has the only truth or the whole truth but only a partial truth or something of the truth; 2) each participant, conscious of his partial or imperfect truth, will not intend to impose his truth to other participants as if his truth were the only truth; 3) each participant, conscious of his partial or imperfect truth, has the disposal to open himself to others in order to profit and to accept that part of the truth or something of the truth others may have so that he can complete and improve his own partial and imperfect truth.

Western liberal nations, in Rawls's project, have not entered into a true dialogue with non-Western and non-liberal nations. Western nations have no intention to exchange roles; they accept only to be "I" and refuse the possibility of becoming "You." At the same time, they accept that the others, the non-Western, be only "You" and do not consider the possibility for the non-Westerns to become "I." Western nations are not ready to be "You," to listen, that is, they are not ready to open themselves to the truths, values, and proposals coming from non-Western, non-liberal nations. Western-liberal-nations are not ready to listen because they do not satisfy the previous quoted requirements to be able to enter into a true dialogue. In fact, Western-liberal-nations are conscious—as always before—that their culture is the most perfect expression of humanity and, therefore, they do have the whole and the only possible truth; that is why they want to share and, even, to impose that truth to other cultures and other peoples. Since they are proud of possesing the whole and only possible truth, they do not need any disposal to open themselves to others' truths, values, and proposals because these non-Western cultures have no truth, no values, and no proposal to make and share.

The only possible relation, according to Rawls's project, between the Western-liberal-democratic nations and the rest of nations (qualified as well-organized, hierarchical societies), is the relation of Western nations offering and sharing only their truths (e.g., human rights), to well-organized, hierarchical societies that accept those Western truths, Western human rights. And that relation, according to Rawls, is not ethnocentric or Eurocentric.

The only procedure to attain a proper and contractual foundation for the universal validity of human rights will be when the authentical representatives of all peoples and nations—all with the same rights and the same duties, with the same disposal for exchanging roles and for being "I" and "You"—sit around a table ready to build a true and real dialogue on human rights. Only then will the rights coming from that true and real intercultural dialogue become true human rights acceptable to all. Part of those human rights, of course, will be Western rights: the right to life and to personal security, the right to personal property, the right to the requirements of a legal rule, the right to a certain amount of liberty of conscience and association, and finally the right of emigration.

Antonio Perez-Estevez, Maracaibo, Venezuela; estevez@cantv.net

NOTES

1. With respect to the philosophical foundations that underlie human rights I recommend: Guy Haarscher, *Philosophie des Droits de l'Homme* (Editions de l'Université de Bruxelles, 1989); and G. H. Sabine, *A History of Political Theory* (Hunsdale, Ill.: Dryden Press, 1973).

2. Jürgen Habermas, "Kants Idee des ewigen Friedens: aus dem historischen Abstand von 200 Jahren," *Kritische Justiz* 3 (Frankfurt am Main 1995), 293–319.

3. John Rawls main works are: *A Theory of Justice* (Cambridge, Mass.: Harvard University Press, 1971); and *Political Liberalism* (New York: Columbia University Press, 1993).

4. John Rawls, "The Law of Peoples," *Critical Inquiry* (Autumn 1993), 36, fn 2.

5. Ibid., 45.

6. Ibid., 50–53.

7. Ibid., 57.

8. John Rawls, *A Theory of Justice,* op. cit., 19. It seems reasonable to suppose that the parties in the original position are equal. That is, all have the same rights in the procedure for choosing principles; each can make proposals, submit reasons for their acceptance, and so on.

9. To be objective, Rawls does accept the possibility of working out a law of peoples, human rights being a part of such law of peoples, by starting with an all inclusive original position with representatives of all the individual persons of the world, such as Brian Barry does in his *Theories of Justice* (Berkeley: University of California Press, 1989). Rawls thinks that both ways should lead to the same law of peoples (see "The Law of Peoples," op. cit., 54–55).

CONSUMERIST CULTURAL HEGEMONY WITHIN A COSMOPOLITAN ORDER— WHY NOT?

William L. McBride

The issue that I wish to address is, why protest and criticize the increasing hegemony of what has been called the "culture of consumerism"? This "why not?" objection encompasses three distinct sets of questions. First, is not resistance to it akin to playing the role of King Canute by the sea? Second, is not acceptance of it dictated by the current liberal philosophical consensus that acknowledges and endorses an inevitable diversity in different individuals' conceptions of what is good, and must not this consensus itself be taken as a given by all who are opposed to political and religious totalitarianisms? Third, does not cosmopolitanism, regarded as a value-orientation favorable to the dissolution or at least minimization of national boundaries and the practices of exclusivity associated therewith, make common cause in the present historical conjuncture with this same trend? I will argue for a "No" answer to all of these questions.

The brief history of a previous paper of mine, entitled "Coca-Cola Culture and Other Cultures—Against Hegemony"[1] is germane to my present reflections. It goes back to two enterprises in which I was involved a few years ago. The first was an effort, on behalf of the American Philosophical Association, to support some young analytic philosophers at the Zadar liberal arts campus of the University of Split against Croatian nationalist initiatives to have them fired for their alleged lack of an appropriately patriotic orientation. The second was a brief "Citizen Ambassador" philosophers' tour of Russia and Hungary that I led in October 1995. Part of the documentation that I accumulated in the first of these enterprises was an issue of the newspaper, *Slobodna Dalmacija*, in which an article strongly attacking the young philosophers, on the grounds both that they still had some sympathy for Marxism and that they also had been influenced by American liberal thought and values, was headlined (in loose translation) "Marx and Coca-Cola: A Challenge and a Provocation."[2] The source of this, one presumes, was a *bon mot* of Jean-Luc Godard's from the 1960s: "*Ni Marx ni Coca-Cola*," that is, neither the one nor the other. As for the tour, the relevant documentation comes in the form of a photograph that I took in front of the former Winter Palace in Saint Petersburg, now the principal building of The Hermitage Museum, on a beautiful Sunday morning during our group's initial introduction to that city. There in front, plainly visible, is a blown-up replica of a Coca-Cola bottle that reaches nearly to the height of the edifice. There is even a second, smaller replica to the left, lest someone miss the point by not looking up to the heights. The occasion for which I originally prepared my resulting paper on "Coca-Cola Culture" was a conference in Saint Petersburg the following spring.

The second occasion on which I presented much of the same material was a conference held in Calcutta in August 1997. In the final part of the Indian version of the paper, I talked about the positive value, as I saw it, of cultural diversity, saying that this seemed obvious enough to me, but that it might not be an easy task to offer solid, convincing arguments in its support. I then talked about what I had seen in India, this having been my first visit to that country, and asked somewhat rhetorically whether the new hegemony of Coca-Cola culture was already on its way to being realized there as well.[3] I remarked: "When I viewed the Taj Mahal I could not help but wonder when *its* time would come to serve as an attractive backdrop for a hugely inflated bottle similar to the one in front of The Hermitage, bought by one or the other of those multinational soft drink giants [Coca-Cola or Pepsi-Cola] at a price sufficient hugely to inflate the coffers of state and federal governments."

"Perhaps," I continued, "this grotesque image of mine is a sufficient argument in itself; I do not intend to offer a longer one here." Perhaps, but perhaps not. Immediately after the session, attended as it was by my friend, the esteemed Professor Jitendra Mohanty, who informed me that he had just recently accepted a Woodruff Professorship—one of the named chairs donated by the family with the principal shareholding interest in the Coca-Cola Company—at Emory University, I entered into a friendly discussion with a Calcutta resident who is married to an American philosopher with whom I have a long-standing acquaintance and who had also been in the audience. She could not see why the implementation of my proposal should seem so problematic. I was taken aback. I now realize, of course, that the more conventional response would have been for me to ask her, as someone more familiar than I with Indian law, what steps I should take to file a suit to defend my interests if the company were ever to implement my idea without according me due compensation.

This, then, is the issue that I wish to confront in the present paper: Why not? Why protest, why criticize, the increasing hegemony of what in a somewhat vague, less colorful, less brand name-oriented language is called the culture of consumerism? This "why not?" objection can be parsed into three distinct sets of questions, which I shall address in turn: first, is not resisting this increasing hegemony akin to playing the role of King Canute by the sea? Second, is not acceptance of it dictated by the current liberal philosophical consensus that acknowledges and endorses an inevitable diversity in different individuals' conceptions of what is good, and must not this consensus itself be taken as a given by all who are opposed to political and religious totalitarianisms? Third, does not cosmopolitanism, regarded as a value-orientation favorable to the dissolution or at least minimization of national boundaries and the practices of exclusivity that are associated therewith, make common cause, in the present historical conjuncture, with this same trend? I, of course, wish to argue for a "No" answer to all of these questions.

I shall not spend much time on the first set of questions. I have devoted considerable effort, especially at a period when Marxist thought enjoyed more widespread popularity than it currently does, to showing that the internal logic of Marx's analysis of the capitalist system in *Capital* argues against the thesis of historical inevitability—in this case the alleged inevitability of a replacement of that system, within a predictable time frame, by a worldwide "society of associated producers"—that was and still is generally assumed to be a central ingredient of that worldview.[4] In doing this, I thought of myself as absolving Marx of the charge of adhering to an untenable thesis, admittedly one about which he was not always perfectly clear himself, that distracted attention from his powerful socioeconomic criticisms and made it easier for defenders of the system under attack to dismiss them. But today it is the defenders of that system, in its contemporary form, who typically uphold the thesis of historical inevitability, sometimes quite brutally. For example, commenting recently on the International Monetary Fund's decision, in light of the widespread riots and deaths in Indonesia, to soften some of its original requirements that popular subsidies of basic goods be completely eliminated immediately, a United States Senator stated his opposition to this retreat on the grounds that obsolete practices of the past should simply not be permitted to survive, regardless of circumstances or consequences. The implication of this sort of attitude is that history is dictating the form of economy and related practices, including consumerist cultural practices, that must dominate the future, and that it is unacceptable, perhaps even immoral, to try to thwart the tide of history. (Of course, the more intellectual version of this ideology was formulated a few years ago by Francis Fukuyama in his work extolling the combination of free market capitalism with political liberalism as constituting the "end of history.")

It may seem unbearably ironic that the implementation of such a savage "consumerism," which insists that henceforth only free market methods of distribution are to be considered acceptable both by those who hold power and by those over whom it is held because this is the message of history, is bound to exacerbate malnutrition and other serious forms of under-consumption among poor would-be consumers, especially in countries undergoing severe inflation and other phenomena of economic crisis. And so it is. However, this fact does not necessarily entail its rejection by some intellectuals or by the general population. I have observed what might be called a "consumerism of lack," which embraces this irony, being preached and to some extent believed in the newly-underdeveloped, or negatively developing, country in which I recently spent three months, Bulgaria. Her citizens were, until quite recently, being indoctrinated with the *other* version of historical inevitability and *other* promises about the supposedly "radiant future of mankind."[5]

But, to put it very simply, I have never seen convincing evidence to the effect that future human history has been predetermined. And there is a great deal of evidence supportive of the opposite hypothesis that freedom plays a role, however strongly free decisions may be mediated by the effects of reciprocal interactions and however frequently they may be "counterfinalized" at the level of very large groups across time and space which *is* the domain of history. A corrupt but seemingly entrenched dictator over the fourth most populous country in the world may suddenly find himself forced to resign office. Just so, the allegedly rigorous mechanisms, with which, as we are constantly being warned, one interferes only at the greatest peril, of what is ironically labeled the "free market" are in fact, as human creations, quite subject to reconstruction and deconstruction. In short, the culture of consumerism, however overwhelming the financial resources that support it may seem and however widely seductive its advertising techniques may be, lacks the inevitability of the tides of the sea and *is* ultimately susceptible, though only at great cost and through painful effort, to criticism and change. An illustration of this is the global rethinking currently underway with respect to what was once a supremely successful consumer product, tobacco—which even Marx himself classified as a "consumer necessity," as distinguished from a luxury, on the ground that it was habitually regarded as such in his day.[6] So much, then, for my first question, concerning the allegedly Canute-like nature of resistance to consumerist culture.

However, the very example that I have just cited raises fundamental questions of definition. What I have here been calling "consumerist culture," elsewhere "Coca-Cola culture," is of course not capable of being defined with extreme precision. No one, I think, would—or at any rate should—demand that. And most people, I further think, would admit that there has to be some element of "I know it when I see it" in any discussion about it and yet agree that it names a collection of real phenomena, not just some fantasy of mine and of a few like-minded victims of illusion. At the same time, there should be limits to permissible vagueness (especially among philosophers), and this notion seems to approximate if not exceed those limits, especially when an illustration drawn from a nineteenth-century writer such as Marx can be cited concerning what was supposed to be a quintessentially contemporary reality. The reference to Marx may in fact be useful in making a few points of clarification. For there are elements of his analysis, in the portion of the less frequently studied Volume II of *Capital* in which he makes his remark about tobacco, that are completely outdated and inapplicable to the present-day situation. And there are other, background elements of it that are of use in making sense of this same situation. The outdated part consists in his relegation of luxury consumer goods exclusively to the capitalist class. His point about tobacco is that it, as a culturally-proclaimed "necessity of life," is part of what even the proletariat normally consumes—a point which, incidentally, some Republican members of Congress, posing as defenders of the working class as part of their effort to reduce the tobacco corporations' future liabilities, tried to stress during the recent debates about possible tobacco legislation! But what is central to contemporary consumerist culture, by comparison with the culture of Marx's day, is the global corporate effort to entice the whole world's population into lusting after goods of the sort that Marx and other writers in his time would have consigned to the "luxury" category and into buying them to the extent of their resources and beyond, that is, to the extent of their credit card limits. What, on the other hand, remains relevant about Marx's account is the exploitativeness and manipulativeness of the system, which of course relies heavily on locating and employing the cheapest labor possible, wherever in the world it is to be found, and employing well-known advertising techniques to maximize consumption, all with a view above all to optimizing the profits of those who are the major owners of the means of production.

That this is indeed the way in which the system works, including the razzle-dazzle aspects of it of which my vignette from Saint Petersburg is a good illustration, is unlikely to be seriously denied by most of those who would ask, "Why not?" The latter tend, however, to invoke some version of the famous Invisible Hand in order to make the case that the system, however exploitative, unvirtuous, or even squalid a description of it may make it appear, is the best imaginable for realizing the ultimate goal of liberal theory, which is the maximum possible realization of different individuals' diverse conceptions of the good. And this brings me to my second set of initial questions. To begin with, is this claim about the maximum possible realization of preferences in fact true? On the surface, perhaps, yes. The Coca-Cola Company and the soft drink industry as a whole are as good illustrations as any of the plurality of diverse possibilities—regular, diet, caffeine-free, diet *and* caffeine-free, and so on. These have been developed in order to cater to the most minutely divergent consumer preferences among those—perhaps at this point a majority of the world's population—who regularly consume the industry's products. I am not trying to make the claim that such practices are in themselves ethically suspect. This particular case could be regarded, in fact, as an instance of particularly skillful Invisible Handiwork, increasing company profits while at the same time catering to consumers' often very legitimate health and dietary concerns. But I would like to contend that, when compared with larger, more global aspects of contemporary consumerist culture, such practices are relatively trivial in import.

On a global scale, it seems to me, a very good case can be made *against* the claim that consumerist culture generally realizes the liberal dream of permitting diverse conceptions of the good to be enjoyed to the maximum extent. While not wishing to retrace all the steps that I took with regard to this issue in my earlier paper, I can mention a couple of the ways that I discussed there in which, as I see it, contemporary consumerist culture reinforces pressures toward standardization and uniformity. This is the case, for instance, in the area of language, in which a bland, business-oriented English is becoming the global standard, and in the area of the media, particularly television news, newspapers, and book publishing. It is becoming the case in the transportation industry, in which, at least in North America, an entire alternative mode to flight, namely, the passenger railroad, has been encouraged gradually to die through a rather complex, intricate process, while the airline industry itself is reconsolidating after a temporary venture into diversity. I could devote the remainder of this paper to generating additional examples. What is happening in so many aspects of our culture is that certain transnational corporations, committed single-mindedly as they are to improving their bottom lines, are becoming increasingly dominant and powerful, so that they are able to dictate the range of preferences that will be honored. Preferences that fall outside this range receive no public consideration; this is the *meaning* of cultural hegemony. In other words, the common expression, "Thank you for choosing x," which of course is intended to flatter the putative choosers, is today all too often spoken with barely concealed sarcasm and can all too often only be properly understood ironically. There are, then, whole possible worlds of theoretically realizable conceptions of the good, which, contrary to the liberal ideal, are systematically kept out of the reach even of the relatively affluent, to say nothing of the situation of the poor, in a global society in which possession and consumption are treated by those who dominate the mass media as the most important, almost *exclusively* important, human activities.

But there is, I acknowledge, a certain air of unreality or at least of indeterminacy about all that I have just written concerning theoretically realizable but actually unrealized diverse conceptions of the good. For how, it may be asked, do I know that these assertions are true for anyone except my own, perhaps highly idiosyncratic, self and perhaps a few others like me? The only possible answer to this question is that, like any other theorist engaged in generalizing about society, I am proposing a certain interpretation of what is the case and hope that it will be recognized by some, or perhaps many, others as having a certain validity. Because, contrary to what some assertions about the purely individual nature of conceptions of the good might suggest, none of us can really be treated as a total isolate. This brings me to the second part of my initial questioning about what I called the "liberal philosophical consensus" in favor of inevitable diversity in conceptions of what is good, namely, "must not this consensus itself be taken as a given by all who are opposed to political and religious totalitarianisms?" No, I think not. For it seems evident to me that the standard distinction between the right and the good that is accepted by Rawls, Habermas, and a number of other recent and contemporary philosophers—a distinction that Rawls celebrates when he says that "it is, in general, a good thing that individuals' conceptions of their good should differ in significant ways, whereas this is not so for conceptions of right,"[7]—is based on a profound though unacknowledged individualist ontology that makes it difficult to deal intelligently with *public* goods. It is thus untenable in the absolute form in which it is often put forward and has contributed to a failure of philosophical nerve in the domain of cultural and political criticism.

Cultural phenomena, together with a number of other types of phenomena not usually categorized as cultural such as information, transportation, and health services, are in large measure public goods (or sometimes "public evils," so to speak), especially in highly technological societies such as our own. At the same time, it would be difficult to deny that there are many ways in which decisions to deliver or not to deliver public goods and in what specific form they are to be delivered involve issues of justice, *even* if we narrowly restrict our considerations of justice, as Rawls generally does, to distributive justice. (The word "decisions" here should be taken broadly and variously to include actions or omissions on the parts of governments, transnational institutions, private corporations, community groups, *and* individuals.) But then an obvious problem arises for anyone who treats the right, the domain of justice, and the good as dichotomous and the latter as having to do primarily with diverse *individual* conceptions. That it is a serious problem is evident in the early work of Rawls, where the discussion of public goods, centered though not exclusively concentrated in a section of *A Theory of Justice* entitled, significantly, "Some Remarks about Economic Systems,"[8] is brief, for the most part derivative, and surprisingly restrictive in terms of the criteria to be invoked for public expenditures. Rawls' interpretations of the implications of his theory for culture are, as I have shown elsewhere,[9] extremely ungenerous and may be regarded as reinforcing an ideological climate (ours today) in which investments in public goods (with the single major exception, perhaps, of new stadiums and arenas that are designed to bring enormous profits to the corporate owners of professional sports teams) are considered highly suspect unless undertaken by private corporations. They are then of course regarded as having the right to exercise control over almost every aspect of their delivery. The paradoxical outcome of this chain of thinking is that, from a view of the good as primarily individual, a theory and practice have been derived which sanction control of the extent and nature of public goods, including in particular cultural phenomena, by the rich and powerful few. And this is said to be most in keeping with justice and right. In this way of thinking, hegemonic consumerist culture finds a powerful ideological ally.

There is, to be sure, a noble motive that is frequently invoked to justify this self-induced aporia in liberal theory, namely, a fear that totalitarian consequences, whether of a religious or a political nature, may ensue once it is admitted that conceptions of the good cannot be construed on a purely individualistic basis. It is this motive, I think, that helps account for what I have just called liberal theory's "failure of philosophical nerve in the domain of cultural and political criticism." (It may also help, incidentally, to explain Rawls' own retreat, in his later work, from any strong claims to universality even about his conception of justice.) Yes, it is true, the Nazis had their diabolical conception of the good, and the self-styled Orthodox Communists theirs, and the Taliban have theirs, and other groups for which I feel comparable loathing have repeatedly attempted, often with considerable success, to impose their conceptions willy-nilly on entire societies over which they have been dominant. But it is self-deceptive folly, in my opinion, to pretend that we can engage in social theory—or even worse, as I shall discuss shortly, to offer social criticism and commentary and at the same time insist that one is not engaging in theory—while, in the name of openness and out of the fear of totalitarian consequences that I have cited, avoiding commitment to a conception of the good.

For example, I would like to see a broadly, genuinely democratic regime—democratic in the economic sphere, not merely in terms of the political procedures upon which liberal theorists focus—tolerant and even supportive of diversity and differences in all spheres including in particular that of culture, and global in scope, come into being. And I am willing to argue for it and to do whatever else is feasible to bring it about. In such a regime, there would be maximal opportunity for others to pursue most of whatever may interest them as individuals and as members of groups. But the scope of this opportunity would not be so broad as to include, for example, Nazi or Orthodox Communist or Talibanic "conceptions of the good." So my vision is at once unitary and comprehensive—total or even "totalistic," if you will—and yet it certainly clashes with *their* visions. But I do not apologize for thinking that mine is superior and trying to advance as good reasons as possible in its favor. These reasons, as far as I am concerned, can only be premised on the belief that human values, of which my and others' visions are constituted, are human creations. While such values must respect physical and other limitations of the human condition, they cannot ultimately be dictated—contrary to what all three of the groups that I have chosen as illustrations have held in one way or another—by "the nature of things." In what I have just said, it should be noted, I have made or implied some significant claims about ontology as well as about values, and I simply do not see that it was possible to avoid doing so. Just so, I cannot accept Rawls's and other liberal theorists' claims to the effect that *they* have managed to avoid ontological commitments. It seems evident to me that the mantra about the necessarily individualistic nature of most conceptions of the good in fact implies just such commitments, as does the related mantra about the strong distinction between the right and the good. It is only after challenging mantras like these, it seems to me, that we may begin to be in a position to articulate philosophically informed answers to my title question about consumerist cultural hegemony, "Why not?"

But Rawls has at least admitted, beginning with the title that he gave to his first book, that he is engaging in *theory*, even if he does not think it is of an ontological sort. There is, however, at least one highly influential writer on the contemporary scene who insists that he is not doing theory at all and we would be well advised not to do so, either: this is, of course, Richard Rorty. He has done much in the past, as I have argued, to endorse the hegemonic culture that I am deploring, even though he does not appear to be particularly enamored of its grosser materialist forms. There was a time, not so many years ago, at which Rorty disdained talk of politics, at least in terms of his role as a professional non-theorist. I remember that time well. For it was just such an attitude of disdain that came through with great clarity in his plenary address to the Inter-American Congress of Philosophy in Guadalajara, Mexico, in 1985, which I heard and which served as the target of an angry attack by Ofelia Schutte on North Americans' attitudes toward philosophers of the "periphery."[10] It is this same Richard Rorty who has defended the market economy as "the Great *Good* Thing"[11]— no hesitation here about identifying what is universally good!—to the intense annoyance of one of the better-known philosophers of the periphery, Enrique Dussel. But more recently Rorty has become politically engaged, or perhaps reengaged, in what can best be described as an eccentric, quirky way. His short new book, *Achieving Our Country*, is essentially a collection of three lectures with a couple of appendices added to make it long enough for Harvard University Press to publish it as a book. Complete with a breathless blurb on the inside of the jacket proclaiming it to be a "galvanizing" piece in the evolution of the American Left, Rorty's book vents much spleen and attacks enough different targets to permit virtually anyone with an opinion about politics and/or culture—even Frederic Jameson, the writer whom he most frequently takes to task—to agree with at least a few of the statements that it contains. Among the most prominent targets is, as always, theory, especially Marxist theory, but also the theories of academics whom he stigmatizes as the "cultural Left" and castigates for turning their backs on politics, the theories of those who advocate a "politics of difference" or an identity politics (which presumably does not fall under what he here understands by "politics"), theorists of "multiculturalism," and on and on. He has compiled a long hit list. "The Left," he says there, "should put a moratorium on theory. It should try to kick its philosophy habit."[12]

What I find especially fascinating about this unique display of eccentricity is the extent to which Rorty, intelligent and politically informed as he is, nevertheless refuses to explore or even, for the most part, to acknowledge the close *interconnections* between the cultural and the political that are presupposed here in my paper and, I think, in much that is currently being written about global ethics. This refusal, I suppose, is of a piece with his profoundly self-contradictory contempt for theory. Closely related to this, and perhaps the most blatant of all of the book's themes, is its constant call to revive American patriotism, to renew a love of American myths and ideals despite all the well-known and admitted ways in which actual historical reality has fallen short of them—in short, to "start trying to construct inspiring images of the country."[13] On the first page of his text, it is true, Rorty pays lip service, citing Tennyson, to the distant ideal of a "Parliament of man," but only in order to dismiss it as irrelevant to the foreseeable future. In a few places he *mentions*, as a concern that he feels but without knowing quite what to say about it, the tension between the increasing insecurity of American workers and gulf between the rich and the rest in this country, on the one hand, and the gap between the United States as a whole and the poor nations, on the other. But his sympathies clearly lie with those who would concentrate on "achieving *our* [*sic*] country." This brings me, by way of contrast to so much of what Rorty stands for, to my third initial question, concerning the cosmopolitan ideal and its relationship to the hegemonic culture of consumerism.

Rorty mentions cosmopolitanism on only one page of his book, where he briefly makes a distinction between "economic cosmopolitanism," that is, economic globalization, which he ultimately finds as "frightening" (his word) as do many of us, and "an agreeable cultural cosmopolitanism," which he sees as a by-product of the other kind, whereby "paunchy professors" like himself, seated in economy class on airplanes while vigorous young economic cosmopolitans occupy the front seats, go "zipping off to interdisciplinary conferences held in pleasant places."[14] In his book, he makes no more of this distinction than what I have just indicated, and at this point I shall take leave of him for the moment with my thanks, because he has placed some of the dilemmas implied by my original question, "Why not?" in a new and useful perspective. It is obvious, as Rorty also stresses, that "cultural cosmopolitans" are privileged, though not as privileged as the entrepreneurs in the business class seats, because what those of the cultural type are doing in such situations is beyond the reach of most Americans, to say nothing of individuals in poorer countries. The entrepreneurs are the flag-bearers of the consumerist culture, crisscrossing the world in the pursuit of deals to enrich their companies, themselves conspicuously consuming as they go. They normally have few "national boundaries" problems—that is, problems with passports and visas—and so in a very significant sense they live the cosmopolitan ideal. The paunchy professors jetting to international conferences can be seen as aping them from a distance, consuming slightly less conspicuously, sometimes experiencing "boundaries" difficulties at international airports, but still enjoying a taste of cosmopolitan existence.

My question here is whether the cosmopolitan ideal, as a set of values to which I would like to claim adherence, is not inextricably interconnected with the hegemonic consumerist culture at this moment in history.

To sharpen the question, a citation from a recently completed doctoral dissertation that I had the honor of directing, Jason Hill's *Becoming a Cosmopolitan: What it Means To Be a Human Being in the New Millenium* (which has now been published in a revised edition), may be in order. At one point Hill distinguishes between what he calls strong or "first order" cosmopolitanism and a "second order" or transitional kind, of which he takes the ideal epitomized in an article by Kwame Anthony Appiah, "Cosmopolitan Patriots,"[15] as an illustration. Hill begins his description of the presumably more robust form of cosmopolitanism as follows: "A first order cosmopolitan is one who refrains from fixating on tribal (racial/ethnic/national) loyalties. The first order cosmopolitan is especially suspicious of employing such loyalties as criteria involved in moral deliberations. Such an individual would not attach any sense of superior value to his or her cultural, ethnic or racial identity . . . ."[16] Now, Hill is certainly not a proponent of consumerism, and yet, as we see, his strong cosmopolitan ideal rules out any special loyalty to the culture from which one originates. (In his case, this happens to be Jamaican culture, and "happens to be" is the appropriate language, for he regards it as a dispensable contingency.) But may it not be the case that to adopt such a stance is to cede the field to consumerist culture, for what *other* alternative is there?

Another angle from which to approach this problem of a possible co-implication between cosmopolitanism and consumerism is that of the generally-acknowledged desirability of preserving and/or reviving civil societies, especially in Eastern Europe. The independence of these civil societies was formerly undermined and suppressed by dictatorial political regimes. Nowadays, it seems evident to me, that independence is being most threatened and undermined precisely by the transnational corporations which are the carriers of the culture of consumerism and their institutional allies such as the IMF. A portion of the title of a paper that I recently presented at a conference on civil society in South East Europe captures this new trend, as I see it, and the dangers that it holds: ". . . Creating Space for Civil Societies: From the Struggle against Nation-State Despotisms to the Critique of Despotic Transnationalisms."[17] Both local and regional cultures, and local and regional business enterprises in small, impoverished countries fare poorly indeed when confronted with razzle-dazzle consumerism. The appeal of the latter particularly to young people, who in countries with unhappy, "totalitarian" recent pasts may tend to be even more strongly motivated to turn their backs on the past than are young people generally, seems virtually irresistible. (The "dissing" of the Winter Palace, site of the October Revolution of 1917, carries an obvious symbolic message along these lines.) Does it even make sense today to counter that appeal in the name of some small, local civil society of which the culture seems destined, to a degree of probability verging on certitude, to total obscurity in the global context of our increasingly "One World"?

In response to these deep and very legitimate concerns, I can offer only a few demurrers and some faint hope. After all, multiculturalism and the politics of difference have enjoyed and are enjoying at least some occasional successes within the territorial boundaries of the United States without tearing the country apart, as Rorty seems in some vague way to think they are doing. Why could this not occur on a global scale, as well? The recent history of former Yugoslavia, where ethnic nationalism wrought such terrible havoc in recent years, is often cited as decisively proving the case for hopelessness. But even there a multiethnic federation functioned reasonably well for several decades until a complicated combination of factors—one which I, as an individual who had a certain familiarity with the situation despite my outsider status, refuse to see as having been inevitable—unleashed the worst elements in that society. In other words, it seems clear to me that it is quite possible in principle to preserve and strengthen particular civil societies, including especially their cultural aspects, without necessarily fanning the flames of particularistic nationalist patriotisms.

In fact there is a deep discontent and, yes, resentment, among so-called "ordinary people" in many parts of the world, with the superficiality and reductionism of human values that are characteristic of consumerist culture. Although sometimes assuming grotesque forms, such as religious fundamentalisms, strenuous efforts to respect and cultivate the realm of the spirit—art, literature, and other aspects of what has more traditionally been meant by "culture"—nevertheless continue and are being abetted in many ways by the new information technologies even as the latter are also being harnessed in the service of super-consumerism. It is this sense of respect that the Coca-Colization of The Hermitage and of the Taj Mahal has deeply violated or would violate. And in fact just such a perception of violation is still the reaction—a healthy one, as I see it—that most people have to my visual image of the former.

Militating against these healthy countercurrents is, precisely, the glorification of particularistic patriotism, especially patriotism directed toward the principal nation-state base of the global hegemon, the United States. In this respect, obviously, I think that Rorty is profoundly misguided, as he promulgates a mitigated and intellectual version of the xenophobia that has been experiencing something of a revival here of late. It is, of course, always a delicate matter to oppose an attitude of glorying in American-based consumerist cultural hegemony while at the same time not simply decrying the achievements of genuine American culture, such as the pragmatist tradition in American philosophy with which Rorty has come to identify himself. But he has deliberately refused to maintain the needed balance.[18] Why, for example, when referring to William James's faith in American democracy, did Rorty not feel it important to mention James' strong opposition to the American aggression against Spain, which was the equivalent in his day of the Vietnam War that Rorty sees as the great turning-point in recent history? One can only surmise that Rorty feared it would weaken somewhat his predominantly chauvinist claims. It seems to me, on the contrary, that contemporary American thinkers, even as they share jet airplanes flying to "pleasant places" with their globalizing entrepreneurial counterparts, have an especially strong moral responsibility to criticize such claims, in the interest of a diverse and robust, *genuinely* cosmopolitan future. Why not make it a matter of *our* faith that such a future, despite the present horrors of potential nuclear and other ecological disasters on the one hand and of an imminent totally dominant, one-dimensional consumerist culture on the other, is possible? Why not?

William L. McBride, Department of Philosophy, Purdue University, West Lafayette, IN 47907; wmcbride@purdue.edu

NOTES

1. W. McBride, "Coca-Culture and Other Cultures: Against Hegemony," *Labyrinth of Culture*, ed. L. Moreva (Saint Petersburg: Centre "Eidos," 1997), 154–68.

2. "Marx i Coca-Cola prkose i provociraju," *Slobodna Dalmacija* (December 12, 1992).

3. Ironically enough, given the standard Western stereotypes about Indian passiveness and non-aggressivity, the recent events of Indian nuclear bomb tests and ensuing Western sanctions may well have slowed this evolution. As if to reinforce this projection, a news report from Delhi shortly after those events related a decision made at the behest of the student organization at the university in that capital city to ban campus sales of both Pepsi-Cola and Coca-Cola.

4. McBride, *The Philosophy of Marx* (London: Hutchinson, 1977), 116–26.

5. The allusion is to Aleksandr Zinoviev's satirical work about the Soviet Union, *The Radiant Future* (London: Bodley Head, 1981).

6. K. Marx, *Capital*, Vol. II, chap. XX, sec. 4 (Moscow: Foreign Languages Publishing House, 1957), 403.

7. J. Rawls, *A Theory of Justice* (Cambridge, Mass.: Harvard University Press, 1971), 447.

8. Ibid., section 42, 265–74.

9. W. McBride, "Culture and Justice and Cultural Injustices," *Actes du XVIIe Congres mondial de philosophie*, Vol. II: *Philosophie et Culture*, ed. V. Cauchy (Montréal: Éditions Montmorency, 1988), 208–212.

10. O. Schutte, *Proceedings and Addresses of the American Philosophical Association* 59:5 (1986): 747–59.

11. This is reported and discussed in E. Dussel, *The Underside of Modernity: Apel, Ricoeur, Rorty, Taylor, and the Philosophy of Liberation*, ed. and trans. E. Mendieta (Atlantic Highlands: Humanities Press, 1996), 116.

12. R. Rorty, *Achieving Our Country: Leftist Thought in Twentieth-Century America* (Cambridge, Mass.: Harvard University Press, 1998), 91.

13. Ibid., 99.

14. Ibid., 85.

15. K. A. Appiah, "Cosmopolitan Patriots," *Critical Inquiry* 23:3 (Spring 1996): 617–39.

16. J. D. Hill, "Creating the Self: Toward a Cosmopolitan Identity" (Ph.D. diss., Purdue University, 1998), 157; idem, *Becoming a Cosmolpolitan: What it Means To Be a Human Being in the New Millennium* (Lanham: Rowman and Littlefield, 2000).

17. W. McBride, "Clarifying 'Civil Society' and Creating Space for Civil Societies: From the Struggle against Nation-State Despotisms to the Critique of Despotic Transnationalisms," *Resurrecting the Phoenix: Proceedings from the International Congress on Civil Society in South East Europe: Philosophical and Ethical Perspectives*, ed. Durst and Gungov (Sofia: EOS Publishing House, 1998).

18. One person who, also strongly influenced by the tradition of pragmatism, always *has*, in my experience, maintained the requisite balance is Lewis Hahn. I recall his frequent, always very judicious, remarks to Russian and Hungarian colleagues on the trip mentioned at the outset of this paper, as well the superbly diplomatic tenor of his discussion of the nature and purposes of the Library of Living Philosophers during a panel discussion that he organized on the topic of global philosophy, and on which he accorded me the honor of participating along with Vladislav Lektorsky and Paul Ricoeur, at the August 1993 World Congress of Philosophy in Moscow.

JUSTICE AND TOLERATION: A WESTERN PERSPECTIVE ON PHILOSOPHY AND SOCIAL JUSTICE

Jonathan L. Gorman

Are there independent standards of justice by which we are to measure our activities, or is justice itself to be understood in relativistic terms that vary with locality or historical period? I wish to examine briefly how far two inconsistent positions can both be accepted. I suggest that perhaps our ordinary understanding of reality itself—and in particular political reality—is essentially the outcome of a time of contest, and that there are areas of political reality where matters may be best seen as still being contested. I thus question the need for a single internally consistent point of view, as if it alone were *the* answer to any particular political problem, and propose that a shared belief that reality is inconsistent may be a viable solution. Using the political scenario of Northern Ireland, I argue that justice requires the deliberate and institutionalised toleration of inconsistent views of the world.

It is almost thirty years since the beginning of the latest—and I hope we will be able before long to say with some confidence the last—round of "Troubles" in Northern Ireland. The nature and grounds of this period of violence and misery have been a particular test for Western conceptions of democracy and justice. While justice has commonly been thought to involve or require a mutually supporting respect for both democratic majorities and human rights, in Northern Ireland these familiar foundational concepts have been contested throughout. In this, the Province reflects contests in academic political philosophy. It is also almost thirty years since political philosophy became once again philosophically influential among analytical philosophers with the publication of John Rawls's *A Theory of Justice*.[1] Are there independent standards of justice by which we are to measure our activities, as he claims to find? Or is justice itself to be understood in relativistic terms, varying with locality or historical period?

What is the right answer here? The many difficulties suggest that Bryce Gallie may have been right in understanding justice, in part, as what he called an "essentially contested concept."[2] Some of the conceptual conflicts that concern justice are due to ambiguity. It is characteristic of ambiguity that, once it is pointed out, conceptual conflict based on it comes to an end. By contrast, certain conflictual discourses do not come to an end once their variety of meaning has been pointed out. As Gallie puts it, *essentially* contested concepts are those "the proper use of which inevitably involves endless disputes about their proper uses."[3] "To use an essentially contested concept means to use it against other uses and to recognize that one's own use of it has to be maintained against these other uses."[4] While it is not one of Gallie's examples, consider whether the word "Ireland" refers to a place geographically or politically identified. It is not enough to point out the ambiguity in the reference of the name "Ireland." Conflict does not end when that simple fact is pointed out. "Ireland" is an essentially contested concept.[5]

Gallie's notion was widely appreciated by political scientists. It was less appreciated by analytical philosophers. It may be a helpful portmanteau term, but it seems to dissolve into other familiar ideas when examined. Gallie analysed an essentially contested concept as having a number of elements: as "appraisive," as "internally complex," as "permitting a number of possible rival descriptions of its total worth," and as being recognized as contested. None of this makes the idea of an "essentially contested concept" into an independently clear notion, and it seemed to add little to the philosopher's familiar understanding of the pragmatic force of moral terms. While Gallie tried to show that there was some rationality in a given individual's continued use or change of use of an essentially contested concept,[6] such "rationality" was understood by him in terms of the explanatory intelligibility or "followability" of the individual's doing so, and had no apparent connection with the deeper issues of whether moral terms can be truly applied or reasoned with in logical ways. In particular, it provided no understanding of how far contestants in a discourse could justifiably see themselves as expressing something *true*.

Jack Higgins, the author of many adventure thrillers about the undercover military world in Northern Ireland, regularly quotes at the beginning of his novels some lines from Justice Oliver Wendell Holmes, that great son of Boston: "Between two groups of men that want to make inconsistent kinds of worlds I see no remedy except force . . . . It seems to me that every society rests on the death of men."[7] Ireland, north and south, has long rested on the death of men, but our present understanding requires a way of living with inconsistent kinds of worlds without force. What we have, sociologically, is an internally complex ongoing conflict in which rival positions are used against each other, each recognizing that one position has to be maintained against others. In various ways the hopes of the rival positions are recognized as flatly inconsistent.

I wish to examine briefly here how far two inconsistent positions can both be accepted. Perhaps reality itself—and in particular political reality—is an essentially contested concept. However, it will not do to think only in terms of vague appraisal, and it is necessary to understand how far the world can really be inconsistent.

Many conflicting histories have been written purporting to express the political reality of Ireland. The truth about this reality is something that each history may be taken as having tried to present. Where two histories conflict both commonsense and simple logic tell us that not both conflicting histories can be true. The term "conflicting" may indeed be analytically taken to mean "incompatible" or "cannot both be true." Conflict between different political histories will then imply a failure to represent political reality correctly on the part of one or more of them, and also imply that some means of deciding correctly between the different historical points of view has to be found. So when we eventually hit upon historical truth, if we have not done so already, existing conflicting histories are superseded. A single comprehensive historical point of view comes to overtake the unsuccessful conflicting points of view of the past. This may seem just as it should be. It would be a mark of final historical truth that conflicts are resolved in the one true history. That would be our proper goal, even if we have not yet achieved it. The existence of many conflicting historical stories is then seen as a mark of failure and not success in representing reality.

Contrast this with the position of Sir Isaiah Berlin. Berlin makes clear that the attitudes of people to each other differ profoundly:

> The world of a man who believes that God created him for a specific purpose, that he has an immortal soul, that there is an afterlife in which his sins will be visited upon him, is radically different from the world of a man who believes in none of these things; and the reasons for action, the moral codes, the political beliefs, the tastes, the personal relationships of the former will deeply and systematically differ from those of the latter.[8]

However, these beliefs are not just theological or moral but include *factual* beliefs: "The facts," Berlin says, "are not at all identical for all men at all times,"[9] for they are classified and arranged against the background of their general conception of the world. Berlin'sworld is in part a *factual* pluralism.

Given factual pluralism, when we allow that there are many conflicting histories, we are not referring merely to conflicts between different accounts about a single fixed historical reality. We are in some way referring to the historical reality itself. Historical reality is in some way inherently and essentially inconsistent. That being so, any attempt to formulate historical understanding into a single consistent historical point of view is a move away from understanding the nature of history and not a move towards it.

The power of Berlin's *moral* pluralism is familiar to many of us. He was one of the great opponents of totalitarianism. But his somewhat shallowly expressed *factual* pluralism is, at best, heroic. One might object that the consistent unity of truth makes factual pluralism impossible. This objection to factual pluralism presupposes our ordinary commonsense belief in a determinate—that is, a fixed and logically consistent—reality. Given this, the factual pluralist idea that reality might be truly represented by two incompatible descriptions may well seem unintelligible. It cannot be correct, it might be argued, since "incompatible" means "cannot both be true," so two incompatible descriptions cannot both truly represent reality. The analysis of pluralism is therefore itself inconsistent.

Commonsense is typically "realist." "Realism" supposes that reality is "out there" beyond us, and exists as some fixed or unchanging consistent conflict-free entity which is independent of us and of the beliefs we have about it. Yet we know that we cannot unreflectively rely on realism. Most Western philosophers, even if they are not empiricists, commonly adopt the knowledge-based agenda set by empiricism, and the view that reality is as we experience it to be is a widely understood one. Within empiricism, the atomistic approach of Hume has yielded much ground to the pragmatic holism of Quine. In contrast with Hume's position, on Quine's approach we may hold that our beliefs look for their warrant, not to particular experiences, but to experience as a whole.

Experience alone then warrants no particular beliefs as certain. There is room for conscious and deliberate decision regarding which statements we propose to hold true and which we propose to discard as false. It is open to us to amend our knowledge claims as we find pragmatically convenient, and there are, in principle, many ways of effecting any required change. As Isaiah Berlin put it, "Any one proposition or set of propositions can be shaken in terms of those that remain fixed; and then these latter in their turn; but not all simultaneously."[10] As Quine perhaps more famously put it, "Any statement can be held true come what may, if we make drastic enough adjustments elsewhere in the system."[11] It should be understood that such decision to believe is a possibility *in principle*. We cannot choose between alternatives that are not available to us, and most of our ordinary beliefs face no rivals. Most of our ordinary beliefs, and thus what we suppose the world to be, are thereby fixed and in practice unrevisable. But not all.

For the sake of the argument, I shall assume this kind of pragmatism. Let us also suppose, for a moment, the first-person singular point of view as a foundation for this holistic epistemology. On this view, the world is what I count it to be. If the world is a function of *my* actual beliefs, then it is also in part a function of *my* actual judgements of inconsistency, and I cannot believe things which I judge to be inconsistent, because inconsistency expresses what I count myself as able to believe. Inconsistency is understood in the following way: when I judge that one thought is "inconsistent" with another I thereby believe that they cannot both be "true." When I believe something I believe it to be true. A belief is "true" when it corresponds to or expresses what I count as reality. I thereby hold that two thoughts are inconsistent in so far as I believe that they cannot both express "reality."

"True" and "reality" in this context are superficial words. The ground of my judgement of inconsistency is really my judgement about what I can believe. When I judge that one thought is inconsistent with another, I judge that I cannot believe both. Each thought is connected to my perceived range of practically possible actions in what I take the world to be in such a way that I judge that I cannot at the same time act or plan my life on the basis of both thoughts. I would typically make that judgement on the basis of the relationship I would perceive between each of those beliefs and some proposed course of action of mine, an action characterized intentionally from my own internal point of view. As Peter Lipton put it, "beliefs are guides to action that help us to get what we want and avoid trouble."[12] I cannot, in an everyday sense, do two things at once. Unsurprisingly the foundation of truth here is *pragmatic*. So, assuming the first-person singular position, "reality" is what I seriously believe it to be. A thought is "true" if and only if I believe it. When I judge that one thought is "inconsistent" with another I thereby believe that they cannot both express "reality." I thereby believe that they cannot both be "true." It is this last claim that is commonly understood to express the nature of inconsistency. Thus reality, from the first-person singular point of view, is not inconsistent.

Let me now deny the assumption of the first-person singular point of view. Reality is now understood as expressed by "our" beliefs, where the reference of "our" is comparatively clear. We may now ask, how far can *we* believe inconsistent things? It is clear, since consistency within a point of view is perceived consistency within that point of view, it is not possible for those holding that point of view to believe those things that they perceive to be inconsistent. If we all hold the same beliefs then in effect "we" is merely "I" writ large, and we get the same result as achieved on the first-person singular point of view. However, "we" cannot be treated in this way, since it is plain that "we" includes at least both you and me, and we may each count reality in different and inconsistent ways. That you and I in this way may believe inconsistent things is completely intelligible. That people sometimes believe inconsistent things is, on one interpretation, trivial, for in most cases, when I ascribe to another person a belief inconsistent with one of my own, I will not take their belief seriously. Sometimes, however, I may have to do so. It is intelligible for me to decide not to reject the inconsistent belief of another person, and decide that reality is such that a decision between them and me need not be made. Realism forces a decision here; anti-realism does not. The limits of choice in this context are what expresses the main distinction between realism and anti-realism.

Once the first-person singular position is denied, the links between inconsistency, belief, truth, and reality as perceived from that point of view— or any single point of view—are broken. Reality is not just what I seriously count it or believe it to be, but also what other people seriously believe it to be. It is not true that a thought is "true" if and only if I believe it. Just because I cannot believe two thoughts p and q, thereby judging them inconsistent, does not imply that they cannot be believed by others, at least in the sense of one person believing p and another person believing q. Moreover, I cannot refuse to ascribe belief in both p and q to another single person merely because I cannot empathize with that mind-set, for my own criteria for the ascription of belief to others do not require such empathy. Once the first-person singular position is denied, then *inconsistency*, understood in terms of my judgements about what I can believe, may remain under my control, but *truth* and *reality* do not. Each of us individually may count reality as being in part what is expressed by the beliefs of other people, even though the beliefs in question may be inconsistent with the beliefs we ourselves have. We may choose to do so in so far as we believe that we share the same world with other people. This makes the inconsistency of reality a perfectly intelligible position, although it should be understood that this is not in itself a claim that reality is inconsistent. One shares reality with other people, and reality is a function of what we all believe when we know that we share it with other people.

The relationships between social decisions and individual decisions are as rationally and practically problematic in the case of decisions to believe as they are in democratic theory. Moreover, it is contingently possible for *authority* and *privilege* to exist in the determination of what counts as reality, and we see such things in, for example, the decisions of juries in courts of law, or in the funding of scientific research. Sharing the world requires *co-ordination* of beliefs about what that world is, if the shared world is what *we* count it to be. But note, in particular, the crucial point here. Does sharing the world, and so co-ordination of beliefs about the world, require consistency? If you believe that *p*, and I believe that *not p*, can this be amalgamated into a single belief that we share? Can there, more briefly, be *agreement* about how to count reality when we have such beliefs? Reality is what *we* count it to be. Does the individually perceived inconsistency between *p* and *not p* preclude social agreement that reality is such that both *p* and *not p*? Given that reality is a function of actual human choice, understood holistically, are we forced to count reality as consistent?

What counts as the world is the solution to a co-ordination problem. I cannot count the world as inconsistent, but "we" can. That being so, it is perfectly intelligible that "reality" might be an essentially contested concept. Essentially contested concepts are those the proper use of which inevitably involves endless disputes about their proper use, including the maintenance of one's own use against other uses. There is little doubt that our ordinary proper understanding of reality is such that endless disputes are not *inevitably* involved. Yet it is possible to regard our ordinary understanding of reality as itself the outcome of a time of contest, and there are areas of reality—particularly political reality—where matters may be best seen as still in that period of contest. What can bring such a contest to an end? Victory for one side is one answer. Compromise is another. Both of these presuppose the need for a single internally consistent point of view, as if it alone were *the* answer. But why insist on this totalitarian universality of the requirement for a single consistent point of view? A shared belief that reality is inconsistent will also end the contest, embodying as it does the explicit toleration of inconsistent points of view.

The serious beliefs we have established are the solution to a co-ordination problem. The main issue is, under what conditions is the best solution to a co-ordination problem the adoption of inconsistent beliefs about reality? In Northern Ireland our new political reality,[13] out of justice to all sides, involves an attempt to create institutions which are such that no answer is *the* correct answer. Justice requires the deliberate and institutionalised toleration of inconsistent views of the world, a world that just is what those views inconsistently count it to be.

In Northern Ireland we have sought to create a political world in which people can justifiably believe inconsistent things about their identity, their citizenship, and the grounds and object of their allegiance. It is a world in which people can justifiably believe inconsistent things about the constitutional authority of the laws and powers that frame the rights and obligations which govern their lives. There is an increasing sense that it is an inconsistent reality that we can rely upon.

Jonathan L. Gorman, School of Philosophical Studies, The Queen's University of Belfast, Belfast, BT7 1NN, Northern Ireland; jgorman@clio.arts.qub.ac.uk

Notes

1. John Rawls, *A Theory of Justice* (Oxford: Oxford University Press, 1972).

2. W. B. Gallie, *Philosophy and the Historical Understanding* (London: Chatto and Windus, 1964), 182. The relevant chapter derives from work first published in the late 1940s and the early 1950s. Bryce Gallie was Professor of Logic and Metaphysics at the Queen's University of Belfast. He died in August 1998.

3. Ibid., 158.

4. Ibid., 161.

5. I do not mean to imply that "geographical identification" and "political identification" are the only grounds of conflict. "Ireland" is much more complicated than that.

6. Ibid., 184.

7. Various, for example, Jack Higgins, *The Savage Day* (Harmondsworth: Penguin, 1972); see also Oliver Wendall Holmes, *Justice Holmes to Doctor Wu: An Intimate Correspondence, 1921–1932*, ed. John Wu (New York: Central Book Company, 1947).

8. Isaiah Berlin, "The Purpose of Philosophy," *Concepts and Categories: Philosophical Essays* (Oxford: Oxford University Press, 1980), 8.

9. Ibid.

10. Isaiah Berlin, "The Concept of Scientific History," *Concepts and Categories*, op. cit., 115.

11. W. V. Quine, "Two Dogmas of Empiricism," *From a Logical Point of View*, 2nd ed. (New York: Harper and Row, 1961), 43.

12. Peter Lipton, *Inference to the Best Explanation* (London and New York: Routledge, 1991), 23.

13. Deriving from the so-called "Good Friday Agreement."

Rhetoric and the Rule of Law

Neil MacCormick

The thesis that propositions of law are intrinsically arguable is opposed by the antithesis that the Rule of Law is valued for the sake of legal certainty. The synthesis considers the insights of theories of rhetoric and proceduralist theories of practical reason, then locates the problem of indeterminacy of law in the context of the challengeable character of governmental action under free governments. This is not incompatible with, but required by the Rule of Law, which is misstated as securing legal certainty. Defeasible certainty is the most that is desirable or achievable.

I. Thesis: The Arguable Character of Law

Law is an argumentative discipline. Whatever question or problem one thinks about, if we pose it as a legal question or problem we seek a solution or answer in terms of a proposition that seems sound or at least arguable, though preferably conclusive, as a matter of law. To check whether it is sound or genuinely arguable, or perhaps even conclusive, we think through the arguments that could be made for the proposed answer or solution. We can test such arguments by constructing all the counter-arguments we can think of. If *this* said on one side of the argument, *that* will be said on other side. By thinking out what seems to be the strongest argument or strongest arguments on that side, we test the strength of the arguments on this side. By figuring out the counter-case they have to meet and, if possible, defeat, lawyers get their arguments into the best shape possible.

This is not an exact science, for it is not a science at all but a practical skill, a practical art. Yet it very much depends upon knowledge and learning (law is not inaccurately called a "learned profession"). Legal arguments are always in some way arguments about the law, or arguments about matters of fact, of evidence, or of opinion, as these have a bearing upon the law or as the law has a bearing on them. To know—and indeed, to be intimately familiar with—a great body of legal learning is essential both to the making and also to the evaluating of high quality arguments in law. So legal science, the structured and ordered study of legal doctrine, is one essential underpinning of law as praxis. Many persons of deep learning evince little flair for forensic argumentation; some persons of considerable flair and skill lack the application fully to master the law. It is the combination that is required.

A process of evaluating the relative strength of competing arguments is bound to be a matter of more-or-less, a matter of opinion, calling for judgment. If arguments often seem close-matched how can we tell for certain which is the stronger? Probably the answer is that we cannot say with certainty, not as we can in demonstrative arguments,[1] where acceptance of premises as axiomatic or as contingently true allows us to derive from them a conclusion which cannot be doubted so long as its premises stand. In law, subjective conviction is possible on occasion, where for you or for me a certain body of arguments points firmly to a certain conclusion, and all the counter-arguments that have been put to us or that we can think of seem fatally weak by comparison. And this can be a shared or inter-subjective certainty, when a community of experts[2] shares such a view, to the point even of treating it as practically axiomatic. But such a shared conviction, such a shared attitude of being certain about something, is not what is meant by certainty in the other sense: that which is certainly true, whether anyone actually believes it or not.

All this is relatively commonplace among those who have any interest in law, whether as a subject of study or as a practical profession. It is the kind of common opinion which leads into related positions such as: that the law is not logical; that logic contributes nothing to legal argument; that law has nothing to do with truth, only with what can be proved according to the law's processes and standards of proof applied to whatever evidence the law characterizes as relevant and admissible. Whether such derived positions really are necessary corollaries of our commonplace starting point is far from obvious, and will be disputed in this work. But the starting point itself will stand as one key element in what must be grasped by one who would understand the nature and character of law as practical activity.

II. ANTITHESIS: THE RULE OF LAW

This, then, we take as an opening thesis about law: so far as law is that which underlies legal claims or accusations and legal defenses, law is something

arguable, sometimes, but not always, conclusively, always at least persuasively. To this an antithesis must be posed at once, which also belongs to
the merely commonplace: where law is faithfully observed, the Rule of Law
obtains; and societies that live under the Rule of Law enjoy great benefits
by comparison with those that do not. The Rule of Law is a possible condition to be achieved under human governments. Among the values that it
can secure, none is more important than legal certainty, except perhaps its
stable-mate, security of legal expectations and safety of the citizen from
arbitrary interference by governments and their agents.[3]

Where the Rule of Law is observed, people can have reasonable certainty in advance concerning the miles and standards by which their
conduct will be judged, and the requirements they must satisfy to give
legal validity to their transactions. They can then have reasonable security in their expectations of the conduct of others, and in particular of
those holding official positions under law. They can challenge governmental actions that affect their interest by demanding a clear legal
warrant for official action, or nullification of unwarrantable acts through
review by an independent judiciary. This is possible, it is often said, provided there is a legal system composed principally of quite clearly
enunciated rules that normally operate only in a prospective manner, that
are expressed in terms of general categories, not particular, indexical com-
mands to individuals or small groups singled out for special attention. The
rules should set realistically achievable requirements for conduct, and
should form overall some coherent pattern, not a chaos of arbitrarily conflicting demands.[4]

Many people, and certainly I for one, find attractive both thesis and
antithesis as stated above. I do believe in the argumentative quality of law,
and find it admirable in an open society. We should look at every side of
every important question, not come down at once on the side of prejudice
or apparent certainty. We must listen to every argument, and celebrate, not
deplore, the arguable quality that seems built in to law. But I also believe in
the Rule of Law, and think that our life as humans in community with
others is greatly enriched by it. Without it, there is no prospect of realizing
the dignity of human beings as independent though interdependent participants in public and private activities in a society. Dignity of that sort and
independence-in-interdependence are, to my way of thinking, fundamental moral and human values.

How is it possible to believe in both? Can this be anything other than
wishful believing? These are the questions that lie before us. Can we reconcile the commonplace of the 'Arguable Character of Law' with the
ideology of the 'Rule of Law'?

III. TOWARD SYNTHESIS

A. Rhetorical Theories

The strategy of trying to reconcile thesis and antithesis that I shall adopt here depends on acknowledging a fundamental constraint on the process of legal argumentation. This lies in the so-called "special case thesis" suggested by Robert Alexy.[5] That is to say, legal argumentation must be acknowledged to be one special case of general practical reasoning, and must thus conform to conditions of rationality and reasonableness that apply to all sorts of practical reasoning. This implies at least that there may not be assertions without reasons—whatever is asserted may be challenged, and, upon challenge, a reason must be offered for whatever is asserted, whether the assertion is of some normative claim or a claim about some state of affairs, some "matter of fact."

Thus it is a restricted version of the Arguable Character of Law that will be reviewed and defended here. The argument will be confined to considering what is rationally arguable. To say this is to distinguish between the use of words as mere weapons of intellectual coercion or deceit, and their use as instruments of reasonable persuasion, where coercion appears only in the sense of the compelling force of an argument. It is the latter—argument as rational justification—that will be reviewed here. And the issue will be whether there can be a "Rule of Law," if "law" is a matter of what is arguable in this sense. It will remain an open empirical question whether or how far actual attorneys and judges in any particular state confine their use of argumentation to the domain of the practically reasonable.

Notwithstanding the restriction to what is rationally arguable, the very idea of law as arguable leads us at once to consider the rhetorical character of legal argumentation. Wherever there is a process of public argumentation, there is rhetoric. The modern rediscovery of rhetoric as a discipline owes much to reflection on legal reasoning. Theodor Viehweg, drawing on Aristotle, has drawn attention to the significance of *topoi*, or 'commonplaces' in rhetorical arguments.[6] An argument for a particular rule or proposition can be supported by reference to some accepted *topos*, and arguments progress by working towards, or from, such commonplace positions. In law, there are maxims and long-standing principles and presumptions, such as "a person is to be presumed innocent until proven guilty," "no one can give a better right than he has himself," or "a later law derogates from an earlier one," and so forth. Likewise, there are well-established argument forms such as *argumentum a fortiori, argumentum a maiori ad minus, argumentum per analogiam*, and the like. An argument in such a recognized form starting from or working toward a recognized *topos* is well-calculated to be persuasive in its given context.

In a not dissimilar way, Duncan Kennedy suggests that common law arguments typically proceed through the adduction of standard 'argument bites' of a kind that frequently can be found in matching pairs. This means that a persuasive legal argument will be an aggregation of argument bites relativized to the fact-situation in question. But a counter-argument can be constructed using a similarly contextualized set of counter-arguments in the form of matching 'bites'.[7] James Palmer has shown that this insight may be exploited in harnessing information technology and artificial intelligence to assist in processes of legal reasoning. Intelligent knowledge-based systems can be envisaged that would generate a battery of relevant argument bites for adduction in relation to problems in given domains of law. So far, at least, there is no suggestion that the evaluation of competing arguments constructed in this way could or should be delegated to computers. Rather, the hope would be to ensure that lawyers and judges would come to the task of constructing their final arguments to lay before a court, or to deploy in justification of a decision, with a thoroughly worked-over checklist of available arguments based on prior practice (precedent) and, where appropriate, statute-law.[8]

In relation to all this, one should bear in mind Josef Esser's teachings concerning the importance of *Vorverständisse* 'pre-understandings'. These are the taken-for-granted assumptions that enter into any judgment of what is acceptable in the setting of legal argumentation, and into the preference of one method of arguing over another in a particular case. Once premises and mode of argument are settled, it is relatively easy to produce an argument that satisfactorily justifies the conclusion reached. But the problem then becomes one about the reasonable choice of premises and method, so there must be inquiry into pre-understandings.[9] Aulis Aarnio has suggested that in the end these may simply have to be assessed as the 'form of life' that they constitute.[10]

La Nouvelle Rhétorique of Chaim Perelman emphasizes that arguments are necessarily addressed to an audience, and that persuasiveness is audience-relative. This is specially obvious in legal practice, where trained advocates put cases before courts as persuasively as possible, and judges decide after weighing their rival arguments on points of law. In systems where juries are responsible for the determination of facts, or of legal conclusions reached through their own findings of fact in the light of law as explained by the presiding judge, the rhetorical character of forensic argumentation is yet more salient. But from the point of view of practical rationality, the immediate and concrete persuasiveness of an argument is not necessarily the same as its soundness. The issue for a theory of reasoning-as-justification is not what argument actually persuades a particular judge or jury, but what ought to convince any rational decision-maker. In this connection, Perelman postulates a 'universal audience' as providing the ultimate test: whatever argument would convince the audience of all intelligent and concerned persons, evaluating issues in a disinterested way, is a sound one.[11]

More or less contemporary with Perelman's work on rhetoric was Stephen Toulmin's *The Uses of Argument.* This offered a way of narrowing the apparent gap between the supposedly timeless pure rationality of formal logic and the context-bound character of rhetorical argumentation and persuasion. Toulmin proposed a reinterpretation of traditional logic as a sort of normative ordering of thought processes and public presentations of reasons, a process that regulates moves in the play of arguments. Rather as a ticket entitles one to undertake a certain journey by train or plane, appropriate forms of argument supply warrants that entitle one to move from premises to conclusions. The validity of the move depends on the soundness to its context of the warrant produced.[12]

The rhetorical turn in analysis of practical reasoning is unserviceable to the present purpose if (or in so far as) it reduces the rational acceptability of an argument to its actual persuasiveness. One of the things that gets rhetoric a bad name is the notorious possibility that a good speaker can win an audience round with a bad case. To counter this with appeals either to the universal audience or to some supposed consensus of reasonable contemporaries seems question-begging, since in fact we work out what would persuade the universal audience by reference to what is sound, not vice versa, and we have no guarantee that a contemporary consensus, where it exists, is correct. Yet again, the 'critical' approaches to legal thought urge that the claim to an objective soundness of legal reasons is the grandest rhetorical turn of all.

This point of the 'Critics' has in part been noted already. Often a set of persuasive reasons or 'argument bites' can be built up to give wrong support for one solution to a legal problem or controversy. But in any actually or imaginably controversial situation we can find a matching counter-reason or counter-bite for each of them. So the problem is not to uphold a soundly arguable case at the expense of a manifestly weaker case. Rather, it is all too often a matter of choosing between two strongly arguable and strongly argued cases, in a dialectical situation in which each argument made by either party is firmly countered by a good argument proposed by the other. Perhaps, therefore, it is only by reference to considerations of ideology extraneous to law that one can come to a justified decision at all and the ultimately justifying ground is ideology, not law.[13] Hans Kelsen's brief discussion of interpretation in *The Pure Theory of Law* points in the same direction as this.[14]

B. Proceduralist Theories

A procedural approach to practical reasoning may, however, provide a partial solution to the problems posed concerning rhetoric. There are various 'proceduralist' approaches, but they have in common a concern with understanding the constraints on practical reasoning that have to be acknowledged if it is to yield rationally acceptable conclusions in an interpersonal context. So a starting point is indeed the rhetoricians' emphasis on the interpersonal context of argumentation. In its light, the concept of universality has two uses. First, it demands universalizability of reasons— for the present instance of circumstances C to count as a reason now for reaching decision D, and acting on D, it would have to be acceptable to hold a decision of type D appropriate whenever an instance of C occurs. Second, it suggests a way of testing whether it is warranted to assert that D is appropriate whenever C obtains. This universalized reason, by its terms, will be applicable to all instances of C, not just the single instance now under attention. The interests, feelings, and opinions of all human beings are therefore potentially at stake, and one can ask whether the formula '*Whenever C, then D*' could be rejected by anyone who is willing for everyone to have the same opportunity to challenge practical principles of decsion.[15]

As Jürgen Habermas and followers like Robert Alexy argue, it may be possible to test practical propositions by reference, at least in principle, to the interests, feelings, and views of the totality of persons in any way affected by or concerned with them. Habermas's move is to propose a test by reference to dialogue in an 'ideal speech situation', envisaged as one in which all forms of coercion or interpersonal power or domination are put aside for the purposes of conducting (or imagining the conduct of) interpersonal discourse. Analysis of the necessary constraints on such a discourse yields a procedural approach to testing the kinds of principles that rational discourse-partners could accept, acknowledging the types of desires and interests they actually have.[16] Important in this is the idea that accepted principles or commonplaces (*topoi*) should be subject to challenge, but are considered acceptable until successfully challenged, e.g., on the ground that they cannot pass the test of universalizability or on the ground that they owe their origins to past or present social power-relations that would themselves have been rejected in the ideal speech situation.[17] A similar, but simpler and thus more persuasive, idea is that of T. M. Scanlon,[18] who suggests that an action is wrong if any principle that permitted it would be one that, for that reason, someone could reasonably reject even if that person were moved to find principles for the general regulation of behavior that others, similarly motivated, also could not reasonably reject.[19]

It is doubtful whether any such procedural approach wholly disposes of recourse to personal feelings or subjective intuitions. For one has to interrogate the grounds that would lead one to reject a certain principle oneself and still the question has to be faced what it is 'reasonable' for anyone to reject given the feelings and pre-understandings that each person brings to the judgment seat. The procedure of procedurally testing arguments cannot be infinitely regressive. But it is surely a merit of such procedural approaches that they both postpone and narrow appeals to intuition[20] and to gut-feeling. They enable us to scrutinize claims about what is reasonable in the light of acknowledged constraints of rational discourse. Commonplace principles are still needed as starting points, but they are changeable within the argumentation.

Rationality of argumentation introduces another significant constraint. Although any particular practical dilemma or topic of concern fails to be considered on its own merits, and subjected to procedures such as we have considered so far, one must recall that the universals (*whenever C, then D*) that we work toward cannot be envisaged as once-off isolated commitments. We who decide them do so as part of an ongoing and interpersonally engaged social life in which decisions and dilemmas are recurrent in character. This has a strong bearing on what one can reasonably accept or reject in terms of the Scanlonian meta-principle or the Habermasian ideal speech situation. So one's principles and rules of decision and of conduct have to belong in a body of practical thought and commitment that is internally consistent, and characterized also by a certain overall coherence.[21] This implies at least some guidelines about priority-rankings and procedures to determine relative weights of practical reasons in order to resolve *prima facie* conflicts.

Here, it is useful to remind oneself of the starting point of the present train of reasoning, namely in a puzzle about the apparent antinomy between law as that which is arguable, and law as that which guarantees security and stability in social life within a *Rechtsstaat*. So far, we have considered in a somewhat abstract way the idea of a rhetorical engagement in the practice of the law, and how far a procedural or discourse-theoretical development of ideas from the 'new rhetoric' offer the hope of an acceptable rational framework for our argumentation in law and indeed in other practical domains.

The legal context, however, is one in which the recently mentioned idea of coherence has a particular and obvious significance.[22] In a legal argument, no one starts with a blank sheet and tries to work out a reasonable conclusion *a priori*. A solution offered must ground itself in some proposition that can be at least colorably presented as a proposition of law, and such a proposition must be shown to cohere in some way with law as already determined. Legal argument-makers and decision-makers do not approach problems of decision and justification in a vacuum, but rather in the context of a plethora of material that serves to guide and to justify decisions, and to restrict the range within which the decisions of public agencies can legitimately be made.

The material in question comprises constitutions, treaties, statutes of national parliaments, regulations and directives of supranational entities, and the multitudinous reports of decisions by judicial tribunals, recognized in some systems as 'precedents' in the sense of a 'formal source of law', and used in practically all systems of law[23] as at least a repertory of available guides to interpretation of statutes, constitutional articles, and other formally binding legal provisions. It also includes treatises and other scholarly writings on law by acknowledged legal experts.

C. Laws

It is trite to say that this mass of material is not and cannot be imagined to be self-interpreting and self-applying. In the perspective of the 'Rule of Law' ideal it has to be comprehended as the raw material of a 'legal system', organized in intelligible bodies of material relevant to particular human concerns within traditionally understood branches or domains of law, such as property, contract, family law, criminal law, administrative law.[24] In the context of states as coercive associations of human beings, governments and thus the human beings who perform governmental roles are empowered to act authoritatively towards others, and can back their assertions of authority with decisions to deploy organized coercive power. Here, the demand for rational justifiability of governmental action is an urgent one if government is not to be the mere mask of tyranny. Hence it has come to be generally understood as legitimate to demand that any governmental act be warranted by explicit provisions mandating, permitting, or authorizing decisions in specific terms (or involving some bounded discretion) only when certain clearly specified circumstances obtain. Provisions of this kind, especially when specifically enacted by some legislative process, but also when they can be derived in reasonably definite terms from other materials such as precedents, are typically called 'roes', in contradistinction to other kinds of norms, such as conventions, standards, values, or principles.[25]

A legal rule is a normative provision stated in or constructed from a recognized legal source that has the form of linking a determinate normative consequence to determinate operative facts. It is in the nature of a rule to provide that whenever a certain state of facts obtains, a given normative consequence is to follow therefrom. To put this in a standard form: '*Whenever OF then NC*'.

At the heart of the liberal idea of free government, and at the heart of the distinction between free and despotic governments is the idea that when governments act towards citizens, their action must be warrantable under a rule in this sense of the term. And this holds good also when government, usually through the agency of the judiciary, purports to regulate or pass judgment on claims and complaints and demands levied by citizen upon citizen. Here too the Rule of Law demands that there be some rule to warrant the claim of one person against another if adjudication of the claim is liable to issue an enforceable order against that other, for example, an award of compensatory or punitive damages or an injunction or interdict.

Codes and statutes of the modern period, and other like materials, represent an institutional response to the ideology[26] of the Rule of Law as a condition of liberty. The state that governs through law takes care to provide in advance the rule-texts which warrant public interventions in private lives, whether such interventions be prompted by public authorities or by private litigants. The security for individuals that is thus guaranteed consists in the fact that rule-application evidently requires the prior existence of specific facts instantiating the relevant rule's generically stated operative facts 'OF'. Thus, for example, if a statute provides a remedy for persons who suffer discrimination in their employment 'because of sex', no action to implement the normative consequence(s) that the rule provides for can be justified unless in a particular case some act of discrimination has occurred, has occurred in the context of an employment relationship, and is attributable to the sex of the person discriminated against.[27] Or if a rule provides for nullification of a driver's license and for some other penalty within a range determined at a judge's discretion when a person drives a motor vehicle while impaired by the consumption of alcohol beyond a specified proportion in her bloodstream, no penalty is legitimately exigible against a particular person except if warranted by her having been in the condition specified and having 'driven' a 'vehicle' while in that condition.[28]

If the Rule of Law is to be actually a protection against arbitrary intervention in people's lives, it seems clear that it is not in practice enough to demand that the operative facts did on some occasion actually happen or obtain. It is necessary that some specific and challengeable accusation or averment of relevant facts be made to the individual threatened with action, and that it be supported by evidence in an open proceeding in which the party charged may contest the evidence item by item and in its cumulative effect, and may offer relevant counter-evidence as she chooses. Moreover, it must also be possible to challenge the relevancy of the legal accusation or claim on the ground that, whatever be the facts, the legal materials that supposedly warrant the assertion of a rule governing the case do not warrant it at all in the alleged, or the actually proven, state of the facts.

Here we are on the familiar terrain of the relative indeterminacy of law.[29] This indeterminacy is in a curious way magnified by the very same considerations that lead to the demand for determinate law. For the dialectical or argumentative character of legal proceedings is a built-in feature of a constitutional setting in which citizens are able to challenge the allegations of fact and the assertions of law on the basis of which government agencies of their own volition or at the instance of private litigants threaten to intervene coercively in their lives or affairs. A vital part of the guarantee of liberty in the governing conception of the Rule of Law is that the opportunity to mount such a challenge on fair terms and with adequate legal assistance be afforded to every person. And yet that same governing conception calls for relatively clear and determinate law in the form of pre-announced rules.

Hence legal indeterminacy is not merely (though it is also) a result of the fact that states communicate their legal materials in natural ('official') languages, and that these are afflicted with ambiguity, vagueness, and open texture.[30] It also results from, and is in some measure magnified by, the due recognition of the 'rights of the defense' in every setting of criminal prosecution or civil litigation. Every doubt that can be raised against prosecutor or plaintiff whether concerning fact or concerning law, is a doubt that may be raised by the defense. On the other hand, wherever there seems to be a significant point of justice or of public order in issue, the plaintiff or prosecutor has reason to seek in the materials of the law some provision that will, upon some reasonably arguable interpretation, justify the civil action or criminal prosecution brought in the given case. And the defense will then again challenge what it characterizes as a strained or illegitimate reading of the law according to how courts, lawyers, and citizens have previously understood and acted upon it.

Thus emerge contests over proper interpretation of legal materials, over the proper drawing of inferences from evidence, over evaluation of conflicting pieces of evidence, over the proper characterization of facts proven or agreed, or over their relevance to the legal materials adduced.[31] These contests are not some kind of a pathological excrescence on a system that would otherwise run smoothly. They are an integral element in a legal order that is working according to the ideal of the Rule of Law, so far as that insists on the production by governments of an appropriate warrant in law for all that they do, coupled with the right of the individual to challenge the warrant produced by government.

This leads to an obvious conclusion. Although it may be possible to formulate rules in a verbally straightforward formula, '*Whenever OF then*

NC', in any contested case a challenge can be raised in one or more of these ways:

1. No instance of '*OF*' as alleged in indictment or pleadings has been proven (up to the required standard of proof) to have existed, taking account of all relevant and admissible evidence, including any evidence in rebuttal adduced by the defense. (We may call this the 'problem of proof'.)

2. What has been alleged, whether or not proved, is not properly characterized as an instance of '*OF'* in the sense proper to the law. (We may call this the 'problem of characterization', 'classification', or of 'qualification'.)

3. The case as presented depends on reading the acknowledged rule '*Whenever OF then NC'* according to a particular interpretation of '*OF*', or of '*NC'*, or both. But this is a misinterpretation, and there is, in fact, a more legally acceptable interpretation according to which the defense ought to be absolved from the accusation OT claim laid against it. (We may call this the 'problem of interpretation'.)

4. Success in the claim or prosecution depends on reading authoritative legal materials as though they generated a rule '*Whenever OF then NC'* such that the allegations of criminal guilt or civil liability are relevant given the facts alleged, or even the facts proven. But no such norm can properly be read out of the adduced materials as a reasonable concretization of them or determination from them. (We may call this the 'problem of relevancy'.)

We may now move towards a conclusion. What we see is how legal processes move through a chain of putative certainties that are at every point challengeable. No claim or accusation may be made without proper citation of the legal warrant that backs it and without giving notice of the allegations of fact in virtue of which it is asserted that the law warrants the conclusion proposed (by prosecutor or by plaintiff). This has the full logical certainty that inheres in syllogistic form.[32] There is a rule '*Whenever OF then NC'*, cited by prosecutor or plaintiff in indictment or in pleadings, and it is there also alleged that *OF* has occurred in a concrete case at a specified time in a way that materially involves the accused person or defendant. So the relevant normative consequence ought to be implemented as demanded. This is the standard legal syllogism[33] variously embodied in criminal or civil pleading and procedure.

But the conclusion is only as good as the premises, and these may be problematized. The challenge can be on proof on characterization, on interpretation, on relevancy (one, some, or all of them). But the idea of the Rule of Law that has been suggested here insists on the right of the defense to challenge and rebut the case against it. There is no security against arbitrary government unless such challenges are freely permitted and sub-jected to adjudication by officers of state separate from and distanced from those officers who run prosecutions. In private law litigation, a similar re-quirement appears in the need for visible impartiality of the judge.

After hearing evidence and argument, the court must decide. In de-ciding matters raised in the problems of characterization, or of interpretation, or of relevancy, the Court may find it necessary and proper to develop a new understanding of the law, and set a new precedent that may confirm or qualify prior understandings. At the end, the case is either dismissed as inconclusive, the defendant being absolved, or some order is made by the court and justified in the light of law as clarified through resolution of the problems posed. And then there is in effect a concluding syllogism. But it is rarely, if ever, identical with the starting syllogism. It is a new defeasible certainty that has emerged from posing problems about the old defeasible certainty and resolving them by rational argument.[34] From confronting law's arguable character, we move to restating a new putative certainty after admitting and dealing with doubts about the old.

In the upshot, it has to be recognized that the original representa-tion of the Rule of Law as antithesis to the Arguable Character of Law was a misstatement in the emphasis it gave to certainty in law. Whatever care is lavished on the source materials of law by legislators, drafters, or judges writing opinions that attempt to state a holding or *ratio* with exemplary character, the rule statements these yield as warrants for governmental action aimed at vindicating public or private right are always defeasible, and sometimes defeated under challenge by the defense. Law's certainty is then defeasible certainty. Its being so is not, after all, something that contrasts with the Arguable Character of Law, but something that shares an underlying ground with it. That ground is a conception of the rights of the defense built into the ideology of the Rule of Law in its guise as protector from arbitrary action by governments.[35]

Neil MacCormick, Faculty of Law, University of Edinburgh, Edinburgh, Scotland EH1 8YY, UK; N.MacCormick@ed.ac.uk

NOTES

1. Ronald Dworkin is a particularly forceful proponent of the well-taken point that the non-demonstrative character of legal arguments is not a bar to their being nevertheless sound arguments, in a context in which one sound argument can genuinely defeat another; see Dworkin's *Law's Empire* (London: Fontana

Books, 1986), 9–15, and cf. Stephen Guest, *Ronald Dworkin* (Edinburgh: Edinburgh University Press, 1992), 141–44.

2. Compare Aulis Aarnio, *The Rational as Reasonable: A Treatise on Legal Justification* (Dordrecht and Boston: D. Reidel, and Norwell, Mass.: Kluwer Academic, 1987), 221–25.

3. Compare Joseph Raz, "The Rule of Law and its Virtue," *The Authority of Law: Essays on Law and Morality* (Oxford: Clarendon Press, 1979), 210–29.

4. The *locus classicus* for this type of account remains Lon L. Fuller, *The Morality of Law*, rev. ed. (New Haven: Yale University Press, 1969), chap. 2.

5. See Robert Alexy, *A Theory of Legal Argumentation*, trans. Ruth Adler and Neil MacCormick (Oxford: Clarendon Press, 1989), 5–10, 212–20, 294–95; cf. Neil MacCormick, *Legal Reasoning and Legal Theory*, 2nd ed. (Oxford: Clarendon Press, 1994), 272–74 making substantially the same point. Alexy's *Theorie derjuristischen Argumetitation* was first published in 1978, almost exactly contemporaneously with *Legal Reasoning and Legal Theory,* so we each came to much the same view by independent processes of discovery.

6. See Theodor Viehweg, *Topik und Jurisprudenz*, 5th ed. (Munich: Beck, 1974); also "Some Considerations concerning Legal Reasoning," *Law, Reason and Justice: Essays in Legal Philosophy*, ed. Graham Hughes (New York: New York University Press, 1969), 266–68; here, 'topoi' is translated as 'points of view'; see also Alexy, op. cit., 21–24.

7. See Duncan Kennedy, *A Critique of Adjudication* (Cambridge, Mass.: Harvard University Press, 1997), 137–56, and note other 'CLS' authors and works cited at 393. As Kennedy fully acknowledges, the fundamental insight here goes back at least as far as the early work of Karl Llewellyn; see, e.g., Llewellyn, *Jurisprudence: Realism in Theory and Practice* (Chicago: Chicago University Press, 1962), 70f.

8. See J. Palmer, *Artificial Intelligence and Legal Merit Arguments* (Oxford: Oxford University D. Phil. Thesis, 1998), 109–28.

9. Josef Esser, *Vorverstandnis und Methodenwahl in der Rechtsfindung* (Frankfurt/Main: Suhrkamp, 1970), 3–20.

10. Aamio, op. cit., 213–18.

11. Chaim Perelman and Lucie Olbrechts-Tyteca, *La Nouvelle Rhétorique* (Paris: Presses Universitaires de France, 1958); ET, *The New Rhetoric*, trans. John Wilkinson and Purcell Weaver (Notre Dame: Notre Dame University Press, 1969), see 76–86 on the 'universal audience'.

12. Stephen E. Toulmin, *The Uses of Argument* (Cambridge: Cambridge University Press, 1958), 94–145.

13. See J. M. Balkin, "The Crystalline Structure of Legal Thought," *Rutgers Law Review* 39 (1986): 195; idem, "Nested Oppositions," *Yale Law Journal* 99 (1990): 1669; idem, "Ideological Drift and the Struggle over Meaning," *Connecticut Law*

Rev 25 (1993): 369; cf. also Kennedy, *Adjudication*, 133–38, and Peter Goodrich, *Reading the Law: A Critical Introduction to Legal Method and Techniques* (Oxford: Blackwell, 1986), 213–23.

14. See Hans Kelsen, *The Pure Theory of Law*, trans. Max Knight (Berkeley and Los Angeles: University of California Press, 1967), 251–54 on the 'political' character of interpretative decisions taken within the framework of statute law.

15. Compare Alexy, op. cit., 65–69, 146–47, 267–77, and MacCormick, op. cit., 76–86.

16. On this, see Jürgen Habermas, *The Legitimation Crisis*, trans. Thomas McCarthy (Cambridge: Polity Press, 1976), 109–12; cf. Alexy, op. cit., 11–37.

17. See Alexy, op. cit., 151–53, 204–05.

18. See Thomas M. Scanlon, "Contractualism and Utilitarianism," *Utilitarianism and Beyond*, ed. Amartya Sen and Bernard Williams (Cambridge: Cambridge University Press, 1982), 103–28; and idem, *What We Owe to Each Other* (Cambridge: Harvard University Press, 1998). Since no actual agreement or contract is involved in such reasoning, and obligations generated by or under it are not in fact contractual in character, it seems to me regrettable that this style of procedural testing of practical principles has been dubbed 'contractualist'; but its value as a mode of reasoning is unaffected by the name it bears; cf. Neil MacCormick, "Justice as Impartiality: Assenting with Anti-contractualist Reservations," *Political Studies* 44 (1996): 305–10.

19. Quoted from Thomas M. Scanlon, "Promises and Contracts," preliminary draft of a paper prepared for *Philosophy and Contract Law*, ed. P. Benson (Cambridge: Cambridge University Press, forthcoming).

20. Michael J. Detmold, *The Unity of Law and Morality* (London: Routledge and Kegan Paul, 1984), rightly stresses the element of intuition in judgment, but leaves too wide open the scope for its exercise.

21. See Aleksander Peczenik, *On Law and Reason* (Dordrecht, Boston and London: Kluwer Academic Publishers, 1989).

22. See Kennedy, op. cit., 33–34; compare also Neil MacCormick, "Coherence in Legal Reasoning," *Theorie der Normen*, ed. Werner Krawietz (Berlin: Duncker und Humblot, 1984), 37–53; idem, "Time, Narratives, and Law," *Time, Law, and Society, Archiv für Rechts und Sozial-philosophie Beiheft* 64, ed. Jes Bjarup and Mogens Blegvad (Stuttgart: F. Steiner, 1995), 111–25.

23. See D. Neil MacCormick and Robert S. Summers, *Interpreting Precedents: A Comparative Study* (Aldershot, England, and Brookfield, Mass.: Ashgate/ Dartmouth, 1997).

24. See Jerzy Wróblewski, *The Judicial Application of Law*, ed. Zenon Bankowski and Neil MacCormick (Dordrecht and Boston: Kluwer Academic, 1992).

25. For a clarification of these distinctions, see Neil MacCormick, "Norms, Institutions, and Institutional Facts," *Law and Philosophy* 17 (1998): 301 ff.

26. Of course, 'ideology' in this context is not used in its pejorative sense; cf. Wróblewski, op. cit.

27. See the *Oncale* decision, where the Supreme Court held that same-sex harassment could amount to a breach of the anti-discrimination provisions in Title VII of the Civil Rights Act 1964.

28. See *State v Blower*, Utah 1989, on the question whether a person riding a horse while drunk can be said to be in charge of a 'vehicle'. Palmer, *Artificial Intelligence and Legal Merit Arguments*, 36–38, cites a fascinating run of precedents from various jurisdictions illustrating the indeterminacy of the predicate 'drive' in the context of judicial determinations about the statutory offence committed by those who 'drive' a motor vehicle while disqualified from doing so.

29. See Steven J. Burton, *An Introduction to Law and Legal Reasoning*, 2nd ed. (Boston: Little, Brown, 1995), 27–28, 54–58, 77–85.

30. Compare H. L. A. Hart, *The Concept of Law*, ed. Penelope A. Bulloch and Joseph Raz, 2nd ed. (Oxford: Clarendon Press, 1994), chap. 7; Brian Bix, *Law, Language, and Legal Determinacy* (Oxford: Clarendon Press, 1993), 7–35; and Neil MacCormick, "On Open Texture in Law," *Controversies about Law's Ontology*, ed. Paul Amselek and Neil MacCormick (Edinburgh: Edinburgh University Press, 1991), 72–84.

31. Compare MacCormick, *Legal Reasoning*, op. cit., 65–72.

32. But for an opposed view, see Bernard S. Jackson, *Law, Fact, and Narrative Coherence* (Liverpool: Deborah Charles, 1988), 37–60; in response, see Neil MacCormick, "Notes on Narrativity and Normative Syllogism," *International Journal for the Semiotics of Law* 4:11 (1991): 163–74, "Legal Deduction, Legal Practices and Expert Systems," *International Journal for the Semiotics of Law* 5:14 (1992): 181–202, and "A Deductivist Rejoinder to a Semiotic Critique," *International Journal for the Semiotics of Law* 5:14 (1992): 215–24.

33. Compare Kennedy, *Adjudication*, op. cit., 101–04, and Burton, *Introduction*, op. cit., 43–58.

34. On defeasibility, see H. L. A. Hart, "The Ascription of Responsibility and Rights," *Proceedings of the Aristotelian Society* 49 (1948–49): 171–94; disowned by Hart in *Punishment and Responsibility* (Oxford: Clarendon Press, 1968), Preface. But see also G. P. Baker, "Defeasibility and Meaning," *Law, Morality and Society*, ed. P. M. S. Hacker and J. Raz (Oxford: Clarendon Press, 1977), 26–57. Cf. Neil MacCormick, "Law as Institutional Fact," Edinburgh University Inaugural Lecture No. 52, 1973; *Law Quarterly Review* 90 (1974): 102–29; now in Neil MacCormick and Ota Weinberger, *An Institutional Theory of Law* (Dordrecht and Boston: D. Reidel Publishing Company, 1986), chap. 2; this has now been superseded by MacCormick, "Defeasibility in Law and Logic," *Informatics and the Foundations of Legal Reasoning*, ed. Zenon Bankowski, Ian White, and Ulrike Hahn (Dordrecht: Kluwer Academic, 1995), 99–117.

35. This paper was written while I was a Visiting Professor at the School of Law of the University of Texas at Austin in the Spring Semester of 1998. I am deeply indebted to Dean M. Michael Sharlot and to faculty colleagues in Texas for their generous hospitality and the provision of an ideal environment for the production and discussion of scholarly work.

ON THE LIMITS OF LAW AT CENTURY'S END

Olúfẹ́mi Táíwò

In this paper, I examine the generally accepted idea that law has definite limits to what it can be used to achieve. Toward this end, I discuss the limits of law as suggested by the Truth Commissions and the Truth and Reconciliation Commissions (TRC), and summarize the divergences between law and the TRC. I suggest reasons why law may not serve or may underserve the purpose of healing and reconciliation in our time and conclude that the TRC is at best a reminder to us of the limits of law as a principle of social ordering.

This paper is based on a belief that I do not defend here. The belief is that however good a social order that has law as its organizing principle is, it will always be second best to one that is able to secure all that law delivers without employing the instrumentality of law. That is, however much good law embodies or ensures, there is evidence of a widespread unease in most societies with law such that if they could secure the same amount of good without law, their inhabitants would prefer it.[1] But I hasten to concede that even though many feel this way, there is also widespread skepticism about the possibility of a world without law. Although many find the idea of a world without law eminently desirable, few would concede that such a world is attainable. Yet, even among those who insist that law is indispensable, very few deny that there are real limits to what law can do and that, on occasion, law is radically insufficient for the enthronement or inauguration of a good society.

On that score, there is agreement between those who are skeptical about the necessity of law and those who are skeptical about the desirability and or attainability of a world without law. It is this generally accepted idea that law has definite limits to what it can be used to achieve that I propose to examine in this paper. That is one part of my task. The other part is traceable to the specific historical conjuncture—century's end—presaged in the title.

There are few more opportune times than now to raise questions about the limits of law. In the first place, the twentieth century has witnessed two global wars, several other wars that have evidenced incredible cruelties and unspeakable evils, genocidal movements in Cambodia and Rwanda, apartheid in South Africa, the operations of bloody regimes in different parts of the world, and the list goes on. Second, the century has witnessed some of the boldest and farthest reaching attempts at deliberate social transformation and the creation of new human beings and the subsequent disastrous failures of such experiments. Third, the century started with a revolution, the Russian Revolution, that challenged the dominance of the global capitalist system and the hegemony of its political twin, liberalism and the Rule of Law. It is ending with capitalism resurgent and liberal democracy, however many distortions afflict it in practice, triumphant. It is precisely this proclivity towards triumphalism and its attendant elevation of the law and its attributes to near sacred status on the part of their enthusiasts that provoked the inquiry undertaken here. At the present time, in the historical conjuncture of which I speak, Capitalism Resurgent has become deified and Liberalism Triumphant with the Rule of Law as its beloved offspring has become dominant. The rest of the world now bows before them in adoration and mimics them in its design of institutions and practices. It is ironic that the present tendencies towards the deification of law completely miss or misapprehend various other phenomena which, more than at any other time, serve to remind us who are mindful of it of the limits of law.

The specific phenomena I have in mind are those of *Truth Commissions* and *Truth and Reconciliation Commissions* in different parts of the world. Such commissions have been struck in the aftermath of some of the ugly realities of the century: genocide, apartheid, bloody civil wars, murderous totalitarian/authoritarian rule by military and civilian despots. It is very easy for us to assimilate these Commissions to instances of the operations of law and to nascent steps towards the entrenchment of the Rule of Law in the societies concerned. They may well be that in some or all of the cases. But that is not all that they are or may be. What tends to mislead us is that they are usually set up through the instrumentality of law and their *modus operandi* often enough mimic the operations of a properly constituted court. This is what a commentator said of the South African version:

> The Commission sometimes functions as a quasi-court: it has the judicial trappings of sworn testimony, subpoena power, investigators,

cross-examination at amnesty hearings. And, like courts, it often hears many truths about the same events. But, [and what big BUT it is!] *the Commission is not a juridical body; it cannot mete out punishment, nor can it transform truth into justice.*[2]

I shall come back to this last sentence in a moment. What I am concerned to point out at this stage is that once we get past the quasi-judicial character of the Commission, to the fact that it is empaneled to uncover truth as a precondition for reconciliation; that its main aim is to facilitate healing and not mete out punishment; to enhance forgiveness while shunning amnesia; to ensure that the future does not witness any similar excesses rather than retrospectively to punish perpetrators. I suggest that in placing truth above justice and, sometimes, in shunning altogether the justice that law promises, the constitution of Truth Commissions and the goals that they are set up to achieve are founded on a basic realization that law may not be an appropriate means or institution through which to bring about the kind of society that those who embrace the idea wish to see incorporated in their communities. It should be easy to see why this is the case.

Recall that this is the century that gave us Nuremberg as well as the International War Crimes Tribunal that sat in Paris in 1972 to examine United States' involvement in Vietnam and that saw the active involvement of Bertrand Russell as chairman. What was significant about these earlier commissions and the current ones sitting at the Hague and Arusha, dealing with Bosnia-Herzegovina and Rwanda respectively, is that they were/are set up to "mete out justice" and punish those found guilty. In all such cases, the perpetrators involved had either lost in war to those who tried them, as in Nuremberg or Rwanda, or had lost in the bar of public opinion and morality, as did the United States in Vietnam and, in the main Serbia and Croatia, in Bosnia-Herzegovina. In such countries, the triers and the tried do not have to live together or work out any *modus vivendi* for future interaction within the context or, perhaps one should say, within the confines of a single geopolitical entity and unitary citizenship. This is a key difference. Let us explore it.

The fundamental difference between the countries where Truth Commissions have been used and those where Court trials have been held is that in the former, the crucial challenge is not so much to bring offenders to book but to go beyond to life after trials shall have been concluded. How are those who may have escaped trial but are easily identified as perpetrators go on, within the context of a common geopolity and shared citizenship, to live, interact, and commune with those who are victims but do not feel redressed? Lingering resentment, undischarged frustration, unsoothed hurt are not exactly the stuff of which peaceable social living is made.

A related difference is that the societies concerned have become so popularized and the net of perpetrators in Truth Commission countries is so widespread that to require trials along the lines of Nuremberg is to engage in an impractical exercise: putting entire segments of the population on trial. We must not make light of this impracticality. To put that many people in jail, even if it were possible, would ultimately bankrupt the country and slow down, if not arrest, its progress. But even if these costs were affordable, the costs in terms of further damage to the country in lingering resentment harbored by future generations must make us pause. I am aware that some might object that I seem to place more premium on the lingering resentment of the perpetrators or their descendants than I do on that of the victims whose hurt I said earlier would not be assuaged if trials were not all encompassing. Unless we wish to risk the makings of interlocking feuds or feud-like situations, we must take seriously the challenge to break the cycle of recriminations and revenge. Truth commission countries do not cover all cases of the perpetration of crimes against citizens nor do they operate to make the perpetrators go untarnished. What is important to note is that the punishment may be of a different kind and the moral censure that attaches to being identified as perpetrators of crimes against their fellow citizens is not washed away by the granting of amnesty. I shall say more about this later. It suffices to point out here that it is only an attitude that sees incarceration or execution as the only acceptable options for punishing perpetrators that will discountenance the force of moral opprobrium in the context of social living.

Meanwhile, even in countries where Truth Commissions have not been impaneled but where similar atrocities have been alleged, their inhabitants have considered it not worth the costs (in terms of being further traumatized) to set up tribunals to try perpetrators of crimes against the populace. I have in mind here most countries of Eastern Europe where whole societies would be rocked to their foundations were they to insist that all those who collaborated with the defunct communist regimes that brutalized them in the recent past should stand trial.

What has transpired in the countries that I have been describing is that there has been a trade-off between the goals set by desert and retribution that might have been served by trials under law, and those set by the need for national reconciliation anchored on knowing what happened to whom and when, who did what and when, and what was it that allowed those things to happen, which is what the Truth Commission is meant to supply. Archbishop Desmond Tutu, the Chairman of the South African Truth and Reconciliation Commission, put it best when he wrote, "the Commission remains a risky and delicate business, but it remains the only alternative to Nuremberg on the one hand and amnesia on the other."[3] I am suggesting that in consciously rejecting the Nuremberg model, the designers of Truth Commissions repudiated the legal model and, in so doing, brought to the fore the limits of law in addressing the goals for which the commissions were created. Although I use the South African Truth and Reconciliation Commission as the focus of my discussion, what I say of it can be applied, *mutatis mutandi*, to other countries that have used the instrumentality of a Truth Commission. Such countries include El Salvador, Guatemala, Argentina, and Chile.

What has been done in each of the above cases is to separate out the most egregious cases of infliction of harm as beyond the pale; identify a category of cases where the inflictions of harm are not necessarily less deleterious but are committed in the process of facilitating a political objective. It is only acts of the latter type that are candidates for *amnesty* in the specific case of South Africa. As Beth Lyons puts it, an act that is a candidate for amnesty is defined according to principles drafted by

> Carl Aage Norgaard of Denmark and president of the European Commission on Human Rights, for use in the 1989 settlement in Namibia that foreshadowed events in South Africa. These principles require an examination of the: (1) motivation of offender; (2) circumstances; (3) nature of the political objective; (4) legal and factual nature of the offense; (5) object (state vs. private entity); and (6) relationship between the offense and the political objective, its directness or proximity or proportionality.[4]

Based on these criteria, "amnesty shall be granted if, in short, it is with respect to an act associated with a political objective committed in the course of the conflicts of the past and if the applicant has made a full disclosure of relevant facts."[5]

It should not be forgotten that the acts elegible for amnesty include murder as well as the infliction of torture. So we are not talking about petty offenses here. The question that such a recourse raises is: Why would a people, represented in a state and its institutions, forswear the demands of justice and deployment of law when serious crimes have been committed and confessed to and opt instead for amnesty as long as there is full disclosure of relevant facts? Beth Lyons asks: "Are truth and justice in opposition in this process . . . ?"[6] I answer, yes, they are. It is an acknowledgment of the limits of law and the justice it promises that South Africa opted for truth over justice. It remains to spell out what these limits are that render law unsuitable for the task of delivering what truth is adjudged to enable in this case. The answer lies in what goals are considered to be crucial in a polity in which truth is held to trump justice. It is time to examine the objectives of the Truth and Reconciliation Commission.

The fundamental aim of the TRC is to "promote national unity and reconciliation in a spirit of understanding which transcends the conflicts and divisions of the past."

> The objectives are to (1) establish as complete a picture as possible of gross human rights violations perpetrated between 1960–1994 by conducting investigations and hearings; (2) facilitate granting of amnesty in exchange for full disclosure of truth for acts with a political objective within guidelines of the Act; (3) make known the fate of victims and restore their human and civil dignity, and allow them to give accounts and recommend reparations; (4) make a report of findings and recommendations to prevent future human rights violation.[7]

The overriding consideration that determined the objectives just iterated is articulated in different ways by some of the principal actors in this process. There is continual emphasis on "healing," "forgiveness," "reparation," "reconciliation," "unity," "understanding," "transcending the conflicts of the past," and so on. Here is the South African Minister of Justice, Dullah Omar, speaking on the significance of the TRC:

> The people of South Africa [can] transcend the divisions and strife of the past, which generated gross violations of human rights, the transgression of humanitarian principles in violent conflicts and a legacy of hatred, fear, guilt and revenge . . . these can . . . be addressed on the basis that there is a need for understanding but not for vengeance, a need for reparation but not for retaliation, a need for *ubuntu* [the essence of being human], but not for victimization.[8]

Again, I cite Archbishop Tutu who insists that, "We [the TRC] are meant to be a part of the process of the healing of our nation, of our people, all of us, since every South African has to some extent or other been traumatized. We are a wounded people . . . . We all stand in need of healing."[9] It is easy to argue that Archbishop Tutu's submissions are consistent with his professional calling and general moral outlook. What is remarkable is that the principal enforcer of the South African law, the Minister of Justice, would elect to support an alternative that seems to detract from most of what the law is ordinarily taken to enjoin. This is a significant departure. After all, were the Nuremberg model to be adopted, it would have meant the invocation of the processes and outcomes of criminal law and, to a limited extent, of constitutional law. Some of the victims of apartheid might also have had recourse to tort law for reparations for personal injury. The principal motivation for the criminal law is to punish the wrongdoer and mete out just desert, with the hope that the hurt of the victim will be vicariously assuaged by her seeing the person who hurt her put behind bars or made to pay in some other way. While this may satisfy the thirst for vengeance, it would be a stretch to suggest that it would promote understanding, or unity, or reconciliation, or any of the other lofty principles for the achievement of which the TRC was constituted.

In light of the objectives of the TRC and the expostulations of its principal actors, I would like to argue that the recourse to the TRC mechanism is a repudiation of law as an appropriate or effective instrument for the achievement of the understanding, unity, reparation, healing, forgiveness, and transcending of the conflicts of the past that South Africa needs to move forward as one country in the aftermath of the depredations of apartheid. It is an admission that the Nuremberg model with its recourse to law was inappropriate for the more fundamental goals of the new South Africa. Such an admission may have been prompted by the general recognition in South Africa that law was a principal instrument of the apartheid state and was, for that reason, a suspect tool to repair the damage done by apartheid while it lasted. Additionally, there seems to be a feeling that the objects of law—desert, punishment, and so forth—are at variance with the objectives of the TRC. These elements combine to yield the conclusion that law may fall considerably short of what would facilitate the healing of a wounded people. In the rest of this essay, I shall summarize the divergences between law and the TRC and why law may not serve or may underserve the purpose of healing and reconciliation. Needless to say, I do this at the risk of oversimplification, but it is a risk worth taking.

(1) Had law been the preferred mode of realizing the aim of the TRC described above, what law might it have been? Recall that, under apartheid, law was the handmaiden of a brutal regime whose principal mode of operation was characterized by the United Nations as a crime against humanity. That law was useless, if not worse, once the apartheid regime unraveled. But how about the sort of legal fiction that was deployed at Nuremberg where Nazi laws were dismissed as non-laws? That option was not available because, unlike the Nazi state, the apartheid state had not suffered total defeat. Furthermore, the principal operators of the apartheid state led by their last leader were also the principal negotiators of the terms of the dismantling of apartheid. Their participation in the latter process, as representatives of the apartheid state, in a supreme irony required that they be recognized as legitimate negotiators on behalf of the rogue state that, in different circumstances, would have made them defendants in a criminal trial. So the path of constitutional law was not available. How about criminal law? This would have been most intractable. First, the prosecutors would have had to be manufactured anew. By what authority would they have been appointed? That of the apartheid Constitution? As it turned out, the new Constitution that was worked out allowed for a transitional program under which the new one was accepted as a successor to the apartheid one. Then the question arose as to what to do with those who might argue that in committing various crimes under apartheid, they

were merely obeying orders, or carrying out the law as it then was in the apartheid state. One significant way out was the TRC.

Had the choice been made for a full blown Nuremberg model, given what we said earlier about the crucial difference between apartheid South Africa and Nazi Germany, the prosecutors would have had to pay serious attention to considerations of due process and the rights of the accused. One must not take lightly the gravity of these considerations. Yet one must remark the fact that their observance often impair or hinder the possibility of truth-finding. I shall say more about this anon. Worse still, most white South Africans and many black South Africans would have had to face charges. Might tort law have offered a less problematic way out? I do not think so. The requirement of identifiable parties who must prove that they possess *locus standi* by showing that they have been injured, and that they deserve compensation, would have been extremely difficult to meet for most victims of the apartheid state. Secrecy and anonymity were fundamental traits of the operations of the South African state under apartheid. So identification of possible defendants would have been extremely difficult. Meanwhile, given that the onus of initial fact-finding rests on the plaintiffs, the costs to potential black plaintiffs would have been prohibitive. Simultaneously, the overwhelming material advantages of white South Africans would have made this option inoperative for most black South Africans. The consequence would have been that most perpetrators of political crimes under the apartheid regime would have been able to hide their records. While a few black South Africans might have been able to secure justice through the courts, most would have had to trust their cases to the care of God!

(2) The motivating force of the law, especially of municipal legal systems, is that of desert, its principal form of resolution is that of punishment or retribution. A basic aim of the polity that adopts the Truth Commission model is to promote national unity and reconciliation. In the example of South Africa, it might have served the cause of justice, legally understood, to have locked up F. W. de Klerk, the last President of apartheid South Africa, for crimes committed under his direction. How would that have helped a South Africa that not only acknowledges a common citizenship for all its inhabitants but is, at the same time, desirous of creating a civic culture out of this broad cloth? In place of desert, the society elects to amnesty some perpetrators as *an unavoidable cost for the attainment of a future devoid of the rancours that wracked the past.*

(3) It can be argued that legal processes may not be the best or most efficient means of truth-finding. In the typical legal process, "lawyers calling attention to picayune legal technicalities"[10] may obscure rather than unmask the truth. For example, anyone who is familiar with the intricacies

of the Fifth Amendment under the U.S. Constitution knows that its invocation is a peremptory way of stopping the search for the truth on the part of the party that invokes it. At the same time, the American version of amnesty—the granting of different degrees of immunity from prosecution—is used to aid the cause of truth-finding. That is, on occasion even in the United States, notorious for the litigiousness of its citizens, considerations of truth-finding trump the concern with desert.

(4) Were law to be used instead of the TRC, the victims will not be restored, their agency will remain maimed or unrecognized, and they will remain without voice, without language. Except for the most rudimentary levels of the legal system, e.g., small claims court, litigants must employ the services of an *alágbàwí*, literally one who accepts to speak for them. In the proceedings themselves, the *alágbàwí* substitutes his or her voice for those of the victims, the latter remain voiceless, sometimes nameless or without a face, and the telling of their stories is bereft of the cadences of natural speech, shorn of whatever poetry cannot be forced into the narrow registers of legalese. In short, the victims become silenced again.

Consider the alternative TRC context. In that context, the agency of the victims is restored, they are given back their voices—a significant gesture in light of the fact that that was the first thing that their tormentors took away. They are enabled to tell their stories in their own inimitable ways without the intercession of an *alágbàwí*. Testifying in their own person, telling their truth to power, as it were, is evidence of the recognition of their agency, of their entitlement to the dignity that is theirs by virtue of their humanity. One must not underestimate the significance of this process of restoration for the recovery of what the Minister of Justice called *ubuntu* (the essence of being human).[11]

More importantly, they compel the perpetrators of political crimes to shed the cloak of anonymity that permits them to claim to be mere cogs in an impersonal machine. I suggest that tremendous moral force is generated when evil is forced to disclose its name and record its address. Particular torturers are no longer mere state representatives, they are fathers, brothers, sisters, and, sometimes, neighbors. The daughter of a murdered activist was reported to have told the TRC at a sitting in East London in April 1996: "We want to forgive, but we don't know who to forgive."[12] To ensure that the dialectic of forgiveness is not preempted, under the terms of the TRC, in order to qualify for amnesty, perpetrators must come forward, accept responsibility for what they did, describe in painstaking, exhaustive details what they did, where and when. One consequence of their stepping forward to accept responsibility is that they have to confront some of their victims, those who survived, who could then ask them to explain why they did what they did and have an opportunity to ask for forgiveness. In so doing, the perpetrator has to listen to the voice that he had silenced, hear stories that in the past he had considered *infra dignitatem* for him to hear and, finally, concede the equal humanity of his victims.[13] With the unmasking of the perpetrators and their acts comes the removal of what Beth Lyons calls the "Privilege of Not Knowing" under which white South Africans of all persuasions expiated their guilt from complicity in the crimes of the apartheid regime.

What I have done from (1) through (4) is to show, at the risk of over-simplification, how a preference for law as symbolized by the Nuremberg model might have underserved or might not have served the purpose that motivated the adoption of the TRC mechanism. I conclude that even though the TRC came about through the instrumentality of law, beyond this formal genesis, it is at best a quasi-legal institution. In its operation, even when it uses some of the tools that a legal tribunal would use, it ought to be clear that it proceeds in a manner that shows that it does not consider the legal way an adequate or efficient one for attaining the objectives set for it by its designers. This is the basis for my contention that the TRC model serves to remind us of the limits of law as a principle of social ordering. That such a recourse would be had at the close of a century in which we have witnessed law in both its glory and its infamy is proof that law is seriously inadequate for the realization of the good society.

The TRC model has not been without critics. Even among those who are sympathetic to the model, they have interpreted it as a legal institution and have, accordingly, seen it as part of the process of implanting the Rule of Law in the societies where it has been adopted.[14] I have presented arguments for the claim that this view is inadequate. Others have objected that the empaneling of the TRC has cheated some victims out of their day in court where they would have confronted their tormentors and secured criminal convictions as a matter of justice and desert. I do not wish to suggest that some people may not be underserved by the TRC model. My rejoinder is that, without falling into the snare of crass utilitarianism, what is at issue in the debate over which model to embrace is the question of what kind of society is to emerge from the ruins of apartheid and how South Africa might move forward as a multiracial society, whose inhabitants, in spite of the conflicts of the past, must learn to interact, even in disagreement, as bearers of a single, indivisible citizenship. While selective prosecution, and it cannot be other than selective, may serve the yearnings of some for just desert for perpetrators of some crimes, the larger issue of moving the society past its conflicts and divisions is unlikely to be served by this manner of proceeding. It is significant that it is for similar reasons that the Constitutional Court in South Africa rejected the challenge to the installation of the TRC. The Court said, *inter alia*: "The erstwhile adversaries of such a conflict inhabit the same sovereign territory. They have to live with each other and work with each other and state concern is best equipped to determine what measures may be most conducive for the facilitation of such reconciliation and reconstruction."[15] I do not interpret the Court as making light of individual claims. Nor is it to be read as giving the state unlimited power to determine what measures may be most conducive for the facilitation of such reconciliation and reconstruction. Rather it is a classic case of what the court has to do every day in every municipal legal system: that is, in light of contending social purposes and interests, come up with the best arguments for what it deems to be, on balance, the best interests of the polity. The judges too chose truth over justice.

The choices made by South Africans have implications for societies elsewhere. I will mention only one. Much of the debate about affirmative action in the United States has revolved around the issue of fairness and the issue of equal protection under the Constitution. This is as it should be. But it is only on the assumption that the justice of law is the highest form of justice attainable that one can continue to claim that affirmative action is unwarranted. In South Africa, there is a deliberate adoption of the view that if the new society is to be created in which no group will be inferior to another, then those who have been hurt must be made whole and those who have hurt others must be made whole, too. But the latter must concede that they had done wrong in the past as a precondition for forgiveness. In a similar way, the United States, too, can affirm its commitment to affirmative action as a necessary, even if insufficient step, on the road to building a better society in which those who are descended from those who had inflicted pain in the past acknowledge that wrong had been done to some segments of the population whose descendants deserve to be made whole. Affirmative action then becomes one of the necessary steps towards the building of a future society in which the need for it will no longer exist and where all of America's peoples shall be reconciled. That the justice promised by law for some white applicants might be abridged must not be denied. But that the country cannot be whole until it has made its historically disabled minority whole will be the ultimate, even if legally inconvenient, justification for upholding affirmative action and similar remedies. The issue is not whether it violates the law, but whether we can arrive at a good society without it.

Olúfẹ́mi Táíwò, Department of Philosophy, Loyola University, Chicago, IL 60626; otaiwo@luc.edu

Notes

1. The case for this belief is made in Olúfẹ̀mi Táíwò, *Legal Naturalism: A Marxist Theory of Law* (Ithaca: Cornell University Press, 1996), ch. 6.

2. Beth S. Lyons, "Between Nuremberg and Amnesia: The Truth and Reconciliation Commission in South Africa," *Monthly Review* 49.4 (September 1997): 7–8; my emphasis.

3. Quoted in Lyons, ibid., 22.

4. Ibid., 19.

5. Ibid.

6. Ibid., 10.

7. Ibid., 9.

8. Quoted in Lyons, op. cit., 8.

9. Quoted in Richard A. Wilson, "The Sizwe Will Not Go Away: The Truth and Reconciliation, Human Rights and Nation-Building in South Africa," *African Studies* 55.2 (1996): 15.

10. Ibid., 16.

11. Ibid.

12. Quoted in Lyons, op. cit., 13.

13. "Identifying perpetrators—putting names with the descriptions of clothing, physical attributes, demeanor, brutalities and obscenities of the state's footsoldiers—is one of the Commission's key tasks." See ibid.

14. Lyons seems to me to see it in this way.

15. Quoted in Lyons, op. cit., 21.

RAWLS ON CONSTITUTIONAL CONSENSUS AND THE PROBLEM OF STABILITY

Rex Martin

This paper lays out the background and main features of Rawls's new theory of justice. This is a theory that he began adumbrating about 1980 and that is given its fullest statement in his recent book *Political Liberalism*. I identify the main patterns of justification Rawls attempts to provide for his new theory and suggest a problem with one of these patterns in particular. The main lines of my analysis engage Rawls's idea of constitutional consensus and his account of political stability.

I. RAWLS'S NEW THEORY

In 1971 John Rawls published his monumental treatise, *A Theory of Justice* (hereafter TJ). The book has been widely discussed, both favorably and unfavorably. Over the years Rawls responded to many of the criticisms that were made. Indeed, to the list of criticisms, Rawls himself has recently added one of his own.

He claims that his basic account of stability in TJ is wrong or, at least, seriously off center.[1] In any event, in his more recent writings, Rawls seems very concerned with the problem of assuring political stability in a pluralist or multicultural social environment. And, as might be expected, Rawls gives his current preoccupation—and his new theory of justice—its most complete elaboration in *Political Liberalism* [PL], a paperback version of which Rawls brought out in 1996.[2]

Perhaps, the most significant feature of Rawls's current theory (his "new theory," as I have called it) is that he takes the public political culture of a contemporary democratic society to be the deep background of the entire theory. For the leading ideas out of which the political conception of justice is to be constructed and by reference to which it is to be justified are said by Rawls to be implicit in that culture.

More specifically, political justification, in Rawls's post-1980s writings, sets out from four "model conceptions" or "fundamental ideas": (1) the idea of the person or citizen (as having two distinctive capacities or moral powers),[3] (2) the idea of social cooperation for mutual (or, better, reciprocal) benefit, (3) the idea of the well-ordered society and its basic institutional structure, and (4) the idea of a linking or mediating conception which lays out the standards for discussion and decision-making to which fellow citizens could be expected to adhere in reaching a decision respecting the governing principles of political justice (that is, the principles of justice for the basic structure of their well-ordered society, in which they could expect to live their entire lives). This fourth idea is linked with what Rawls called "the original position" in his earlier book. Herein would be included such ideas as limited information (the so-called veil of ignorance), publicity, and unanimity. Technically, the mediating conception is not implicit *per se* in democratic political culture; rather, its function is to help unify the other fundamental ideas into a single coherent whole from which one could then reason, with some effect, to certain principles and institutional arrangements.

The main object of Rawls's new *political* conception of justice is to establish terms of social cooperation for mutual benefit—principles for a fair distribution of certain primary goods (including such things as liberties, opportunities, social and economic positions, income, and wealth). In this account, the principles that emerge as preferred (from among a small set of historically available candidate principles) are, presumably, the principles that are best supported from within the nexus formed by the model conceptions. The preferred principles are the ones that, upon reflection and given the balance of reasons, are the most appropriate ones with respect to the starting point itself. That is, they are the principles most appropriate to the fundamental ideas themselves, under the assumption that there is and is going to be, in a continuing free and open society, an irreducible pluralism of reasonable comprehensive moral and religious and philosophic doctrines.

Rawls thinks that those best-supported principles will be his own preferred two principles of justice, understood now as *political* principles.[4] Or, to be precise, he thinks the preferred set will actually be a "family" of principles, among which are included the two he emphasizes. This "family," for want of a better name, we can call the set of 'generic' liberal principles. Generic liberalism, as Rawls conceives it, has three main features: (1) certain familiar rights, liberties, opportunities are to be singled out and specified and maintained; (2) a certain priority is to be given to these rights, etc. over against "the claims of the general good (understood aggregatively) and of perfectionist values"; (3) measures to help citizens make effective use of these rights (etc.), by having an adequate base of income and wealth, are to be set in place.[5]

The "political conception of justice," as Rawls calls it, is not limited to such principles alone. It also includes certain of the institutional arrangements that are required to put the principles into effect in a given society. These institutions—political, economic, social—are the sort of thing Rawls had in mind when he referred to the basic structure of a society.

But he tends to emphasize only the basic political institutions. And, I would add, to emphasize the rights, liberties, and opportunities mentioned in his account of generic liberalism. Thus, the principles of justice that identify and specify these important rights and the basic political institutions are, Rawls says, the "constitutional essentials."

II. Problems of Justification

It is convenient to view Rawls's account of justification in PL as having two main stages.[6] The first stage is the one we have focused on up to now. The main project here is to settle on that principle or set of principles for distributing primary goods which is optimally appropriate, given the fundamental democratic ideas from which we start. Thus, Rawls argues, more or less straightforwardly, that the generic liberal principles (a family of principles in which are included his own preferred two principles) are peculiarly well designed to specify a democratically acceptable distribution of primary goods in the context of existing democratic political arrangements.

This first line of justification (justification from democratic principles in a democratic context) is said by Rawls to be "freestanding," in the sense that it draws only on these implicit ideas, presumably shared already to a large degree by fellow citizens. It does not draw on the ideas or values of any comprehensive moral or religious doctrine *per se*.

What Rawls calls overlapping consensus is a second stage of political justification in which the antecedently established "freestanding" justification is endorsed from the respective points of view of a variety of comprehensive ethical doctrines (such as Kant's moral theory or Mill's utilitarianism) and religious doctrines (such as contemporary Catholic Christianity). On this view, the political conception is a common focal point—a "module, an essential constituent part, that fits into and can be supported by various reasonable comprehensive doctrines that endure in the society regulated by it."[7] But it is not *presented* by reference to such support initially; rather it is established independently of direct consideration of any and all such doctrines. Even at the second stage, it is not regarded as a part of any one of them in particular (to the exclusion of all or most others).

Here we contemplate the justification of the political conception from *within* the confines of a variety of comprehensive views: (a) In some of these cases such justification will follow a deductive pattern; (b) in others it will be more like a justification on the instantiation model—here the claim is that the political conception counts as a nearest practical approximation (or at least as a feasible real-world exemplification) of the comprehensive view in question—and (c) in yet others it will be justification only in the very weak sense given by the notion of consistency; here the political conception is said merely to be compatible with—that is, not incompatible with—the comprehensive doctrine in question. In any event, where several different comprehensive doctrines can justify a single political conception in one of these ways, we say that there is an overlapping consensus among these comprehensive doctrines; each for its own reasons endorses one and the same political conception.

There is one feature, though, of Rawls's account of the first sort of justification ("freestanding" justification, as he called it) that has continued to puzzle me greatly. My problematic can best be put in the form of a question or two. First, can the model conceptions or fundamental ideas generate, on the balance of reasons, support for the generic liberal principles? Presumably, given Rawls's argument throughout PL, such support clearly can be generated. Second, can the model conceptions also generate, on the balance of reasons, support for the two principles *in particular*? This second question is the one that gives puzzlement.

If the answer to this second question is *yes*, then why does Rawls privilege generic liberalism in his exposition throughout PL? It would seem an illegitimate and pointless procedure to do so. (For, though it is true that what is the case for the genus is also the case for the species, the reverse is not true. So if the argument pattern picks out one species *in particular*, then that is sufficient and it is conclusive. There is no need to elevate the generic over the specific but, rather, the reverse should be the case.) On the other hand, if the answer is *no*, then where does the support for the two principles *in particular* actually get generated? And what is Rawls's basis for preferring them throughout, as the best in the lot?

III. CONSTITUTIONAL CONSENSUS

I think the answer to this question lies in what Rawls has to say about constitutional consensus, one of the most important and certainly one of the least understood new ideas in PL. Constitutional consensus is introduced in Rawls's argument at the point where he is addressing the issue whether overlapping consensus is a utopian notion (as some have claimed).[8] He attempts to deal with this issue by showing how it is possible to move from a political *modus vivendi* to a detailed set of constitutional essentials, the features of which "all citizens may reasonably be expected to endorse."[9]

In a *modus vivendi*, certain principles and practices are accepted as a way for people to live together without constant fighting and disruption. In its crudest version a *modus vivendi* is simply an institutional matter, simply an agreement on political procedures.[10] In a more realistic version a *modus vivendi*, at least one sustainable over a long period of time, would involve a bit more than that. Thus, to give the example Rawls himself uses, there might be "agreement on certain basic political rights and liberties—on the right to vote and freedom of political speech and association, and whatever else is required for the electoral and legislative procedures of democracy . . . ." But there is disagreement even here, about the "exact content and boundaries of these rights and liberties, as well as on what further rights and liberties are to be counted as basic . . . ."[11] And there is agreement about some features of the basic political institutions (e.g., a willingness to accept parliamentary government, based on popular elections) but not on the whole range of basic structural institutions (on the economy or the establishment of religion, to give two examples). In short, the agreement here is not wide (it covers only a fairly narrow range of rights and institutions). It is not deep (in that the reasons offered for the desirability of accepted arrangements does not go beyond the idea of establishing a *modus vivendi*). And it lacks focus (fellow citizens have no shared conception of a public political life—no animating principles, widely accepted, that would take them beyond the status quo—unless we count the fear of a worse alternative, the return to war—as in the wars of religion in the past, and in the present century).

In a real sense, in a *modus vivendi*, there is and can be no *public* conception of justice because there is (in a *modus vivendi*) no shared conception of a public order or entity at all. There are no public reasons for a *modus vivendi* because there is no public. Thus, whatever reasons there are, they are nonpublic reasons—reasons afforded each participant by the values of their own morality or their own religion or their own philosophical view of the world (where such reasons are coupled, as I have indicated, with considerations of prudence and of strategy).

A constitutional consensus (of the sort Rawls had in view) comes about, then, as the agreed-upon area of rights and practices widens. It comes about as the ground under that area deepens (as convincing reasons for having such arrangements, reasons that go beyond the mere utility of a *modus vivendi*, gain acceptance and are taken on board). And it comes about as a conception of public principles of justice, with greater focus and definition, gains widespread support. Thus, a shared conception of a public order or entity is created, as constitutional consensus moves beyond its starting point (in a *modus vivendi*); and with the conception of a body politic (a *res publica*) in place, a shared political conception of justice becomes possible.

In the story told in PL, there are two main stops on the path away from a political *modus vivendi* toward overlapping consensus, at the end of the road. The first stage is the one where Rawls's argument in PL (respecting constitutional consensus) actually begins: with a vigorous version of generic liberalism. It is, presumably, where democratic political culture is at today, in the U.S., Canada, Western Europe, and parts of the Southern hemisphere (to name the favored cases). Here the consensus has become *wide* enough to embrace most of the well-known constitutional rights, liberties, and opportunities and to cover the main democratic political institutions—universal franchise (on a one-person/one-vote basis), contested voting (at both the electoral and legislative stages), and majority rule decision making. And wide enough to embrace such further basic structure institutions as an open and competitive market (but ultimately subject to detailed political overview) and a system of free public schooling. And the consensus has become *deep* enough to draw, as background, on a well-established, viable democratic political culture and to draw on the "model conceptions" latent there as the ultimate ground of justification of a "freestanding" political conception of justice. And this political conception has gained increasing focus and detail—in particular, at the point of economic justice. For here the constitutional essentials now embrace, specifically, some features of equality of opportunity (such as freedom of movement and free choice of movement) and a "social minimum providing for the basic needs of all citizens." Here, the familiar features of Rawls's own second principle—*fair* equality of opportunity and the requirements of the difference or maximin principle—are *not* constitutional essentials, though they are still eligible topics for continued discussion under the heading of "basic justice."

The *second* stage of constitutional consensus is one not yet attained. If attained, it would map Rawls's own preferred political conception of justice in all relevant details. It would be widened to include the idea of the "fair value" of the political liberties.[12] And it would take in more basic institutional detail, going beyond the largely political part (emphasized in generic liberalism) to cover "the basic structure as a whole,"[13] thus including issues of economic ownership and worker participation in management. It would be deepened to include, among other things, a formulation of the "model conception" of society as a cooperative venture that stressed cooperation not just for mutual benefit but for *reciprocal* benefit.[14] And it would become even more fine-grained, more focused. Here the political conception of justice would have as its principles, precisely, Rawls's preferred two principles, including therein both the principle of *fair* equality of opportunity and the maximin principle, which requires that the income and wealth of the least well-off group (the bottom 20%, say) be as high as it can possibly be.

Rawls calls his own political conception of justice "justice as fairness." In the second stage of constitutional consensus, then, justice as fairness would be the focus of the political conception of justice. Justice as fairness would be the point that generic liberalism finally came to center on; it would become, in the end of the day, the "center of the focal class."[15]

There are several important things, in my view, that must be noted to make this reading of Rawls's notion of constitutional consensus at all a plausible one. The first is that constitutional consensus is a temporal notion, a notion of change over time (of development or evolution, if you will).

It seems clear, to me, that it must be seen this way. Rawls presents the generic liberal constitutional consensus as a move away from *modus vivendi*; presumably, such a move takes time. For it involves not only certain changes in practice but also changes in thinking (in particular, as regards the kinds of reasons one argues *from* and the kinds of principles one comes to endorse, that *everyone* comes to endorse). It involves the creation of a certain kind of political culture.

If constitutional consensus involves a temporal move away from something (*modus vivendi*) and, at its most developed end, a temporal move to something (overlapping consensus, as already described), then it itself is probably a temporal process, a process of historical change. Constitutional consensus is, in short, not merely a process in which changes are occurring at each end, so to speak; it is a process in which changes are occurring *within* constitutional consensus itself, over time. There are, in other words, *stages* of constitutional consensus; and I have tried to map two of these stages in this paper (the earlier stage of generic liberalism—in what I described as a vigorous version—and the succeeding one of justice as fairness). But the interpretation of Rawlsian constitutional consensus as a temporal process of historical change, which I have tried to develop here, is not widely accepted. Why not? I think there are two reasons for this.

First, Rawls is not regarded as a thinker who puts much weight on history. I do not mean he's not interested in historical stories or facts; he recounts them himself. I mean that history (understood as a process of change, of development) seemingly plays no integral part in the main argument pattern of his overall theory. This is, perhaps, one legacy of Rawls's initial (and continuing) reliance on the relatively atemporal notion of an original position as a ground point (some would say *the* ground point) of his whole theory. And it reflects things Rawls has said about his own theory, in the past (pre-1985), when he was in his more Kantian mode. For example, in "Basic Structure" he described his position by calling it an "as-if nonhistorical doctrine."[16] My discussion here is meant to suggest a deeper and more integral role for the notion of historical processes of change in Rawls's theory than the common understanding has been prepared to acknowledge.

The second main reason for reluctance to see a crucial role for historical development in Rawls was his discussion of the constitutional essentials. This is the matter that perplexed and in a sense misled me the most. For a long time, I read the term 'essentials' in a rather standard way: as identifying the abiding core of the matter, as something fixed and settled for all time. But as I began to see that constitutional consensus was itself a temporal developmental notion, I concluded that the essentials needed to be given a somewhat different construal, one that captured but that went beyond this standard reading.

Rawls refers to the constitutional essentials frequently throughout PL, but he discusses them in detail only once there.[17] And here he describes them, quite unmistakably, as the basic political essentials of generic liberalism (albeit in what I have described as a *vigorous* version).

The essentials here are what all the species of that genus, justice as fairness included, have in common beyond that point. For each of the species, and again justice as fairness is included, they constitute a minimum agenda. They are the constitutional essentials for the whole *family* of liberal conceptions, from that stage on.

It is not surprising that Rawls laid out the family-resemblance essentials as his point of departure. Since Rawls's first main stopping point (on the trajectory he traces from *modus vivendi,* at one end, to overlapping consensus, at the other) is with a robust version of the family of liberal political conceptions, it is quite natural that he would describe the constitutional essentials at that precise stage (the stage of a vigorous version of generic liberalism) in exactly the way he has done.

But as liberalism gains focus *beyond* this point, it is not expected that the more or less rudimentary generic account will adequately capture what is distinctive and fundamental (essential in *that* sense) in these more specialized accounts of liberalism. Even so, there is a clear sense in which the family resemblances (as identified in the rudimentary version of generic liberalism) are retained in justice as fairness. But we would expect justice as fairness, as a distinctive species of the genus of liberal theories, to include modifications that are appropriate to it as a species.

Here the minimum or rudimentary agenda is retained, though it is gone beyond in the principles and practices laid down in justice as fairness. Thus, the rudimentary idea that there be "a social minimum providing for the basic needs of all citizens" is not denied but, instead, built upon when a "more demanding" standard, Rawls's difference (or maximin) principle, is put in place.[18]

The backdrop to Rawls's thinking here can be put in a familiar idiom. We are thinking of developmental stages that occur in a progression; each stage builds on the one that went before; there is no reversion at a later stage back to some earlier one. Rather, the stages in the process 'build'; they exhibit *cumulative* development. This is, typically, how natural evolution is theorized. And it is the way we should take Rawls's discussion of the constitutional essentials, I think.

The notion of constitutional essentials is, in sum, a variable, ringing a variety of changes upon one and the same generic pattern. What it is in its details (and here we assume, as backdrop, the *family* of liberal conceptions of justice) depends on what stage we're at within a developing constitutional consensus. Each stage presupposes a certain institutional history; and the formation and configuration of basic structure institutions, at that stage, is appropriate to that history (or, more likely, is in tussle to become so). And at that stage, with that particular history in view and with certain ideals and practices in place, as part of the ongoing enterprise there, we will find a certain characteristic citizen mindset.

Rawls's puts this mindset well (and in a simple formulation, so simple indeed that it's easy to glide on by and miss its significance). He says of the constitutional essentials that they are matters which all citizens "may reasonably be expected to endorse."[19]

Rawls is not saying that fundamental principles and practices have been selected *because* they find favor with the citizens on a given day (a view more suited to a Roman circus than to a constitutional consensus). Rather, the fundamental principles and practices are in place *because* they constitute, on the balance of reasons, the best contemporary interpretation and application of the "model conceptions" appropriate to the background political culture (in this case a democratic political culture), given the institutional history embedded in that particular culture and the profile of existing basic structure institutions that this history has currently given rise to. Or at least I take this to be Rawls's claim.

In short, if the first main feature of Rawls's idea of constitutional consensus is that it is a temporal or historical variable, the second is the identification of the appropriate citizen mindset at each stage, at each stage *successfully* reached, of constitutional consensus. Here I have in view, simply, widespread citizen endorsement of the constitutional essentials at that stage.

Citizen endorsement is not *the* rock bottom basis of liberal legitimacy. It has a different role to play here than that. It provides a kind of *evidence* that the ideals and practices, which can be argued for, relying upon the background political culture and its history, are actually congruent with the extant political morality of the body of citizens. It is evidence that these ideals and practices are congruent with existing maxims and paradigm cases (bearing on matters of good government and of bad) that could be cited by one citizen or another, to general concurrence.

Of course, nothing is perfect. Adjustments between the argued-for ideals and practices, on the one hand, and the deeply held maxims and paradigms, on the other, may sometimes be required to bring them into congruence. But congruence, and with it general concurrence, is what is sought.

This ideal of congruence, expressed in the claim that the constitutional essentials are matters which all citizens "may reasonably be expected to endorse," functions in PL in much the way that Rawls's notion of reflective equilibrium did in TJ. They have the same role: each provides evidence that the principles argued for (on the balance of reasons) are congruent with the prevalent workaday standards, at least the deepest standards, of the folks involved. They show that the reasoning (sound on other grounds) has not occurred in a cultural vacuum.

IV. Stability

It seems, then, if all or most citizens may reasonably be expected to endorse the constitutional essentials (in the favored case we have just described), that an important degree of stability is built into any constitutional consensus. Of course, we could expect the stability to be greater for some stages of such consensus than for others. But at its highest stage of development, a constitutional consensus (being wider than before and deeper and more focused) should be stable indeed. After all, the foundational political consensus itself covers more important areas here, for deeper and better reasons, and the principles relied on to make policy decisions are much more focused and fine-gained.

Thus, a vigorous version of the family of liberal political conceptions (as one stage of constitutional consensus) would enjoy considerable consensual support and a high degree of stability, for that very reason. Justice as fairness (as a wider, deeper, and more focused stage than this version of generic liberalism) would have an even thicker layer of consensual support and a considerably higher level of internal stability.

Indeed, if justice as fairness is, as Rawls thinks it is, at the topmost end of constitutional consensus (as the widest, deepest, most focused stage among all the liberal conceptions), then its degree of internal stability would be considerable indeed. It is the most likely arena in which overlapping consensus (if it is to be achieved at all) can be achieved. I take it that Rawls is claiming this.

I will leave this important point unexplored at present. Perhaps our subsequent discussion will bring out reasons why such a claim is plausible.

The question I do want to address at this point is, what more could an overlapping consensus (of the various competing moral and religious doctrines alive at the same time) add to that high degree of stability?

Very little, I would think. If Rawls's main problem in PL is to account for political stability in a pluralist world, then that problem is already solved at the point of a well-developed constitutional consensus. Where justice as fairness is the freestanding political conception, it generates and will enjoy (if what I have said so far is sound) a very high degree of internal political stability. What overlapping consensus can add to that, as regards stability, is marginal at best.

The problem in his first book, TJ, was that Rawls had allowed political stability to rest, almost entirely, on his solution to the problem of moral justification. In sum, both problems were given one and the same solution. But this solution proved to be defective because it would not work—or was not seen to be plausible—under conditions of moral pluralism.

In Rawls's second book, PL, the problem of political stability, in a world of moral pluralism, was tackled first and solved on its own, using political devices: constitutional consensus and the attendant idea of constitutional essentials, which all citizens "may reasonably be expected to endorse." The solution to the next problem, that of critical moral justification, was first tailored to confront the idea of a permanent and irresolvable moral pluralism and was then brought to bear, in the idea of overlapping consensus, on a "freestanding" political conception of justice and on a pre-existing political solution to the problem of internal stability, thereby providing an *independent* critical moral grounding for each—a solution compatible this time with the moral pluralism that had infirmed the original TJ solution. In sum, overlapping consensus (whatever marginal increase in stability it might afford) is directed by Rawls primarily at the issue, not of stability, but of critical moral justification.

V. CONCLUSION

Rawls's idea of constitutional consensus and the attendant idea of the constitutional essentials has another use in Rawls's theory besides solving the problem of internal political stability. It also bears in a definitive way on another of his new ideas in PL. For the idea of the constitutional essentials is the centerpiece, the *leitmotif*, of public reason (as Rawls calls this new idea).[20]

Public reason, for Rawls, is a way of deciding policy disputes in a principled manner within the public arena. Public reason, as Rawls uses that idea, is a sort of schematism: it bids us to resolve policy issues, so far as possible, by using agreed-upon public standards. And where such resolution is not possible, the nonpublic values called upon (for example, particular religious values or those of conventional morality or majority preferences or individual interests) should be compatible with the agreed-upon public values and, more important, should not endanger the great values of comity (of peace on earth) and civility and mutual respect which characterize the relations of citizens with one another in such a society. This schematism is saved from mere formalism and becomes a useful guideline to public reasoning where its informing notion (that of constitutional essentials) has real determinate content.

Now, if we accept my earlier suggestion that the notion of the constitutional essentials is a variable, depending on what stage we're at within a developing constitutional consensus, then it follows that public reason will necessarily be relativized in a similar way to the underlying, fundamental idea of constitutional consensus. In sum, two of Rawls's leading *new* ideas in PL (constitutional essentials and public reason) are not only linked to each other but, more important, are also linked to the idea of constitutional consensus as their grounding principle. And this consensus is itself a historically developmental thing.

It is not clear, however, whether Rawls has adequate grounds for believing that such an evolutionary passage (to a constitutional consensus focussing on justice as fairness) will occur. If so, its grounds would have to be embedded within his theory. Are they grounded there? Again, this should prove a useful point for discussion.[21]

Rex Martin, Department of Philosophy, University of Kansas, Lawrence, KS 66045; and Department of Politics, University of Wales—Swansea, Swansea, Wales, SA2 8PP, UK; RexMartin@compuserve.com

Notes

1. For Rawls's own account of the matter, see *Political Liberalism* (New York: Columbia University Press, 1993), xv–xvii [hereafter: PL].

2. The pagination of the paperback version of PL for Lectures I–VIII is identical to that of the hardback. To avoid confusion I will refer to the hardback version of PL for all citations to the original introduction and to Lectures I–VI; and to the paperback version (as Rawls, 1996) for all citations to the paperback introduction and to Lecture IX.

3. Rawls claims (in PL, Lectures II and VIII) that there are two fundamental capacities or powers and, correspondingly, two "higher-order interests" of every individual citizen. Thus, each person has, over that person's entire life, (i) an interest in being able to have, formulate, revise, promulgate, live according to, and advance one's particular determinate conception of the good and (ii) an interest in exercising one's "sense of justice" and being motivated by it, providing others do so as well. That is, (to amplify this second point) each person has, over that person's entire life, (ii) an interest in living cooperatively with fellow citizens, on terms of mutual respect and reciprocal benefit, under a unified and stable scheme of basic political and economic institutions that has been organized by a shared set of principles of justice which each citizen can rationally affirm.

4. Rawls's current version of his preferred two principles of justice (from PL, 5–6) reads as follows:

> [1] Each person has an equal claim to a fully adequate scheme of equal basic rights and liberties, which scheme is compatible with the same scheme for all; and in this scheme the equal political liberties, and only those liberties, are to be guaranteed their fair value.

> [2] Social and economic inequalities are to satisfy two conditions: first, they must be attached to positions and offices open to all under conditions of fair equality of opportunity; and second, they are to be to the greatest benefit of the least advantaged members of society.

Conventionally, the first principle is referred to as the principle of equal basic liberties. The first condition or part of the second principle is conventionally described as the principle of fair equality of opportunity; and the second part as the difference principle (or, sometimes, the maximin principle). All these descriptions are used by Rawls himself.

5. See PL, 6.

6. Ibid., 140–41; also 1996, 385–88.

7. PL., 12; see also 145.

8. Ibid., Lecture IV.

9. Ibid., 217.

10. Ibid., 149.

11. Ibid., 159, for the passages quoted.

12. Ibid., 235, n. 22, 324–31, esp. 327–28, and 359–62.

13. Ibid., 164.

14. Ibid., 16–18, incl. n.18; see also 50, 54.

15. Ibid., 168; see also 164 and 167–68.

16. Rawls, "Basic Structure," *Values and Morals*, ed. Alvin I. Goldman and Jaegwon Kim (Dordrecht: Reidel, 1978), 47–71.

17. PL, 227–28.

18. Ibid., 228 and 229 respectively, for the quoted passages.

19. Ibid., 217; cf. 137.

20. As we find it, mainly in PL, Lecture VI.

21. Parts of this paper draw, sometimes verbatim, on my article, "Rawls's New Theory of Justice," *Chicago-Kent Law Review* 69.3 (1994): 737–61. And I have been helped greatly by my discussions with David Reidy, over the intervening years, of ideas contained in the present paper.

BIBLIOGRAPHY OF RELEVANT WRITINGS BY JOHN RAWLS

Rawls, John. 1971. A *Theory of Justice*. Cambridge, Mass.: Harvard University Press.

————. 1978. "The Basic Structure as Subject." *Values and Morals*, ed. Alvin I. Goldman and Jaegwon Kim. Dordrecht, Holland: Reidel, 47–71. (This essay is reprinted, unrevised, as Lecture VII in PL.)

————. 1980. "Kantian Constructivism in Moral Theory." *Journal of Philosophy* 77: 515–72. (A published version of three lectures given as the John Dewey Lectures, at Columbia University, 14–16 April 1980.)

————. 1982. "The Basic Liberties and Their Priority." *The Tanner Lectures on Human Values*, Vol. III, ed. S. M. McMurrin. Salt Lake City: University of Utah Press, 3–87. (This essay is reprinted, unrevised, as Lecture VIII in PL.)

————. 1985. "Justice as Fairness: Political not Metaphysical." *Philosophy and Public Affairs* 14: 223–51.

————. 1987. "The Idea of an Overlapping Consensus." *Oxford Journal of Legal Studies* 7: 1–25. (This paper is the text of the 1986 Hart Lecture in the University of Oxford.)

————. 1988. "The Priority of Right and Ideas of the Good." *Philosophy and Public Affairs* 17: 251–76.

_____. 1989. "The Domain of the Political and Overlapping Consensus." *New York University Law Review* 64: 233–55.

_____. 1993. *Political Liberalism*. New York: Columbia University Press: [*PL*].

_____. 1995. "Reply to Habermas." *Journal of Philosophy* 92: 132–80. (This essay is reprinted, virtually unrevised, as Lecture IX in Rawls 1996.)

_____. 1996. Paperback version of *Political Liberalism*. New York: Columbia University Press. (This paperback version is unchanged from PL, except that it has a second [paperback] introduction, xxxvii–lxii, and adds Rawls, "Reply to Habermas," as Lecture IX.)

_____. 1997. "The Idea of Public Reason Revisited." *The University of Chicago Law Review* 64: 765–807.

LIBERAL DEMOCRACY AND RADICAL DEMOCRACY: THE TWO FACES OF JANUS

Gabriel Vargas Lozano

While the word "democracy" has proliferated in social and political discourse in recent decades, I suggest that the liberal democracy of the past, connected as it is (especially in the West) to the market economy, is insufficient for the challenges facing the contemporary Latin American context. I assess and criticize democratic ideas in order to suggest that the way forward is radical democracy based on socio-economic and political justice. These, however, have to be articulated at a variety of levels, from that of local and indigenous peoples to that of national and international relations.

During the past few years, democracy has become a "good word" in certain parts of the world. This fact is due to several reasons. First, the fall of the so-called "truly existing socialism," in Europe and the Soviet Union (1989–1991) revealed both the importance of political democracy in a society that was intended as an alternative to capitalism, and the theoretical deficit of critical theory—Marxism specifically—in this field. On the other hand, the fall of those regimes and their legitimizing ideology has opened up a void that has cried out to be filled.

The second element that contributed to the rise of democracy's prestige was the beginning of a new stage of the capitalist system called "globalization." I understand globalization as a complex and irreversible process, which is the result of the broadening of the market, the general restructuring of the system, and the use of new technologies in all sectors of society. This process affects cultural and historical identity, the sovereignty of states, representationalist ways, communication systems, culture, and a certain conception of development. Just as liberalism helped in the construction of the state-nations, globalization (now homogenized by neo-liberalism) is supporting the destruction of the former. If we consider, however, that there is an ontological priority of practice and a whole set of contradictions involved, we can say that there are possibilities of generating alternatives in other ways and directions.[1]

The third aspect that helps the prestige of democracy is the transition observed in Latin America during the 1980s and 1990s from dictatorial or authoritarian governments to political democracy. This transition has been possible because the dominating groups have been forced to make their domination conditions more flexible in order to share with other sectors the social and economic crisis which Latin America is undergoing. On the other hand, the same crisis issued forth in a series of social movements looking to defend their rights and political expressions (ethnic, neighbor, feminist, human rights, and ecological groups). Their demands can no longer be restrained by former policies that have been undermined by the globalization process.

In addition, both the fall of the "actually existing socialism" and the failure of the movements which intended to establish a new social order by violent means in Latin America have produced a crisis in the paradigm of the foundational revolution. This has, as a result, opened up the possibility of social change in the long term.

Finally, the theoretical crisis into which several traditions of the political thought—such as liberalism, socialism, and republicanism—have fallen into, has generated an important debate that implies the renovation or transformation of such theories.

By contrast, in those societies where liberal democracy has been developed, a deep skepticism can be found regarding the real possibilities that the form of democracy might have in order to modify society in a certain, more just ways. This is expressed, for example, by John Dunn:

> [T]here are indeed two different democratic theories running all over the world: one is depressingly ideological and other evidently utopic. In the first, democracy is the name given to a determined and tangible form of modern state which, in the most optimistic case, is no more than the least worse mechanism to guarantee, in the modern states, a certain standard of responsibility of the governors over the governed. In the second, the democracy (or as it is sometimes called, participatory democracy) simply has a meaning confined to the good society functioning . . . and in which all social mechanisms authentically represent all the interests of all people.[2]

For Dunn, we are trapped between two incompatible rationalities. Regarding the latter, we cannot help but wish it, yet we cannot have it. We face a dilemma.

A paradox therefore arises. In some areas of the world where there has been no strong democratic tradition because it has been hindered both by local oligarchies and empires, there is growing interest in democracy. However, in other areas where there has been such tradition, there is great disillusion. Does this mean that, e.g., in Latin America we can only "wait" awhile so that we may recognize the limitations and weaknesses of such democracy and thus, the motives for our mistake?

In my opinion, the liberal democracy that implies commitment to the market economy is the concept in crisis. Thus, we must study consciously the modern democratic experience in order to find its mistakes and main problems and open up new paths. For such purposes, we can start with the following. First, we must recover the contributions of liberal democracy.[3] Second, we need to distinguish the various models of democracy, some adequate to capitalism, because—as Marcos Roitman puts it—"no conception of democracy is unbiased regarding the type of state and domination order."[4] Third, we should register the "adaptation and distortion" process regarding democracy understood as "popular sovereignty" and consider it as a domination form (from Bentham and James Mill with democracy as "protection," to Schumpeter with democracy as procedure, and Hayek with his "legal democracy"). Fourth, we must study the struggle for the differentiated rights of the citizens and strengthen civil society. Fifth, we need to look for phenomena that block the decisions of the majority (such as the representation forms, bureaucracy, and technocracy). Finally, we should generate an alternative conception of democracy such as that defined by Carol Gould in her essay "Diversity and Democracy: Representing Differences"—"Governance in a democracy is self-government by means of participation and representation in a context of decision-making."[5] This idea of democracy, however, must be considered as a "regulatory idea" for action.

The binomial democracy and globalization has caused several effects in Latin America, but I shall only point out four: 1) inequality and democracy; 2) crisis of the state-nation; 3) liberalism and communitarianism; and 4) the power behind the ballot boxes.

I. INEQUALITY AND DEMOCRACY

Beyond economic, social, political, and cultural diversity, in words of Pablo González Casanova, "democracy (both as reality and project) is part of the historical development of the nations and peoples of Latin America."[6] But applied modernization has resulted in inequality and extreme poverty both within particular nation-states and with regard to North-South relations. Under such conditions, is it possible to have a political democracy?

Undoubtedly, democracy, understood according to its original meaning, requires basic economic and social conditions—education, constitution of citizenship, and citizens' will—but it is precisely at this point where the type of democracy required is at stake. A limited and excluding democracy such as the one under development would only perpetuate the extreme inequity conditions suffered by our societies. On the contrary, a radical democracy would have to allow not only the defense of political rights, but also that of social rights, in order to achieve the foregoing conditions.

II. CRISIS OF THE STATE-NATION

Political democracy has been part of the constitution process of Latin American nations. Independence was motivated by the ideas of Jean-Jacques Rousseau and the consolidation of the republics took place under the impulse of John Stuart Mill. Liberalism allowed for the struggle against corporations (the church, military groups, and Indian communities) trying to establish homogeneity and egalitarianism. The nation-state was also the form under which a country protected itself from the aggressions of greater potencies. Such strategy, however, resulted in the deepening of the economic, social, and cultural inequality. Today in Mexico there are 40 million poor within a whole population of 91 million, and from those 40 million, 18 million exist in conditions of extreme poverty. In general, such is the current ratio in Latin American countries. The policy of the apparent homogeneity together with an economy which during the last few decades has been struggling to destroy the populist state or welfare state has allowed the emergence of greater injustice and inequalities. Thus, philosophers such as Luis Villoro have supported urged for the constitution of a new symbolic order that recognizes the heterogeneity of the members of a society together with an economy of distributive justice.[7]

III. LIBERALISM VERSUS COMMUNITARIANISM

The foregoing becomes more relevant at the light of the Indian revolt that took place in Chiapas on 1 January 1994. On that date the American expression of the global restructuring, "North America Free Trade Agreement" (NAFTA), was coming into force. In this case, however, contrary to the European Union, two highly industrialized countries were linked with a country undergoing an economic crisis. For this reason, NAFTA was not seen as the construction of an egalitarian economic platform but as subordination of the Mexican economy to the American economy. This resulted in two effects, among others: the intent to reproduce the American political system (which would have been impossible) and a reaction against the neoliberal policies among a sector which had been oppressed during the past five hundred years, namely, the Indian sector.

The rebellion in Chiapas and its later evolution increased awareness of the following issues: 1) the existence of a complex Indian culture integrated by 56 ethnic groups with their respective languages; 2) the great resistance of such peoples against assimilation by liberal society; 3) their purpose of achieving a relative autonomy regarding the na-tion-state; 4) their decision not to accept backwardness but, on the contrary, to incorporate international standards respecting human rights; 5) the achievement, for the first time, of international solidarity by means of the non-governmental organizations; 6) the clash between the neoliberal con-ception of a society formed with autonomous individuals and cooperative collective forms; and 7) their interest in experimenting with a unique way of development together with the State. This conflict poses the following problem to Mexican society: after so many years of repression and inequal-ity, should the neoliberal politics conception be imposed without taking into consideration the millenary traditions that the Indian peoples have kept? My answer is negative. Only a radical democracy will provide the opportunities for the representation of the various groups that integrate Mexican and Latin American societies.

IV. THE POWERS BEHIND THE BALLOT BOXES

But there is a greater problem initially posed by Norberto Bobbio and later by Offe and Schmitter.[8] Behind Bobbio's approach to democracy—in pro-cedural terms, a "(primary or fundamental) set of rules which establish who is authorized to take the collective decisions and under what proce-dures"—here are a number of powers threatening democracy itself.[9] These are corporativism, separation of *demos* and their representatives, oligar-chies, technocracy as an "invisible power," the lack of interest among citizens, bureaucracy, drug dealing, and the interests of the great potencies that have hindered the development of democracy (as in the case of Chile in 1973, and the conditions imposed on Nicaragua in 1990). Bobbio's sug-gestion in this context is to extend democracy to other spheres of society. Notwithstanding the problems posed by his procedural approach because it does not take into consideration the adaptations of democracy to the economic system, his proposition is valid. It is necessary to extend the democracy to the plants, to the church, the family, and so forth, although such spheres require differentiated rulings. But we need a political strat-egy and a theory of the differences of the various action sectors.

Also important is Habermas's thesis that we understand democracy as "procedure and deliberation."[10] He suggests the organization and development of rational debate in the public sphere. But both proposals (Bobbio's and Habermas's) generate skepticism when one becomes aware of how the mercantilization, reification, and alienation processes have become entrenched under the control of the multinational companies and oligarchies within national and international political systems. In my opinion, in spite of the plausibility of their suggestions, their proposals are weakened in part because they retain the liberal distinction between politics and economics.

Consequently, it is not sufficient to support an alternative radical democracy. In addition, the conditions that will sustain a democratic society must be created. Such conditions include strong civil societies at the national and international levels. What is needed is a non-excluding alternative democracy based on socio-economic and political justice and articulated by a variety of forces, institutions, and movements.

I have entitled this paper "Liberal Democracy and Radical Democracy: The Two Faces of Janus." As is well known, Janus was a Roman God, guardian of heaven and God of the beginning and the end. Janus's face towards the past would see that liberal democracy has today come to an end. This God's face towards the future would see the rise of the non-excluding radical democracy.

Gabriel Vargas Lozano, Philosophy Department of the Universidad Autónoma Metropolitana, México

NOTES

1. Cf. Samir Amin, *Los desafíos de la mundialización*, trans. Marcos Cueva (México: Siglo XXI–UNAM, 1997).

2. John Dunn, *La agonía del pensamiento político occidental* (Cambridge: Cambridge University Press, 1996), 43–44 (my English translation from the Spanish edition).

3. As suggested by C. B. Macpherson, *Democratic Theory: Essays in Retrieval* (New York: Oxford University Press, 1973); Norberto Bobbio, *El futuro de la democracia*, trans. J. F. Fernández Santillán (México: Fondo de Cultura Económica, 1986); idem, *Liberalismo y democracia*, trans. J. F. Fernández Santillán (México: Fondo de Cultura Económica, 1989).

4. Cf. *La democracia en América Latina: Actualidad y perspectivas*, ed Pablo González Casanova and Roitman Marcos (México: Jornada Ediciones; Centro de Investigaciones Interdisciplinarias en Ciencias y Humanidades,1995), 63; see also

the further discussion of this dialectical process in Ellen Meiksins Wood, *Democracy Against Capitalism: Renewing Historical Materialism* (Cambridge: Cambridge University Press, 1995).

5. *Democracy and Difference: Contesting Boundaries of the Political*, ed. Seyla Benhabib (Princeton: Princeton University Press, 1996), 176.

6. Casanova and Marcos, op. cit., 12.

7. Luis Villoro, *El poder y el valor: Fundamentos de una ética política* (México: Fondo de Cultura Económica, El Colegio Nacional, 1997).

8. Bobbio, *El futuro de la democracia*, op. cit.; and later by Claus Offe and Philippe C. Schmitter, "Las paradojas y los dilemas de la democracia liberal," *Revista Internacional de filosofía política* (Diciembre 6, 1995).

9. Ibid., 14.

10. Jürgen Habermas, *Facticidad y validez*, trans. M. Jiménez Redondo (Madrid: Trotta, 1998).

THE MEANING OF DEMOCRACY: A WESTERN PERSPECTIVE

Peter A. French

I suggest that part of the reason the on-going debate in the West between the liberal democrats and the communitarians about the future and/or the ills of democracy is futile because both sides are committed to conceptually different accounts of democracy. The roots of communitarianism in the Athenian *polis* and that of liberalism in the atomistic individualism of the Enlightenment are contrasted in order to discern the motivating visions and overarching structures of both. Whereas communitarian democracy is will-dominated, liberal democracy is choice-dominated. My purpose here is not to argue for the supremacy of one over the other, but to call attention to the distinctions between the two that are often blurred in contemporary discussion about democracy.

W hen I was asked to talk about the meaning of democracy from a Western perspective, I worried that I had nothing especially useful to contribute to the vast volume of materials already in the literature on the subject. Also, I have written very little in political theory in recent years and nothing on the concept of democracy. That worry is probably well founded, but I have decided to take a stab at sorting out a bit of a conceptual tangle that my somewhat less than trained eye has noticed in what purports to be debates about democracy in the literature that I have examined. I am not, however, going to survey that literature or pick on any particular pieces for close investigation. Instead, I only want to offer some reasons why we should regard the on-going debate in the West between the liberal democrats and the communitarians about the future and/or the ills of democracy as a non-starter. The two sides are committed to conceptually different accounts of democracy. They mean quite different things by the term "democracy," and are referring to radically different political structures. The fact that the word "democracy" seems to fit both of their conceptions is an indication of how vague that term is in socio-political discourse in the West, and, also, its enormous cash value. No one, these days, touts the virtues of monarchy or various forms of totalitarian political systems. The discussion in the circles of political theory is over various brands and types of democracies. So "democracy," at best, is an umbrella term, and an extremely wide umbrella at that. Although both the communitarian's and the liberal democrat's conceptions of the ideal state may be roughly called democratic, even a cursory examination reveals that their dissimilarities are far greater than their common features. It, however, is worth noting that one feature they do share is that they wrap themselves in thick blankets of political nostalgia, though subscribing to distinctly different conceptions of the "good old days." Unwrapping those blankets is a reasonable way to start.

In the Western philosophical tradition, reflecting the current dichotomy of conceptions, there are two rather different stories about democracy. They are, mistakenly and often, interwoven into a single story that reads as if seventeenth- and eighteenth-century liberals are the progeny of the classical Athenian democrat. The Athenian model, however, is what Benjamin Barber calls a "strong democracy," while the liberal democratic conception requires a rather "thin" democratic political structure that Barber calls "weak."[1] Athenian-style democracy is conceptually thick, building political order and structure out of the very meaning of the term "democracy." It is radically participatory.

> Active citizens govern themselves directly . . . not necessarily at every level and in every instance, but frequently enough and in particular when basic policies are being decided and when significant power is being deployed. Self-government is carried on through institutions designed to facilitate ongoing civic participation in agenda-setting, deliberation, legislation, and policy implementation.[2]

It is proximate self-legislation. Its success depends, as a number of political theorists have told us, on the conversion of a not insignificant amount of individual interests into public goods. The Athenian model is characterized by the transformation of multiple individual conceptions of the good into a commonly held, and rather singular, communal conception of the good towards whose achievement and/or maintenance political processes are directed.

The Athenian conception derives its strength from the fact that the citizens' individual interests are seen to orbit around their shared conception of the good, tending, by exclusion, to produce a homogeneous population. Citizens in the participatory process of governing, in the Athenian-style democracy, formulate the public ends towards which their community will strive and thereby define itself. Barber writes:

> In such communities, public ends are neither extrapolated from absolutes nor 'discovered' in a preexisting 'hidden consensus'. They are literally forged through the act of public participation, created through common deliberation and common action and the effect that deliberation and action have on interests, which change shape and direction when subjected to these participatory processes.[3]

"Good old days" communitarian democracy amateurizes politics and government, creating a community out of a collective. That community, the non-abstract "we," transforms the individual while it sustains itself. It educates its citizens to become effective public participants and to appreciate and adopt its values, its shared vision, and purpose. The sustenance of the "strong" democracy requires the nurturing of an abiding sense of civic responsibility in the members that is developed through training in the arts of citizenship.

Although I associate this "strong" or communitarian conception of democracy with classical Athens, for that is its purported "golden age," there is a heavy doze of Rousseau's political theory in the mix. The communitarian democracy, it is typically maintained, is necessary for individuals to achieve true moral freedom and to live lives of worth. Rousseau, frequently quoted by communitarians, wrote that the primary task in the formation of a democracy is "to change human nature, to transform each individual . . . into a part of a larger whole from which this individual receives, in a sense, his life, his being."[4] The great accomplishment, the goal, of the communitarian conception of democracy was also framed by Rousseau when he wrote: "If each citizen is nothing except in concert with all the others . . . one can say that the legislation has achieved the highest possible point of perfection."[5] As Michael Sandel notes, this conception of democracy is, at heart, coercive.[6] It links the moral improvement of its citizens and, perhaps more to the point of difference with the other conception, the freedom of its citizens, to the formative project of democracy. The political community attends to the moral character of its citizens as a condition of their freedom. Statecraft is a part and parcel of, to use Sandel's term, "soulcraft." Or, within Aristotle's framework, the epitome of virtue requires active citizenship in the *polis*.

Other than sharing some of the basic descriptive terminology of democracy, as I suggested above, there is very little in common between the Athenian/communitarian democratic ideal and the conception of the liberal democrat that has dominated the political scene in the West for the past three or four centuries. Consider the way in which the relationship between the "people" and their government is formulated. Lincoln, famously, talked of "government by the people and for the people," and the Constitution of the United States begins, "We the people." For the communitarian democrat, government is the province of the participating citizen, not the people, definitely not the untutored and uninitiated masses. To be a citizen is to be capable of participation and to be actually involved in government. Barber writes:

> To be a citizen is to participate in a certain conscious fashion that presumes awareness of and engagement in activity with others. This consciousness alters attitudes and lends to participation that sense of the 'we' associated with community. To participate is to create a community that governs itself, and to create a self-governing community is to participate.[7]

For the communitarian, democrat participation and community are the defining characteristics of the citizen. They are not necessarily the properties of the people who happen to make a democratic state their home. Aristotle, it may be remembered, excluded women, slaves, and resident aliens from citizenship in his *polis* because they, he believed, lacked the excellence of virtue required of those in positions of civic responsibility.

The liberal democrat's roots are firmly planted in the individualism that marks political philosophy in the West since at least the seventeenth century. Seventeenth-century political thought stirs the hearts of those who see human society as an aggregate of free individual humans contracting together for individual personal benefit. The great political theorists of atomistic individualist liberalism, Hobbes and Locke, understood individual natural persons to be the elemental parts of society. The civil state, for them, is built on and composed of consenting individual contractors each committed to the protection and preservation of his or her natural rights to life, liberty, and property. Freedom is a precondition of civic association. It is not a goal of the formative project of the state. Methodological individualism, treating talk of communities and organizations as reducible to talk about individual humans who happen to be involved in certain kinds of group or collective enterprises, gained a firm foothold in our conceptual scheme. Collective enterprises, including democratic government, are to be thought of as goal-directed activities in which individual humans freely engage and disengage, usually for prudential (self-interested) reasons. Among the primary aims of the atomistic individualist liberal democrats of the seventeenth and eighteenth centuries were two socio-political transformations: (1) the medieval feudal subject into the independent, prudentially motivated, Enlightenment citizen; and (2) social relations from matters of status to matters of contract. The latter conversion reflects the conceptual chasm between Athenian-style democracy and modern liberal democracy because membership in the citizenry of the communitarian state is, as already noted, clearly an exclusionary matter of status, albeit moral status, not contract. Charles Taylor writes:

> We inherit atomism from the Seventeenth Century. Not that we still espouse social contract theories (although various transposed versions are still popular) . . . . [E]ven though we no longer understand the origins of society as reposing in agreement, we nevertheless both understand and evaluate its workings as an instrument to attain ends we impute to individuals or constituent groups.[8]

This seventeenth-century conception on which liberal democracy is based was not born in full glory out of the heads of either Hobbes or Locke. It culminates an individualist movement in Western thought that appears to have budded in the twelfth century, even within the Catholic Church, and flowered in the sixteenth century with the Protestant Reformation and its rallying cry of the "priesthood of all believers." It embraces individual autonomy, and its politics is the politics of individual interests and interest groups comprised of individuals. The democratic process, for it, is an adversarial encounter of factions, individuals associated into loosely confederated groups that are generally united only with respect to a single issue, likely with quite distinct conceptions of the good, collectively and individually, each seeking majority support. Its basic conception of government is that of decision-making between competing points of view. Though it may seek consensus, it is not interested in the formative project of citizenship. It rejects the notion that moral freedom and character development are crucial elements of the civic enterprise. It radically disassociates the public from the private sphere.

The liberal democrat conceives of the decision, whether it be made by the single voter in the booth choosing over a list of candidates or cast in the vote of the representative in the halls of the legislature, as the heart and soul of the political process. Its magnitude in the liberal democratic scheme of things can be observed, daily during the Congressional sessions, on C-Span as a near empty hall fills only when a vote is taken. Representatives and Senators rush into their respective chambers to have their votes recorded on a bill, then depart with equal haste. It is the vote that matters, not the discussion of the issue. The majority rules, and its rule is not constrained with respect to the outcomes to be reached, except that it cannot infringe upon the Constitutionally established political freedoms of its citizens. Those freedoms include those set forth, for example, in the Bill of Rights. Brian Barry adds two other conditions to the list of constraints: the rule of law will govern and there will be formal voting equality.[9] Robert Dahl adds a third: that citizenship is extended to all adult members, excepting transients and the mentally defective.[10]

This view of popular liberal democracy, however, generates a paradox, as Amy Gutmann notes, "in the tension between popular will and the conditions of maintaining the popular will over time."[11] (This is not Wollheim's paradox.[12]) A liberal democrat should oppose any decision of the majority that restricts any of the basic liberties because it would not be democratic to restrict those freedoms, but the same liberal democrat should support the majority's decision because not doing so would be undemocratic. What then should the liberal democrat do if the majority votes to restrict the freedom, for example, to practice religion by excluding from the protection any religion that forbids its practitioners from seeking medical treatment for their ill children? There is a Rousseauian way of overcoming the paradox involving the contrast between the general will and the will of all. Rousseauian-type solutions, however, should be rejected by liberal democrats for the reasons noted above. So liberal democrats can discover themselves trapped in their own rhetoric once they start using theoretical stratagems to salvage majority rule from its illiberal and undemocratic tendencies. Gutmann writes:

> A practically inevitable tension exists between any actual procedure of popular rule and the corresponding ideal of popular democracy. The ideal requires outcomes—unmanipulated political preferences, the rule of law, formal voting equality, and inclusive citizenship—that can, and do, conflict with the actual popular will as revealed by any procedure designed for the sake of popular rule.[13]

In a communitarian-type democracy the highest premium is placed on what Barber calls "talk."[14] I will borrow his term, though I am not especially happy with it. "Talk" is understood not to be merely speech. It includes listening. Actually, a better term might be "conversation." "Talk" has also been appropriated by the liberal democrats, but for them it does comes to mean something like speech-making or "sound-biting." Looking again at those Halls of Congress, when a vote is not being taken, a C-Span viewer is likely to see a single member of Congress at a microphone rambling on and on about something or other while the rest of the chamber is empty. To whom is he or she talking? To no one, the speech is for the record, a record that is seldom read. "Talk" in the liberal democrat's lexicon is, at best, the expression of an opinion, regardless of whether or not anyone is listening. It achieves its fullest realization on Talk Radio. It is the noise that precedes the vote. The media, especially the electronic media, have reduced talk to the 10–30 second sound-bite in which, at most, a slogan is beamed forth to the less-than-attentive audience. Listening is not required. In fact, listening to talk is something of a lost art, especially in America. Politicians do not listen to their constituents and citizens do not listen to their representatives. Then again, the electronic media does not encourage listening. As Barber notes, "One measure of healthy political talk is the amount of silence it permits and encourages, for silence is the precious medium in which reflection is nurtured and empathy can grow."[15] Silence may be golden according to the adage, but it has only a negative value on television and radio.

Communitarian democracy is deliberation-oriented, and it is deliberation over how the social world, the community, is to be formed and sustained. So it is talk to a practical purpose. It is not merely the statement of preferences. It is, crucially, involved in persuasion and the critical examination of options. It is what Barry calls "decision by discussion of merits."[16] It leads, of course, to the vote, but the vote is not the be all and end all of the democratic process, though it embodies the sense of urgency that marks the process as political. The choice-oriented liberal democrat who sees the political process as a combat between various individual and group preferences can only stave off what could easily become an "anarchy of adversary politics" with the principle of majority rule, despite its potential paradoxes. "Majoritarianism," Barber bemoans, "is a tribute to the failure of democracy."[17] Well, it is the failure of communitarian democracy to sustain itself in the modern Western world, but less so the failure of liberal democracy, which seems prepared to live with the paradoxes in the name of getting to closure on an issue.

It might be fair to characterize communitarian democracy as will dominated and liberal democracy as choice dominated. Barber makes just such a suggestion when he writes: "Strong [read 'communitarian'] democracy decision-making is predicated on will rather than choice and on judgment rather than preference. Strong democracy understands decision-making to be a facet of man as maker and as creator and consequently focuses on public willing."[18] It, in the language favored by certain European philosophers, is to will a world that fits a certain description and therefore permits of certain types of human actions and organizations.

The foundations of liberal democracy are laid on the theory of rational choice. Independent rational preference based on one's conception of one's own best interests drives the political and the economic theory. Political arrangements and choices are the result of aggregated individual choices. Compromise, sometimes called the art of politics, is typically understood as the Pareto optimal choice when one cannot maximize one's preferences, where preferences and their orderings are pre-political and independent of communal relationships and commitments, even unchosen commitments such as those embedded in culture and heritage. The need for compromise arises, of course, when conflicts of interests occur in the social world. Such conflicts are bargainable, but they are always intractable. The conflict does not disappear in the compromise, it is put aside as the competing individuals or groups settle for something less than the realization of their interests in total.

The communitarian democrat requires that citizens develop and practice conversational techniques that allow the forging of a common vision and plan of action for the community. Such techniques are not conducive to a pluralistic or diverse citizenry. But that is exactly the sort of citizenry that dominates the Western democracies. The media has certainly discovered this and has, for example, proliferated special interest channels and programming to appeal only to those who are proficient in the conversational techniques of narrower and narrower topic ranges. The catering to such individual interests and the encouraging of narrow bands of conversational proficiency that marks the West today, in large measure, works against anything like the communitarian's common vision oriented ideal.

Underlying this encouragement of narrow-banding interest development and the virtual obsession with the glorification of diversity that has marked American liberal democracy in recent decades is the rejection of the communitarian idea that the identity of a person and the identity of a citizen are not distinct or separable. The liberal democrat draws a rather thick and clear line between the public sphere and the private sphere of a person's life. One's public or political life is bounded by the obligations of a procedural democracy and the choices one makes as a rational and independent chooser. Those choices are conceived of as not being encumbered by ties antecedent to choice. Sandel, however, comments:

> This vision cannot account for a wide range of moral and political obligations that we commonly recognize, such as obligations of loyalty or solidarity. By insisting that we are bound only by ends we choose for themselves, it denies that we can ever be claimed by ends we have not chosen . . . for example, by our identities as members of families, peoples, cultures, or traditions.[19]

The liberal democrat, however, can respond that his vision does not exclude such obligations. It reserves them for the private sphere.

Governmental neutrality with respect to conceptions of the good is preserved by a procedural conception of democracy that restricts the political sphere to operations within boundaries set by the protection of individual rights. Those rights are, of course, neutral with respect to ends citizens might pursue, provided the gaining of those ends does not violate the boundaries. The ends at which citizens aim, their conceptions of the good, are, at least theoretically, of no real political or governmental interest, provided that in getting to those ends citizens do not overstep the constraints that give teeth to their basic rights or liberties. Democratic proceduralism is merely a constraint theory, and a rather minimal constraint theory at that. It is not a formative theory of democracy.

The West's rejection of formative democracy, in which the civic virtues the communitarian believes essential to effective self government are positively fostered in the citizenry, in favor of pluralistic proceduralism has given rise, the critics stress, to a general discontent with (or disaffection for) democracy. Typically, it is noted that those who vote, even in local elections, represent a very small percentage of the citizens. Jorge Castaneda writes:

> Today, in many cases, those who vote, run for office, get elected, legislate, and rule are less and less a reflection of society as a whole, although they are an increasingly faithful image of the electorate. This could be named the Michael Riordan syndrome: how did the most cosmopolitan, tension-ridden, socially and racially diverse city in the United States elect a Republican, white, over-fifty male millionaire as its mayor? It didn't: the people of Los Angeles did not elect Riordan, the voters did, and the people and the voters are no longer the same thing.[20]

Sandel writes of the procedural democracy: "its vision of political discourse is too spare to contain the moral energies of democratic life."[21] What he means is that the public philosophy of the currently popular conception of democracy in America requires citizens to bracket their moral and their religious commitments and their cultural heritages outside of political debate. Perhaps that is the only way for something resembling democracy to survive in such an utterly complex and diverse country as the United States.

It is not as if anyone is calling for a return to some other form of government. Even though citizens regularly express concern that their government is out of their control and that they have very little trust in their governmental officials, they seems also to gain a modicum of satisfaction from having a government that is virtually hamstrung by its own machinations. There is something to be said for Byzantine governmental structures! The procedural democracy has become the bureaucratic leviathan, and I suspect that is what Hobbes envisioned.

A final point: The communitarian's conception of democracy, rooted in the Athenian model was, and I suspect, still is, place dominated. For

Aristotle, that place was the *polis*, the city-state, a rather small place at that! Loyalty to place, to a way of life peculiar to that place and to a common language and heritage, and a commitment to the maintenance of that place and that way of life are the impetus for the development of the art of self-government and for the fostering of the civic virtues in the residents (citizens). The communitarian ideal of democracy is, first and foremost, a story of place, a narrative of a people in a place. Commitment to that narrative drives the communal conscience to sustain the institutions of self-government. No such narrative is possible in the pluralistic social world of contemporary Western democracies like the United States. That is not to say that we have no stories or that we have no sense of place. Rather, with the help and urging of the liberal democrat, we have come to the realization, though probably regretfully, that it is impossible to compose a single coherent narrative that would make interpretive sense for most of the people of their current conditions, explain their commonality, and bring order and a sense of place to their lives. There are far too many strands in the story of America for the communitarian storyteller to weave a coherent communal identity to provide the exemplar for the formative project of communitarian democracy. Our shared stories are not those that sustain Athenian-style democracy. They are what Sandel calls the "vacant, vicarious fare of confessional talk shows, celebrity scandals, and sensational trials."[22]

The liberal conception of procedural democracy, however, requires little by way of narrative, and its emergence into the Kafkaesque bureaucracy seems to provide a certain amount of comfort, cold though it may be, to the populous. As E. J. Dionne has noted, "The options deemed viable are indistinguishable from the status quo."[23] Of course, the inertia of the contemporary liberal democratic state stifles almost all attempts at political creativity to address great social problems, within the country and globally. Whether or not that will ultimately topple procedural democracy in the West or encourage a Balkanization of the existing liberal democratic states into communitarian democracies is a matter about which I have no opinion. The latter, however, I think is most unlikely in so fragmented a collectivity as the United States. Pluralism and diversity are, perhaps, the salvation of the liberal democracy *qua* bureaucracy.

Peter A. French, Department of Philosophy, University of South Florida, Tampa, FL 33620-5550; french@bayflash.stpt.usf.edu

NOTES

1. Benjamin Barber, *Strong Democracy* (Berkeley: University of California Press, 1984).

2. Ibid., 150.

3. Ibid., 151.

4. Jean-Jacques Rousseau, *On the Social Contract*, ed. and tr. D. A. Cress (Indianapolis: Hackett Publishing Company, 1983), 39.

5. Ibid.

6. Michael Sandel, *Democracy's Discontent* (Cambridge: Harvard University Press, 1996), 318.

7. Barber, op. cit., 155.

8. Charles Taylor, *Sources of the Self* (Cambridge: Harvard University Press, 1989), 195.

9. Brian Barry, "Is Democracy Special?" *Philosophy, Politics and Society*, 5th Series, ed. P. Laslett and J. Fishkin (New Haven: Yale University Press, 1979).

10. Robert A. Dahl, *Democracy and Its Critics* (New Haven: Yale University Press, 1989).

11. Amy Gutmann, "The Disharmony of Democracy," *Democratic Community*, ed. J. W. Chapman and I. Shapiro (New York, New York University Press), 126–60.

12. Richard Wollheim, "A Paradox in the Theory of Democracy," *Philosophy, Politics, and Society*, 2nd Series, ed. P. Laslett and W. G. Runciman (Oxford: Oxford University Press, 1974).

13. Gutmann, op. cit., 130.

14. Barber, op. cit., 173.

15. Ibid., 174.

16. Brian Barry, *Political Argument* (London: Routledge and Kegan Paul, 1965).

17. Barber, op. cit., 198.

18. Ibid., 214.

19. Sandel, op. cit., 322.

20. Jorge Castaneda, "Three Challenges of U. S. Democracy," *Kettering Review* (Summer 1997): 14.

21. Sandel, op. cit., 323.

22. Ibid., 351.

23. E. J. Dionne, Jr., "The Era of Big Government: Why You'd Miss It If It Went," *Kettering Review* (Summer 1997): 34.

RECONCILING PUBLIC REASON AND RELIGIOUS VALUES

James P. Sterba

Philosophers who hold that religious considerations should play some role in public debate over fundamental issues have criticized Rawls's ideal of public reason for being too restrictive in generally ruling out such considerations. In response, Rawls has modified his ideal so as to explicitly allow a role for religious considerations in public debate (others, such as Robert Audi, have also offered accounts of public reason along similar lines). Nevertheless, some critics of Rawls's ideal of public reason, such as Nicholas Wolterstorff, remain unsatisfied. In this paper, I will argue that once Rawls's ideal of public reason is correctly interpreted, it will be possible to reconcile that ideal with much of the role its critics want religion to have in public debate.

In *Political Liberalism,* John Rawls sets out an ideal of public reason according to which "citizens are to conduct their fundamental discussions within the framework of what each regards as a political conception of justice based on values that others can reasonably be expected to endorse."[1] Since all citizens in pluralistic societies, like our own, cannot reasonably be expected to share the same religious values, Rawls's ideal of public reason generally rules out any role for religious considerations in public debate over fundamental issues in such societies. Accordingly, philosophers who hold that religious considerations should play such a role in public debate have criticized Rawls's ideal for being too restrictive.[2] In response, Rawls has modified his ideal so as to allow an explicit role for religious considerations in public debate over fundamental issues.[3] In addition, other philosophers (such as Robert Audi) who are attracted to

Rawls's ideal of public reason, have offered their own accounts of public reason which also allow religious considerations to play a role in public debate.[4] Nevertheless, some critics of Rawls's ideal of public reason, such as Nicholas Wolterstorff, remain unsatisfied.[5] These philosophers want an even greater role for religious considerations than either Rawls or Audi allows. In this paper, I will argue that once Rawls's ideal of public reason is correctly interpreted, it will be possible to reconcile that ideal with much of the role its critics want religion to have in public debate.

I

Originally, Rawls ruled out any role for religious considerations in public debate whenever "matters of constitutional essentials and questions of basic justice" are at issue in pluralistic societies, such as our own. Because religious considerations are typically drawn from comprehensive conceptions of the good, which are not shared by all the citizens of pluralistic societies, Rawls argued that normally such considerations should not be used in public debate.

Yet, Rawls allowed that there could be exceptions to this restriction. In certain cases, Rawls allowed that an appeal to religious considerations could be justifiably used in support of a political conception of justice in pluralistic societies. As examples of such justifiable uses, Rawls cites the American abolition movement beginning in the 1830s and the civil rights movement as led by Martin Luther King in the 1960s. Nevertheless, Rawls contended that normally citizens must be "able" and "ready" to explain to one another how the principles and policies they advocate and vote for can be supported by considerations of public reason.[6] Apparently responding to criticisms, Rawls subsequently modified this requirement, allowing that citizens may propose whatever considerations they like for public policy, including religious considerations, provided that they are also prepared "in due course" to offer considerations that comply with public reason.[7]

Robert Audi also defends a view of public reason that is quite similar to Rawls's.[8] According to Audi, the following principles govern political discourse:

> *The Principle of Theo-Ethical Equilibrium*: Those who are religious should embody a commitment to a rational integration between religious deliverances and insights and secular ethical considerations.

> *The Principle of Secular Rationale*: Everyone has a prima facie obligation not to advocate or support any law or public policy that restricts human conduct, unless he or she has, and is willing to offer, adequate secular reasons for this advocacy.

The Principle of Secular Motivation: Everyone also has a prima facie obligation to abstain from advocacy or support of a law or public policy that restricts human conduct unless he or she is sufficiently motivated by some normatively adequate secular reasons.

Obviously, when compared to Rawls's view, Audi's view is much more detailed in its requirements and, when compared with Rawls's earlier view, which only allowed religious considerations to play a role in public debate in certain exceptional cases, Audi's view allows for a greater role for religious considerations in public debate. This assessment is reversed, however, when Audi's view is compared with Rawls's later view. In that comparison, Audi's view is more restrictive than Rawls's later view since Rawls now has an even more relaxed requirement about providing public reasons.[9] Nevertheless, critics have contended that all these views are still too restrictive, holding that religious considerations should play a still greater role in public debate.

II

A basic criticism that has been raised to the views of Rawls and Audi focuses on the public reasons that each would make centrally important to political discourse. In general, critics question whether such reasons are actually available to the extent that defenders of the ideal of public reason say they are.[10] Obviously, if such reasons are not generally available, the question of whether to require their presence along with religious reasons will not generally arise. If public reasons are not generally available, then, either religious reasons, or other reasons drawn from our comprehensive conceptions of the good, will turn out to be the only reasons that we will generally have on which to ground our coercive public policies.

But what are these public reasons on which Rawls and Audi claim that coercive public policies should be grounded? As Rawls characterizes them, they are reasons that everyone can reasonably be expected to endorse in a liberal democratic society.[11] As Audi characterizes them, they are reasons that all fully rational citizens in possession of all the relevant facts (and so fully informed) would affirm. Both Rawls and Audi agree that citizens should be capable of appealing to such public reasons when advocating restricting human conduct at least with respect to matters of constitutional essentials and questions of basic justice.

As we noted, for Rawls, public reasons are the principles and ideals that are justifiable to every citizen in a liberal democratic society. More specifically, Rawls suggests that these include the ideal of citizens as free and equal, the ideal of a well-ordered society, the ideal of the original position, and possibly his two principles of justice, which Rawls claims can be derived from his original position. But the ideal of citizens as free and equal, and the ideal of a well-ordered society are widely understood to be very formal ideals, from which little, if anything, can be derived with regard to matters of constitutional essentials and questions of basic justice. Thus, political ideals as different as libertarianism and socialism can both be interpreted to be regarding citizens as free and equal, and society as well-ordered. By contrast, Rawls's ideal of the original position is clearly a substantive rather than a formal ideal. From it, either Rawls's two principles of justice or principles similar to them can be derived. But given the contentiousness of this ideal and its derived principles, it is not clear that it belongs to the domain of public reason as one of those values that everyone can reasonably be expected to endorse. Even Rawls acknowledges this when he writes:

> Accepting the idea of public reason and its principle of legitimacy emphatically does not mean . . . accepting a particular liberal conception of justice down to the last details of the principles defining its content. We may differ about these principles and still agree in accepting a conception's more general features.[12]

Yet while Rawls admits in this passage that his two principles of justice cannot be derived from the ideal of public reason alone, he still contends that all citizens in a liberal democratic society in virtue of being reasonable and rational are required to endorse the ideal of public reason.

But is this the case? Are all citizens in a liberal democratic society in virtue of being reasonable and rational required to endorse the ideal of public reason and thus conduct public debate by appealing to values that everyone can reasonably be expected to endorse? Surely, this is one interpretation of what it means for citizens to be reasonable and rational in a liberal democratic society, but is it the only one?

Nicholas Wolterstorff, in his critique of Rawls's ideal of public reason purports to offer another. According to Wolterstorff,

> In a democracy, we discuss and debate, with the aim of reaching agreement . . . . Then, finally, we vote. It cannot be the case that in voting under these circumstances, we are violating those concepts of freedom and equality which are ingredient in the Idea of liberal democracy, since almost the first thing that happens when societies move toward becoming liberal democracies is that they begin taking votes on various matters and living with the will of the majority—subject to provisos specifying rights of minorities.

> We aim at agreement in our discussions with each other . . . . Our agreement
> on some policy need not be based on some set of principles agreed on by all
> present and future citizens and rich enough to settle all important political
> issues. Sufficient if each citizen, for his or her own reasons, agrees on the
> policy today and tomorrow—not for all time. It need not even be the case
> that each and every citizen agrees to the policy. Sufficient if the agreement
> be the fairly-gained and fairly-executed agreement of the majority.[13]

So, according to Wolterstorff, citizens are reasonable and rational in a
liberal democratic society if after all sides have the opportunity to express
their views, they abide by the results of majority voting, provided that the
will of the majority is constrained by certain minority rights.

III

One of the rights that Wolterstorff thinks that minorities do not have in a
liberal democratic society is the right to have matters of constitutional
essentials and questions of basic justice decided in a way that everyone can
reasonably be expected to endorse. To grant minorities this right would be
to endorse Rawls's ideal of public reason, and Wolterstorff objects to Rawls's
ideal of public reason on grounds of fairness. He writes:

> Is it equitable to ask of everyone that, in deciding and discussing political
> issues, they refrain from using their comprehensive perspectives . . . ?

> [This] seems to me not equitable. [For it] belongs to the *religious convic-
> tions* of a good many religious persons in our society that *they ought to
> base* their decisions concerning fundamental issues of justice on their reli-
> gious convictions. They do not view it as an option whether or not to do so.
> It is their conviction that they ought to strive for wholeness, integrity, inte-
> gration, in their lives . . . .[14]

Thus, Wolterstorff thinks that he has provided another interpretation of
what it means for citizens to be reasonable and rational in a liberal democratic society—one which happily lacks the unfairness that he believes
characterizes Rawls's interpretation with its demand for public reason.

Wolterstorff contends that without the unfairness of Rawls's interpretation of what it means for citizens to be reasonable and rational in a liberal
democratic society, religious reasons will function more freely in public
debate. Yet notice that Wolterstorff's interpretation of what it means for
citizens to be reasonable and rational in a liberal democratic society still
does constrain how religious reasons are to function in public debate. First,
before religious reasons can be enacted in public policy, their advocates must

muster a majority of votes. Second, the enactment of such reasons is further constrained by minority rights, which Wolterstorff leaves unspecified here, beyond saying that Rawls's ideal of public reason should not be incorporated into such rights because it is unfair.

But is it unfair to impose Rawls's ideal of public reason on public debate? Presumably, Wolterstorff thinks that there are good religious reasons to support the constraints that he himself wants to impose on public debate—the requirement of majority rule and minority rights—whereas, by contrast, he thinks that Rawls's ideal of public reason is an unfair constraint on those who regard religious reasons as fundamental to their lives. So one might conclude that Wolterstorff regards his view of public debate as supported by religious reasons, whereas he regards Rawls's view as, at best, supported by only secular reasons.

Yet when Wolterstorff goes on to illustrate the difference between his view and Rawls's and Audi's views, he associates his view with what he calls a parliamentary model, which operates by majority rule, but then associates Rawls's and Audi's view with what he calls a Quaker model, which requires some form of consensus to reach decisions.[15] By characterizing Rawls's and Audi's views in this way, however, Wolterstorff implicitly concedes that their views, as well as his own, can be supported by religious reasons; at least he implicitly concedes that their views can be supported by the religious reasons that characterize a Quaker tradition. This means that the choice between his view of public debate and Rawls's and Audi's views can be understood as a choice between views that are all supported by religious reasons. This could explain why Wolterstorff argues for the choice of his own view not by appealing to specifically religious reasons but rather by appealing to an ideal of fairness. Given that Rawls's and Audi's views, as well as his own, can all be supported by religious reasons, Wolterstorff appears to recognize the need to appeal to something that is neutral or common to them all in order to support his religious view over their views. Accordingly, he appeals to an ideal of fairness.

But are Rawls's and Audi's views of public reason an unfair requirement to impose on public debate? Let us grant that Wolterstorff has made a prima facie case that Rawls's and Audi's views are unfair to a religious majority by limiting their use of religious reasons. What needs to be determined is whether this is the only unfairness that is at issue here. It would not due to correct one unfairness by imposing a similar or even greater unfairness. We need to determine, therefore, whether a minority, religious or otherwise, which loses out to a religious majority might also be unfairly treated, and if it is unfairly treated, whether that unfairness needs to be addressed as much, or even more so, than the unfairness to which Wolterstorff has drawn our attention.

Presumably, if the imposition of the majority will on the minority is to be fair, it must be possible to morally blame the minority for failing to accept that imposition. If that were not the case, then the minority could justifiably resist that imposition, and the will of the majority would lack moral legitimacy.[16] But if the imposition of the will of the majority is to be fair, there must, then, be sufficient reasons accessible to the minority, religious or otherwise, to morally require them to accept that imposition. For a group cannot be morally required to do something if they can not come to know and so come to justifiably believe that they are so required. So fairness here requires that there be reasons accessible to a minority that are sufficient to require the acceptance of the will of the majority by that minority.

Surprisingly, or not so surprisingly, Wolterstorff accepts this requirement of fairness, that is, he accepts the need for there to be reasons accessible to a minority that are sufficient to morally require the minority's acceptance of the will of the majority in the relevant cases. Moreover, Wolterstorff thinks that he has provided just those kind of reasons that are needed to morally require the minority's submission to the will of a religious majority in a liberal democratic society. As he puts it, "It need not even be the case that each and every citizen agree to the policy. Sufficient if the agreement be the fairly-gained and fairly-executed agreement of the majority."[17] According to Wolterstorff, then, the fact that an agreement is fairly-gained and fairly-executed by a religious majority should provide the minority with sufficient reasons to morally require their submission to the will of the majority in such cases. Moreover, such a fact should be accessible to a minority in a legitimate state, and its accessibility would render the minority morally blameworthy for failing to submit to the rule of the majority in such cases. Thus, by putting his justification for rule by a religious majority in terms of fairness, Wolterstorff must think that he is providing a moral justification that everyone in a liberal democratic society should regard as sufficient to justify that rule.

Yet notice that if Wolterstorff is successful in providing a sufficient moral justification for both secular and religiously-committed minorities to accept the rule of religious majorities in such cases, he would have succeeded in more ways than he realizes, since he would have also succeeded in satisfying Rawls's ideal of public reason. This is because Rawls's ideal of public reason requires a justification that everyone can reasonably be expected to endorse in a liberal democratic society. Moreover, the sense of reasonable in Rawls's requirement is not epistemological (it is not that we can reasonably predict that everyone will endorse something), nor is it morally neutral (it is not that everyone is required by minimal rationality to endorse something). Rather it is moral: it is that everyone is required by fair terms of cooperation to endorse something.[18] So when Rawls's ideal of public reason is correctly understood in this way, it clearly coincides with what Wolterstorff is claiming. For Wolterstorff is claiming that everyone, religious or otherwise, morally ought to accept the requirements of fair majority rule in a liberal democratic society.[19]

IV

Yet while Wolterstorff's ideal for public debate in a liberal democratic society can be seen to coincide in this way with Rawls's own ideal of public reason, Wolterstorff and Rawls may still be disagreeing about what their ideals, now recognized to be substantially equivalent, require. This is because they are each focusing on different aspects of the application of their ideals. Wolterstorff is focusing on the unfairness of denying members of a religious majority the right to base their decisions on religious reasons, or the unfairness of requiring them to bifurcate their lives between what they are committed to religiously and what they are, or could be, committed to non-religiously. I have granted the prima facie unfairness of such requirements. Surely, fairness would allow religious people to base their decisions on their religious reasons, provided that other requirements of fairness are satisfied. Surely, fairness would also not require religious people to bifurcate themselves between what they are committed to for religious reasons and what they are committed to for nonreligious reasons, provided that other requirements of fairness are satisfied.

By contrast, Rawls and Audi are focusing on a different requirement of fairness for majority rule. They are focusing on the issue of whether minorities, whether religious or otherwise, would have sufficient reasons accessible to them for submitting to the rule of the majority. Wolterstorff seems aware of this problem, and that is why he put the case for rule by a religious majority in terms of an ideal of fairness.[20] But fairness can have both procedural and substantive requirements. Fairness can procedurally require that a minority submit to a majority only after its members have had a chance to speak their mind and been outvoted.[21] But fairness can also substantively require that a minority submit to a majority only when there are certain additional reasons that are accessible to the members of the minority which support the will of the majority.

Now if a majority is only constrained procedurally, its impositions on a minority can turn out to be quite severe. For example, a religious majority could require a minority to financially support its religious activities or to participate in its religious services. The majority also, for example, could impose significant restrictions on women or on homosexuals as demanded by its religious doctrines. Moreover, such impositions typically would be much more constraining than the requirements that Rawls and Audi seek to impose on public discourse. So, if fairness is to be secured, particularly with respect to matters of constitutional essentials and questions of basic justice, there must be substantive reasons as well as procedural reasons that are accessible to the minority for accepting the will of the majority. And while these substantive reasons need not, by themselves, be sufficient to require abiding by the will of the majority, they must, when joined together with the procedural reasons that are also accessible to the minority, provide a sufficient justification to require abiding by the will of the majority. So it turns out that the requirements of fairness go further than Wolterstorff explicitly allowed. To meet the requirements of fairness, procedural reasons that are accessible to the minority are not enough. At least with respect to matters of constitutional essentials and questions of basic justice, there must be substantive reasons that are also accessible to the minority, and taken together these procedural and substantive reasons must constitute a sufficient justification to require the minority to abide the will of the majority.

Nevertheless, fairness does not require that each and every advocate of the majority view be willing to offer, or be motivated by, these procedural and substantive reasons. While these reasons must be accessible to the minority, they can be accessible to the minority without requiring it to be the case that each and every majority advocate not only have these reasons, but also be sufficiently motivated by them. So fairness does not impose on majority advocates the particular requirements that Rawls and Audi endorsed; and Wolterstorff is correct in maintaining that those particular requirements constitute an unfair imposition on a religious majority.

Nevertheless, collectively, the majority does have an obligation to ensure that sufficient procedural and substantive reasons for going along with the majority are accessible to the minority, at least with respect to matters of constitutional essentials and questions of basic justice. To meet this obligation, it generally suffices that the majority has taken sufficient steps to ensure freedom of speech, quality public education, and open debate for people of all persuasions. The idea is that through these institutional structures the needed public reasons will be made accessible. From time to time, however, this obligation will also require that some well-placed majority advocates help make accessible sufficient procedural and substantive reasons for the minority to go along with the will of the majority. By ensuring the accessibility to the minority of sufficient procedural and substantive reasons for their going along with the majority, this collective obligation of the majority is thereby discharged.

V

So far I have argued that once Rawls's ideal of public reason is correctly interpreted, critics of that ideal, like Wolterstorff, can actually be seen to be endorsing that very ideal, while possibly disagreeing with Rawls concerning its practical consequences. I further argued that when the practical consequences of the ideal of public reason are correctly specified, we need to reject Rawls's and Audi's requirement that each and every majority advocate be able to provide the minority with sufficient reasons that necessitate their going along with the will of the majority, and reject Audi's additional requirement that each and every majority advocate be motivated by these reasons. I contend that when such requirements are correctly judged by the ideal of public reason, they can be seen to be an unfair imposition on the majority. It follows that much of the role that critics of Rawls and Audi have wanted religious reasons to have in public debate can be justified. However, I also argued that when the practical consequences of the ideal of public reason, now seen as shared by Rawls, Audi, and Wolterstorff, are correctly specified, they require that the minority have more reasons accessible to them for accepting the will of the majority than the purely procedural reasons which Wolterstorff seems to favor. What is additionally required, I have argued, is that there be both procedural and substantive reasons accessible to the minority, which, taken together, are sufficient to require the minority's acceptance of the will of the majority, and that collectively the majority has an obligation to ensure that such reasons are accessible to the minority. In brief, I have shown that Rawls, his defenders, and critics, like Wolterstorff, all have good reason to modify the practical requirements that they have endorsed in favor of requirements that are actually demanded by the ideal of public reason which they all can be seen to accept.[22]

James P. Sterba, Philosophy Department, University of Notre Dame, Notre Dame, IN 46556; James.P.Sterba.1@nd.edu

NOTES

1. John Rawls, *Political Liberalism* (New York: Columbia University Press, 1993), 226. Throughout this discussion, I will be assuming that all citizens are morally competent, that is, sufficiently capable of understanding and acting upon moral requirements.

2. Nicholas Wolterstorff and Robert Audi, *Religion in the Public Square* (Lanham: Rowman and Littlefield, 1997), 67–120; Philip Quinn, "Political Liberalism and

Their Exclusions of the Religious," *Proceedings and Addresses of the American Philosophical Association* 69:2 (1995): 35–56; Paul Weithman, "The Separation of Church and State: Some Questions for Professor Audi," *Philosophy and Public Affairs* 20 (1991): 52–65; and the contributors to *Religion and Contemporary Liberalism*, ed. Paul J. Weithman (Notre Dame: University of Notre Dame Press, 1997).

3. Rawls, *Political Liberalism* (New York: Columbia University Press, paperback edition, 1996), li–lii.

4. Robert Audi, "The Separation of Church and State and the Obligations of Citizens," *Philosophy and Public Affairs* 18 (1989): 259–96; idem, "Religion and the Ethics of Political Participation," 100:2 *Ethics* (1990): 386–97; idem, "Religious Commitment and Secular Reason: A Reply to Professor Weithman," *Philosophy and Public Affairs* 21 (1991): 66–76.

5. Wolterstorff and Audi, op. cit.

6. Rawls, *Political Liberalism* (1996), op. cit., 217–18.

7. Ibid., li–lii.

8. Wolterstorff and Audi, op. cit., 1–47, 122–44, 167–73.

9. For example, Rawls's constraint on the use of religious reasons in public discourse applies only to matters of constitutional essentials and questions of basic justice, whereas Audi's constraint on the use of such reasons applies wherever laws and public policies restrict human conduct.

10. Wolterstorff and Audi, op. cit., 67–120, 145–66; Quinn, "Political Liberalism," op. cit., 35–56.

11. Rawls, *Political Liberalism*, 24. On one occasion, Rawls characterizes the policies that are favored by public reasons to be policies that are at least not unreasonable in the sense that those who oppose them can nevertheless understand how reasonable people can affirm them (ibid., 253). This seems to be an appropriate way of understanding the ideal of public reason in contexts where public reasons are very difficult to come by.

12. Ibid., 226–27.

13. Wolterstorff and Audi, op. cit., 108, 114.

14. Ibid., 104–05.

15. Ibid., 152.

16. The will of the majority if it is to be morally legitimate must be backed up with more than power. The minority must have a moral duty to accept the imposition of the majority, but that could only be the case if the minority would be morally blameworthy for failing to accept that imposition. Moreover, as noted before (see note 1), I am assuming throughout this discussion is that everyone is

morally competent, that is, sufficiently capable of understanding and acting upon moral requirements.

17. Wolterstorff and Audi, op. cit., 114.

18. Rawls, *Political Liberalism* (1996), op. cit., 48ff.

19. I do not think the same holds for Audi's view of public debate because "rational" in his ideal of what fully informed and fully rational people would endorse is not understood in any moral sense. But then it is does not follow that fully rational but nonmoral people, even when fully informed, will always endorse (even verbally) the requirements of morality, and certainly they will not always abide by them.

20. Procedural constraints are usually opposed to non-procedural constraints, and substantive constraints are usually opposed to formal constraints. So it is possible for a procedural constraint to be a substantive one (e.g., Rawls's original position), and for a formal constraint to be a non-procedural one. Nevertheless, typically procedural constraints will be formal and substantive constraints will be non-procedural, and right now my analysis is only trying to cover typical cases.

21. Except for his important provisos concerning minority rights, Wolterstorff might seem to be committed only to a procedural constraint on majority rule. But what if a majority decides to significantly limit the use of religious reasons in public debate (the outcome of U.S. Constitutional history?), would Wolterstorff rest content, or would he still object that such limitations are substantively unfair to the minority? My guess is that he would still object on grounds of substantive unfairness, and he would be right.

22. An earlier version of this paper was presented at the Fourteenth International Social Philosophy Conference held in Kingston, Canada, July 18–21. I am grateful to Robert Audi, Shyli Karin-Frank, Janet Kourany, Jan Narveson, Robert Van Wyk, and Nicholas Wolterstorff for their comments on this version of the paper.

PHILOSOPHY IN AMERICAN PUBLIC LIFE: *DE FACTO* AND *DE JURE*

Jorge J. E. Gracia

My focus here is on two questions: Does philosophy have a place in contemporary American public life? and should philosophy have a place in American public life? Because my answer to the first question is negative, I also will discuss some of the reasons why I believe philosophy does not play a role in American public life. I suggest that philosophers have been excluded from the public conversation in part because the work of philosophy entails criticism and challenge—activities best accomplished from "outside" of the structures of power. This means that we have a role in public life, but it is an indirect role, as teachers and critics, not as advisers and active participants.

Recent discussions of this issue have centered on the definition of the role of philosophy in American public life and the ways of increasing philosophy's influence in the public arena.[1] This emphasis is prompted by the fact that philosophers are worried about the future of the profession. After a tremendous expansion in the sixties, there has been a steady decline in the number of college-teaching positions open to newly graduated philosophers. The job market is bloated and Ph.D.s in philosophy find it increasingly difficult to secure permanent jobs. The American Philosophical Association has tried to address this situation in various ways and discussions of the state and future of the profession, once rare, are becoming common. I am quite sure that part of the motivation for this panel involved these reasons.

Today, however, I am not going to address the issue of jobs, or the ways in which we can increase the influence of philosophy. Rather, I am going to concentrate on only two questions: First, does philosophy have a place in contemporary American public life? Second, should philosophy have a place in American public life? Because my answer to the first question is negative, I will also discuss some of the reasons why I believe philosophy does not play a role in American public life.

By the first question I mean to raise the issue of whether philosophers, *qua* philosophers, play a role in the discussion of matters which concern the public at large. Are philosophical views given attention by those who are in charge of making decisions that have an effect on the American public? Are philosophers in positions of power where their decisions have an effect on the general population? Are philosophical views discussed in the mainstream media—newspapers, radio, and the ever-increasingly influential television? Are philosophers called to advise politicians, heads of large corporations, and social organizations concerned with the health and well being of Americans at large?

By the second question I mean to address the issue of whether, regardless of the place philosophy actually has in American public life, philosophy should have a place in it and whether philosophers should play a role in the discussion of matters which concern the public at large. Should philosophical views be given attention by those who are in charge of making decisions that have an effect on the American public? Should philosophers be in positions of power where their decisions have an effect on the general population? Should philosophical views be discussed in the mainstream media—newspapers, radio, and television? Should philosophers be called on to advise politicians, heads of large corporations, and social organizations concerned with the health and well being of Americans at large?

Of course, the answers to these questions depend on what is meant by "philosophy" and "philosophers" on the one hand, and "American public life" on the other hand. As everybody knows, philosophers do not agree on what philosophy is or who is to count as a philosopher. The words 'philosophy' and 'philosopher' have been understood in many ways throughout history and carry with them both good and bad connotations which make them desirable and undesirable, depending on context. Socrates already faced this problem and complained that philosophy is a field in which everyone believes himself or herself to be an expert. This means, of course, that everyone thinks of himself or herself as a philosopher of sorts, at least sometimes, and also that almost every idea, at least of a general nature, has been considered to be a philosophical idea at one time or another by someone. One of the most common sports of teachers of philosophy is to reject the credentials of other teachers of philosophy and what they teach. Can you count the number of times a colleague of yours referred to someone else who also teaches philosophy as not a philosopher, or not really a philosopher, and to what he or she does as not philosophy or not really philosophy? Indeed, perhaps you yourself are guilty of this peccadillo! I know I am. If we were going to get into this kind of debate here, we could probably not go beyond it and would never be able to give an answer to the two questions in which I am interested today. Besides, I am sure the American Philosophical Association did not ask me to be a member of this panel to discuss this issue. The APA wants me to say something about the role of the APA and its members in American public life. For, although there are some individuals who truly qualify as philosophers, judged by their own criteria and even by those presumably used by many, if not most, members of the APA, and who are not themselves members of the Association, the largest number of persons who regard themselves as professional philosophers and who are regarded by members of the APA as philosophers are indeed members of the Association. These are people who teach or have taught philosophy mostly at the college level (but some even at the secondary school level), who engage or have engaged in some philosophical research, and who hold some graduate degree in the discipline. Our issue, then, has to do with persons of this sort.

The other expression that needs clarification is "American public life." The first word, "American," should not give us any trouble. We are speaking of philosophy as practiced by philosophers in the United States. Some of these philosophers may be natives of the country, whereas others may not; some may speak and write in English, whereas others may not; some may be of Anglo-Saxon background, and others may not; and so on. The important condition they must all satisfy is that they function as philosophers in the U.S.

The rest of the expression is more complicated, for what exactly is "public life"? In some ways all life is public to the extent that it appears in principle to be open to observation. But, in another sense, no life is public to the extent that each living thing appears to live its own life independently of that of others and this living involves some dimensions that are not open to public scrutiny. But let us not quibble here. The expression is meant to refer to social rather than individual or family matters. In particular, I believe it is intended to refer to those aspects of the life of the nation which have to do with politics and social policy and which are reflected in the media, excluding academic life.

With these clarifications in mind, we can now go back to the first question we raised: Does philosophy have a place in American public life? The answer seems quite obvious: No, philosophy has no place in American public life. There are no discussions of public policy which include philosophy. Philosophers are generally excluded from policy-making bodies or posts in which they can have serious influence on the development of public policy or even its implementation. Seldom have philosophers been called upon by the President or the Congress to be members of blue-ribbon committees. To my knowledge, except for rare instances, there have not been philosophers who have been members of a President's cabinet, members of Congress, governors of states, mayors of important cities, or even ambassadors to the United Nations or to nations with which the U.S. maintains diplomatic relations. Moreover, seldom has a philosopher chaired an important national committee or even been a member of one. Still more distressing to those who crave philosophical involvement in the public life of the nation is the fact that philosophical publications, strictly speaking, do not generally attract attention in the halls of political power or even among the public at large. Yes, some philosophers have had important posts in institutions of higher learning and some have been presidents of colleges and universities. But even here, more often than not, these are exceptions. Although universities always choose academics for their leaders, there is often a bias toward members of professional schools (law, engineering, medicine, business, and the like) and when non-professional academics are chosen, these usually come from the ranks of scientists.

The cold shoulder that philosophers get in the halls of public power, and even from the general population, is not to be perceived as part of an overall attitude toward academics, although it is true that a hostile attitude against academics has been encouraged by some politicians from time to time. The reason for the hostility of these politicians to academics is that the latter are perceived as too divorced from the realities of daily life and, more important, as too liberal. Yet this has not deterred academics in fields other than philosophy—law, political science, economics, art, sociology, medicine, engineering, and the sciences—from being appointed to important posts in the government or from having their opinions on important matters of public policy sought and considered by the country's political leadership.

If we turn to the media, the situation is pretty much the same. Whereas scientists, humanists of various sorts, and artists are regularly interviewed on television and radio, and they are asked to speak on various public contexts, it is very seldom that philosophers appear on television, speak on the radio, or give lectures to which the general public and scholars from other fields attend. This is particularly obvious in programs especially devoted to culture and the life of the mind, where one would expect to find philosophers but they are generally absent, whereas other members of the American intelligentsia regularly participate in them. Indeed, when one sees a philosopher on television, one is almost surprised, if not shocked. A few years ago a popular commentator who had his own television show interviewed a fairly well known philosopher in his program. I remember being surprised, and even puzzled, until I realized the philosopher had been the commentator's teacher at Yale. He was not being interviewed because he was a philosopher whose opinion counted, as was the case with most other persons interviewed in the program; he was being interviewed because of a personal connection to the commentator. Perhaps the commentator thought of it as a favor. How pathetic!

Naturally, one would not expect anything different in the U.S. if the situation were the same elsewhere in the world or had always been so in every culture throughout human history. But matters have not always been so and certainly not in every place. In some countries there has always been considerable interest in philosophy, if not among the general public, at least among the educated classes and even among some of the countries' leaders. This, I think, is the case in many European countries, and certainly has been the case in China and India. Moreover, the role of adviser to rulers has been frequent throughout history. Even the notorious Nero had a philosopher for adviser, although the poor man, Seneca, paid with his life for this honor; Aristotle was Alexander the Great's tutor; and Charlemagne gathered in his court all the philosophical talent he could muster. In more recent times, even in places like Latin America, philosophers have been part of the political life and have held posts of importance. Some have even run, or considered running, for President, and quite a few have held important posts at the ministerial level. Indeed, in many countries philosophers have been responsible for putting into place educational systems and have had a hand in shaping policy with respect to such important topics as human rights. And newspapers regularly publish articles by and on philosophers and about philosophical views. Clearly, we cannot explain the situation of philosophy in the U.S. by referring to the situation of philosophy in the world as a whole or to the history of humankind in general. What is the cause of the marginalization of philosophy in this country, then? Why is philosophy, and philosophers, considered irrelevant?

I do not believe one can point to a single reason for this. Nor do I think that the reasons are to be found only in the character of American philosophy or what American philosophers do. One can easily find factors in American culture that work against philosophy. For example, one can point to the generally pragmatic and practical character of American society. A can-do attitude is often hostile to speculation and anything like philosophy that is perceived as eminently theoretical. Another example can be found in the fact that certain kinds of Protestantism have in some ways set the pace for mainstream American life. The Pilgrims wanted religious freedom, but they did not favor the kind of speculation favored by philosophers. Indeed, if one compares the intellectual life of the American colonies to that of the Spanish colonies, one can easily detect the difference. Barely fifty years after the encounter with America, highly speculative treatises, scientific, theological, and philosophical, were being published in Mexico and other parts of the Spanish empire, whereas nothing of the kind took place in the American colonies until much later.

Similar factors could be found in other aspects of American contemporary culture and society. For example, surely one reason philosophy and philosophers are not taken into account in the U.S. may be that the general public, including the educated public, is not exposed to it. Consider the fact that philosophy is one of the few disciplines that is not taught in high school. Students go through primary and secondary schools without any exposure to the field and when they get to college they tend to gravitate toward fields which are known to them. The result is that even most college graduates have had no exposure to the discipline. Under these circumstances can we blame them for not taking an interest in it later on in life?

Apart from these external factors, there are also others that come from within philosophy itself. These are perhaps of greater interest to philosophers, for presumably we could do something about them, if we wished. One factor that is sometimes heard mentioned is the generally irrelevant topics discussed by philosophers. Abstruse matters of logic, metaphysics and epistemology, indeed, are quite removed from the interests of the general population and could contribute to the isolation of philosophy and philosophers from public life. However, although this explanation may have made sense at some periods of the history of American philosophy, it certainly does not make sense today. A good number of living American philosophers are deeply interested in topics that are also of interest to the public at large. As examples of these topics we need only mention issues of race, discrimination, ethnicity, multiculturalism, political correctness, domination, the interpretation of the law, affirmative action, abortion rights, freedom of speech, the rights of internet users, and so on, to illustrate the point. Perhaps these issues are still not considered central to the discipline by some, and they are not discussed sufficiently according to others, but the fact that they are widely discussed preempts the possibility that irrelevancy is the reason philosophers are not taken into account in America today. It may be true that some philosophers are not taken into account because the issues they discuss are not easily related to the concerns of the general population, but this cannot be the explanation why philosophers in general are ignored.

The factors I find most significant may be divided into three groups: some have to do with substance, some have to do with style, and some have to do with the sociology of the profession. For each of these groups I shall mention three examples. Among factors of substance I will mention the anti-philosophical attitude of philosophers themselves; the skepticism of philosophers concerning the achievement of philosophical truth; and the glorification of the sciences by philosophers. Under style, I will refer to the excessive technical character of philosophical writing; the jargon frequently used by philosophers; and the obscurity that characterizes much philosophical discourse. Under sociology I will note the extreme division among American philosophers today; the almost cult-like attitude of some American philosophers with respect to certain historical figures whose thought they favor; and the nastiness with which philosophers speak to each other and judge the work of other philosophers, let alone non-philosophers and their work. Let me say a couple of words about each of these factors.

The sharpest critics of philosophy and philosophers are philosophers themselves. This is not new to this century or to the U.S. Yet it is true that this century, and American philosophy in particular, have seen the development of a marked anti-philosophical attitude. It is not so much that American philosophers themselves have become founders of anti-philosophical movements. Rather, it is that they have appropriated the thought of anti-philosophers from elsewhere. Consider the current popularity of Nietzsche and Derrida, for example. There is almost an irrationalism that permeates much American philosophy today.

To this we must add a deep skepticism toward the ability of philosophers to find the truth. Indeed, the most influential American philosopher in this century, W. V. Quine, is a good example. Quine's philosophy is based on two extraordinary doctrines. According to one, we can never be certain that we mean the same thing as someone else means when we use the same word.[2] But, if this is the case, then how can we aspire to certainty in anything, and how can we believe in the possibility of truth? According to the other doctrine, our language is theory laden, so that we can never adopt an independent, neutral point of view with respect to the nature of the world.[3]

Finally, in contrast with this skepticism toward truth, we find an almost naive optimism with respect to science. A few years back, many American philosophers gladly embraced the view, peddled by the Vienna Circle, according to which only tautologies and empirically verifiable statements are meaningful. Although the view of meaning proposed by the Vienna Circle did not survive the criticisms labeled against it, it had the effect of establishing a favorable attitude toward science which has endured in this country. A large part of the philosophical establishment in the U.S. is still awed by science, a fact that has been recently transferred to cybernetics.

Form, seems to me, has also been an obstacle to the acceptance of philosophy in American public life. Excessive technicality in philosophy—the use of symbolic language and other technical tools—has closed the doors of philosophy to those who have not been trained in it. And in cases where a technical apparatus is not present, there is frequently a jargon that is impenetrable except to those who have mastered it, and some times even to those who have mastered it. Indeed, the jargon of some contemporary schools of philosophy rivals that of the scholastics and justifies the kind of objection and ridicule that Renaissance humanists heaped on scholasticism.

Joined to this is the obscurity of the writing itself, even when technicalities and jargon are absent. Many philosophers simply do not know how to express themselves clearly. The idea of composing sentences that are unproblematic, and of illustrating subtle philosophical points with easily understandable examples, is not frequent among philosophers, even among those who praise clarity. Indeed, there is a general attitude that favors obscurity because it assumes that clarity means superficiality and only in obscurity is there real depth. If a text is easily understandable, then it must not contain anything of value.

The sociology of the profession also creates obstacles to the reception of philosophy by the general public, for it presents a picture that is anything but flattering. Consider, for example, the extreme division in American philosophy between so-called Analytic and Continental philosophers.[4] Never mind that these terms are not descriptive and at least one of them makes no historical sense. And never mind that some efforts have been made by members of both camps to bring about a rapprochement. In fact, these two groups consistently and regularly disparage each other, undermine the credentials of each other, and seldom, if ever, engage in serious dialogue. A house so bitterly divided cannot justify a positive attitude toward itself by those who do not live in it. Besides, who wants to ask for the opinion of people who cannot come to an agreement on even the most simple matters, including the nature of their discipline, and who behave like hostile enemies whenever the opportunity arises?

To this must be added the cult-like attitude that some philosophers have with respect to certain past philosophers whom they favor. Mind you, this is something we have come to expect of those philosophers who have a religious or political commitment. We are not surprised at finding this attitude when it comes to some Thomists and Marxists. But Peirce? Kant? Hegel? Nietzsche? And let us not forget two of the most influential philosophers in contemporary American philosophy: Wittgenstein and Heidegger. About four hundred years ago, John of St. Thomas listed the five criteria for a good Thomist: (1) look back to the continuous line of succession of previous followers of Thomas's doctrines; (2) be energetically intent on defending and developing Thomas's views rather than disagreeing cautiously with them or explaining them in a lukewarm manner; (3) stress the glory and brilliance of Thomas's doctrines rather than your own opinions and novelty of interpretation; (4) follow Thomas, arrive at the same conclusions, explain Thomas's reasons and resolve any apparent inconsistencies in his views; and (5) seek a greater agreement and unity among Thomas's followers.[5] These criteria can easily apply, *mutatis mutandis*, to many followers of Wittgenstein, Kant, Nietzsche, or Heidegger in the U.S. today. But, seriously, who is going to pay attention to a philosopher, someone who claims to follow reason, but who adopts this kind of slavish and apologetic attitude toward the thought of someone else?

Finally, there is the issue of nastiness. Throughout my career I have been involved in considerable editorial work. Some of this work has crossed disciplinary boundaries, which means that I have often had the opportunity to read referee reports written by scholars from disciplinary backgrounds other than philosophy. In my experience, which of course is limited and anecdotal, philosophers are one of the nastiest, if not the nastiest, referees of all. Some reports I have read clearly did not have for aim merely to point out the faults of the work under consideration, but rather to wound the author. And I must say that in some cases the referee succeeded in giving a mortal blow, for I know some young philosophers who, as a result of these vicious attacks, have given up the profession. This nastiness is evident not only in some referee reports, it is often evident in commentaries of the work of others; in the discussion of the publications of other philosophers; and in other situations in which philosophers are asked to give their opinion about other philosophers or their work. Often this is motivated by a spirit of gate keeping, in turn motivated by self-serving and group-serving attitudes. So this nastiness is not always disinterested or benign, and those outside the profession are not so stupid as to miss its character.

The picture I have painted is pretty bleak, but it does not contain even half of the negative things that could be said about philosophers in America today. (It is also one-sided, for there is plenty of good that could be said about philosophers. I omit this because it would not help explain why philosophy is absent in American public life.) We are contentious, ideological, and callous. Many of us have lost faith in what we do and in the ability to know with any degree of certainty. And yet, here is something that I have not mentioned but which is quite evident to those outside the profession: We are extraordinarily arrogant. Although deep down most of us believe we do not really know anything, and we say so quite frequently, we act as if we did and we constantly tell others that we know more than they do. How petulant! How conceited! How unbearable we are! And we wonder why no one in American public life pays any attention to us! Obviously we are very good at covering the Sun with a finger. It is, indeed, surprising that we still have any students, or any jobs.[6]

This does not mean, of course, that our criticisms need always be negative or that we should never make positive proposals. After all, criticism can be internal or external, and both entail commitments of some kind. But it does mean that our contribution to society should always be based on a critical foundation.

So much, then, for the first question I meant to explore today. Now let me turn to the second question very briefly because I am almost out of time: Should philosophy and philosophers play a role in American public life? We all know the arguments for it. They can be found in almost every college catalogue, under philosophy. "Integration of all knowledge," "critical thinking," and so on, are key expressions which stand for arguments which are used everywhere to justify our existence and request support from generally unsympathetic administrations. These arguments are too well known to need repetition. I would rather mention the arguments against having philosophers play a role in public life. Some of these are also well known, although many of us would rather forget them. Some can be found even in Plato, in spite of his great faith in philosophy and his proposal to make philosophers kings in the just society. Aristotle, however, thought differently, and it is to him that we can turn for what I think is probably the foundation of the best argument against philosophers playing a leading role in public life.

The argument is simple and based on a premise that does not apply only to philosophers: Experience is better than theory when it comes to practice.[7] If you have a plumbing problem, it is better to have someone with experience take care of it, even if the person cannot tell you what she is going to do and why, rather than to have someone who has written a book about plumbing and has never or seldom fixed a problem similar to the one you have. The same applies to philosophers and society. Philosophers may have all sorts of theories about society, how it works, its problems, and what should be done concerning those problems, but nothing can take the place of someone who has been there when it comes to dealing with social problems and issues. Let us, then, keep philosophers where they belong, so the argument goes, enclosed in the ivy walls of academia and turn rather to people with practice when we are dealing with social matters.

Apart from this argument, I think we could make a pretty good case against philosophers playing leadership roles in American public life from what was said earlier concerning some of the obstacles we saw philosophers themselves put on the way of their acceptance in public life. Do we really want people like ourselves taking care of society? Do we even want to listen to the ideological verbiage that some of us put out?

American society may have the right idea about philosophers, unless of course, we decide to change our ways. Politicians are bad enough. But give me a corrupt politician any time rather than a principled, self-conceited, cantankerous, and arrogant philosopher. You can get a politician to move, if you exert the right kind of pressure, but you can never get a philosopher to budge. There is too much at stake: his personal reputation and his pride, often covered up under the guise of principle.

Look at the rest of the world. What have the countries that give a place to philosophers in public life accomplished? And look at the U.S.: Do we not have at least as good a public life, if not a better one, than that of most other countries? The conclusion seems to follow: Keep philosophers out, for they do not have what it takes. And perhaps rightly so, for our job in society is not to participate and pontificate. Our job seems to be rather to criticize and to challenge and we cannot be expected to do this if we are part of the power structure and the ideological mainstream. Let others, then, build in complacency. Our task is not to command or to lead. Is this so bad? Only if one wants power, prestige, wealth, or honor—and indeed there are many philosophers who want these above everything else. But deep down most of us know that they do not really matter. We may be very bad, with our divisions, our arrogance, and our skepticism. But these may be, after all, excesses of what makes us who we are, and in being so, perhaps we are not so bad after all and, in a certain sense, are not so far from what we ought to be. So, yes, we need to correct some of our ways, but we should not compromise our nature. This means that we have a role in public life, but it is an indirect role, as teachers and critics, not as advisers and active participants. Those who find this paradoxical are quite right, but then pointing out paradoxes seems to be one of the tasks of philosophy, so presumably I have done my job here today, and have earned my supper.[8]

Jorge J. E. Gracia, Department of Philosophy, State University of New York at Buffalo, Amherst, NY 14260; gracia@acsu.buffalo.edu

NOTES

1. See, for example, Richard Schacht, "W(h)ither Graduate Study in Philosophy?" *Proceedings and Addresses of the American Philosophical Association* 71.5 (1998): 99–115.

2. W. V. Quine, "On the Reasons for the Indeterminacy of Translation," *Journal of Philosophy* 67 (1970): 178–83; and idem, "Indeterminacy of Translation Again," *Journal of Philosophy* 84 (1987): 5–10. I propose an indirect response to Quine's challenge in chapter 6 of *A Theory of Textuality: The Logic and Epistemology* (Albany: State University of New York Press, 1995), 189–214.

3. Quine, "Ontological Relativity," *Relativity and Other Essays* (New York: Columbia University Press, 1969), 69–90; and idem, "On What There Is," *From a Logical Point of View* (Cambridge, Mass.: Harvard University Press, 1953), 1–19.

4. I have discussed this regrettable situation at length in *Philosophy and Its History: Issues in Philosophical Historiography* (Albany: SUNY Press, 1992), 22–34, where I also refer to the pertinent literature.

5. John of St. Thomas, *Cursus theologicus, Tractatus de approbatione et auctoritate doctrinae d. Thomae*, Vol. 1, Disp. II, a. 5 (Paris: Desclée, 1931), 297–301.

6. Some of these problems actually affect the recruitment of certain students into philosophy, and in particular certain minorities. See chapter 7 of my *Hispanic/Latino Identity* (London: Blackwell Publishers, 2000).

7. Aristotle, *Metaphysics* 981a20.

8. In preparing the final version of this talk, I have profited from comments and criticism offered by the two other members of the panel, Robert Audi and John Perry, as well as several members of the audience, including Woosuk Park and Charles Griswold. and some whose names I did not catch.

COMMUNITARIANISM AND WESTERN THOUGHT

Sirkku Kristiina Hellsten

Within the Western tradition we can find important and interesting philosophical differences between the continental European and the Anglo-American ethical and political outlooks towards biotechnology. The Anglo-American attitude appears based on naturalistic and empiricist views, while continental European viewpoints are built on idealistic liberal humanism. A Northern European view integrates both of the above-mentioned liberal traditions. The main problem is that although these different outlooks can be said to be liberal in their common promotion of equality, autonomy, and individual rights, they still tend to conflict. I purpose to explicate the main differences of these liberalisms and to analyze how they affect the ethical views towards biotechnology in the Western world. Secondly, I will search for the shared values involved in these approaches in order to find common ground for open discussion on the ethical problems involved in biotechnological development.

I. INTRODUCTION

In general, modern Western political and social thought since the Enlightenment has been based on liberal individualism which promotes tolerance, individual autonomy, and individual rights. However, some of these central values of Western individualism have been criticized recently by social theorists and thinkers who have been labeled "communitarians." Communitarians criticize, on the one hand, liberal political theory for its disregard of social circumstances and, on the other hand, communitarians criticize liberal political practice for its rejection of social duties, shared values, and traditions. This communitarian emphasis on the common good in general has been interpreted as a promotion of collectivism rather than individualism and its emphasis on traditions is taken to be particularistic rather than universalistic. However, in this paper I claim that the inner nature of Western communitarian thought is—and must be—universalistic and committed to individualistic rather than collectivist values. This, however, does not mean that other formulations of the communitarian thought would not promote a very different normative agenda. My main argument is that the universalism and individualism of Western formulation of communitarianism actually proves that on the meta-level communitarianism is always particularistic and universalistic. I shall first analyze the particular features which distinguish Western communitarianism from other formulations of communitarian thought appearing in different parts of the world. Then I shall analyze the odd nature of communitarian reasoning which makes it appear to be simultaneously both universalistic and particularistic.

II. DESCRIPTIVE OR PRESCRIPTIVE COMMUNITARIANISM

I want to start my analysis by making an important distinction between two methodologically different formulations of the communitarian thought, that is, between the descriptive and the prescriptive (or normative) communitarianism. The view that I call descriptive communitarianism was most fully first presented by such social theorists as Alasdair MacIntyre, Michael Sandel, Charles Taylor, and Michael Walzer.[1] These descriptive communitarians criticize modern liberalism for its universalism and atomism. They argue that liberal political theory is based on too atomistic and abstract premises that cannot possibly promote the kind of individual morality that we need in order to maintain functioning democracy in practice. Instead liberal emphasis on abstract methodological individualism leads to egoism, moral indifference, political alienation, and social fragmentation. For communitarians particularly, the liberal methodological subject as an image of an individual *qua* autonomous moral agent is philosophically unbearable because it fails to take into account our communal ties and shared values that always affect the choices we make in our everyday life. Thus, on the one hand, descriptive communitarians argue that modern liberal theory and practice have estranged too far away from each other. On the other hand, they seem to claim that the decay of modern liberal societies actually reflects the abstract, theoretical emphasis liberals place on subjective values and formal rights. An important question arises from this apparently inconsistent set of arguments: how can liberal theory and practice be too far apart from each other if they still heavily influence one another?[2]

The other formulation of communitarian thought which I shall call prescriptive (or normative) communitarianism starts exactly where the descriptive communitarian criticism leaves off. The starting premise of the prescriptive formulation of communitarian thought is in the interaction between not only individuals and their societies, but also between theory and practice. A political or social theory born in a particular political tradition inevitably reflects the values of this very tradition. Simultaneously, it justifies these values and thus ends up enforcing their realization in practice. Prescriptive communitarianism attempts first, to redefine theoretically the moral meaning of a democratic regime and, second, to provide some guidelines on how to realize them in practice.[3] This prescriptive approach to communitarianism is currently most clearly elaborated by Amitai Etzioni and the communitarian network he has founded.[4]

The main difference between descriptive and prescriptive communitarianism may be formulated as follows: descriptive communitarians argue, first, that an individual is a product of his or her society and, second, that modern liberal society produces egoistic and asocial individuals who are politically passive and morally indifferent. Prescriptive communitarians, for their part, want to fight against this moral and social decay and provide us with a normative agenda that can guide modern society back on the right track. Since I want to focus particularly on the communitarian normative agenda and its theoretical justification, when I use the term "communitarianism" I refer to prescriptive communitarianism and, particularly, to the views presented by Amitai Etzioni and The Communitarian Network.

III. TEACHING MORALITY AND BUILDING CHARACTER

Communitarians believe that we can avoid the uninvited side effects of modern liberalism if we can create the social circumstances and ethical atmosphere that encourage moral behavior and civic virtue. In order to do so, they emphasize, first, the need for moral education of our children and the civic education of all citizens. Second, they demand that we need to balance freedom with responsibility and individual rights with social duties. Communitarians suggest that we focus on the responsibility individuals have on their own actions as well as on the duties they have towards each other.

Moral education and character education is needed in order to encourage moral behavior, which, for its part, guarantees legitimate and working democracy. For communitarians, the desired political order is constitutional democracy based on responsible market economy. Communitarians have as their goal the realization of a democratic government, which not only formally respects individual autonomy and rights, but also reproduces citizens who are committed to moral behavior and to the maintenance of democratic ideal, that is, democracy as the self-government of autonomous moral and political agents. Communitarians, however, do not see that the state as a political whole should be the ultimate collective moral agency. Instead they believe that "responsive communities" can provide us the motivational moral agency between the state and individual citizens.[5]

Here communitarian views are close to Hegel's criticism of Kant's universalism and his abstract use of such concepts as moral agency and right.[6] Like Hegel, communitarians note that while individuals make the final moral choices, these choices are not based on unlimited freedom. Instead, our moral agency is always tied to our social context and thus relative to social pressure. The only way to promote moral agency is to invest in building a political order which encourages and enforces common morality and shared values. Only within such a political order can individuals identify themselves as moral agents. However, even if communitarians promote the building of civil society, they (unlike Hegel) do not believe a state should be considered our ultimate moral guide.[7] Instead, since we all are born as members of different communities that affect our values and lifestyles, we should use these same communities to strengthen the desired common values and moral behavior.[8] For communitarians, then, the teaching of moral duties, social responsibilities, and shared values is not primarily a political or legal matter but should start at home, in families, neighborhood communities, and other smaller social groups. Communitarians assume that when a community reaches the point at which the social responsibilities are largely enforced by the powers of the state, the state is already in deep moral crisis.

In communitarian thought, the goal set to moral and character education is in general based on sociological and psychological views of human socialization processes rather than metaphysical speculation about human nature. For communitarians, humans are neither innately good or evil, but rather are products of their social circumstance. This means that our minds are morally a *tabula rasa* when we are born, but nevertheless we have some inherent potential for virtue. Here communitarians take an Aristotelian turn and claim that individuals can acquire virtuous behavior from the practices of their communities.[9]

IV. FROM INDIVIDUAL RIGHTS TO SOCIAL DUTIES— OR TO INDIVIDUAL RESPONSIBILITY?

The other goal communitarians have is to find balance between our rights and duties. Communitarians note that whether we speak of a modern market society (such as the U.S. today) or contemporary welfare state system (such as for instance some continental and Northern European societies) there is serious imbalance between rights and responsibilities. However, in order to be able to place communitarian thought politically, we would have to know what communitarians really mean by social duties. After all, if they emphasize the social responsibilities individuals have towards themselves (such as having a virtuous and healthy life, that is, taking care of oneself and not wasting the resources of one's community), their position would not be as far from neo-liberal conservatism as they would like to admit. If they emphasize instead our collective social responsibility (meaning such duties as taking care of and caring for others, contributing to the social resources, and the common good), they are leaning towards collectivist socialism.

In order to show why the attempt to balance rights with duties has made the communitarian position so hard to place on the traditional political map, I want to briefly compare the communitarian idea of social duty with that of three other political traditions: collectivist socialism, welfare liberal democracy (or, put differently, social democracy), and conservative neo-liberalism. First, in a collectivist political system (such as socialism), the obligations that citizens have are primarily for the benefit of the social whole, and only secondarily for the benefit of the individuals within the system. Rights and duties are not in balance because individual citizens have mere duties without any real rights. Second, in welfare liberal democracy, the setting is turned the other way around.[10] Social responsibility is the duty of the state to benefit individual citizens. There is an imbalance between rights and duties, because individuals have most of the formal rights while most of the duties are left to the state. This relieves individuals from their civic duties and alienates them from moral behavior and political participation. Third, the neo-liberal promotion of free market economy, for its part, requires that individuals take responsibility for themselves. Because there is no demand for any wider social responsibility, everybody has mere rights and no one any social duties. This means that there is no real protection of the rights of those who are in the worse-off position. To summarize, for the communitarians the problem of collectivist socialism is in its totalitarianism, and the problem with modern welfare state ideology is in its tendency to transfer too much of social responsibility from individuals to the state. And finally, the problem of neo-liberalism is in its egoism and rejection of social solidarity altogether.

Now, where do the communitarians fit politically? In general, the communitarian prescriptive movement has been vague about its political position, emphasizing instead its non-political nature. Communitarians claim that, for them, it is most important to stress individuals' duties from the moral point of view. This means that they focus on the duties individuals as moral agents have towards each other as members of different communities within the political whole.[11] What makes this emphasis non-political is their claim that our social duties and moral responsibilities are not subjectivist, nor are they universal or objective in a theoretical sense. They are not merely a personal matter, but they should not be forced on us by law either. We cannot always choose what responsibilities we want to accept as our own, nor can we always be definitely told what responsibilities we have as members of a particular political order. Instead, these responsibilities are anchored in the social relations of our communities. Although communitarians believe, much the same way as the liberals do, that the ultimate foundation of morality can be found in commitments of individual conscience, they demand that we need communities to help introduce and sustain these commitments in our social behavior. Hence, it is the duty of communities to articulate the responsibilities that they expect their members to discharge, especially when the understanding of these responsibilities has weakened.[12]

Thus, instead of trying to replace the old political order with a new one (whether this new one would be more collectivist or conservative) communitarians attempt to find the motivational link between individuals' moral choices and the proper functioning of economic, political, and legal institutions in modern democratic regime. That is, communitarians can be said to be working in the gray zone of social ethics, between the public concept of justice and private morality. While politically confusing this attempt is nevertheless philosophically interesting. It not only crumbles the traditional political left-right positioning, but it also seems to abolish some of the old barriers between political, moral, and social philosophy by concentrating on individual relationships between constructive members of different social entities, not in methodological or political senses, but in the moral sense. It also discusses the moral agency of these social entities.[13]

V. ARE COMMUNITARIANS ALWAYS LIBERAL?

The communitarian stress on communal duties, family values and community care is in general done in order to promote the originally modern liberal values of tolerance, individual autonomy and individual rights.[14]

This normative position is only logical, if the communitarian descriptive and methodological argumentation were to be taken seriously at all. After all, communitarian thinkers themselves are always the products of their society and thus tied to its moral tradition.[15] Moreover, communitarians themselves are not only committed to liberal values, but are also quite eager to export these values elsewhere. They note that the balance needed between individuals and groups, between rights and responsibilities, between the institutions of state and the market, is always related to the historical situation of the society in question. Thus, while communitarians demand more social responsibilities in contemporary America, they argue for more individual rights in communist China.[16]

In order not to advocate majoritarianism, communitarians avoid talking about the importance of political consensus or moral agreement. Instead, they refer to those universal moral values which "speak" to us if we listen "the voices of our communities." Communitarians appear to trust that our inner moral sense (rather than pure reason) helps us to find common values despite the differences in our cultural, religious, or social backgrounds.[17] And here again, the values that speak loudest to the communitarians are the values of the modern liberal tradition. The result of this is that communitarians cannot avoid the same conflicts faced by liberals in their attempts to maintain a pluralist democracy that is nevertheless committed to common values, that is, to common individualist values. The main difference between communitarians and liberals is actually in their interpretation of democracy and their understanding of freedom. Liberals in general understand freedom in a negative sense, as freedom *from* something, namely, from legal restrictions and state intervention. The communitarian approach to democracy, for its part, promotes positive freedom, that is, freedom *for* something, namely, for one's self-realization as a moral and political agent. While the liberal "weak" democracy has its roots in Lockean economic liberalism, the communitarian "strong," participatory democracy is inspired by the participatory democracy of ancient Greece, while simultaneously reflecting Rousseau's view of democracy as the realization of the general will.

An interesting question arises from the communitarian position: if Western communitarianism tends towards liberal universalism and individualism, does this mean that communitarian reasoning is never particularistic, resulting in a culturally relativist ethical stand? I believe that this, in fact, indicates quite the opposite. The strong connection between the Western formulation of communitarian thought and liberalism shows quite clearly that communitarianism is always in one way or another relative to the values of the tradition. This means that despite its

universalistic nature, Western communitarianism as such does not suc-
ceed in offering a plausible explanation as to why any other cultures
with different social, political, and ethical system would give up their
own traditions and turn towards liberal values. In other words, while in
a liberal and multicultural communitarian democracy we can demand
that its citizens should commit themselves to the liberal value of tolerance and to the respect for individual autonomy and rights, this does
not explain why, for instance, communist China should demand for
more individual rights if they have no desire to give up their present social system, or why Iran should suddenly turn from fundamentalist Islam
to tolerance and pluralism.

In fact, if we strictly followed the communitarian methodological argumentation, we would have to agree that in traditional, more collectivist
cultures, communitarian reasoning would inevitably lead towards very different normative conclusions. It could easily be used not only to enforce
truly collectivist values but also to justify intolerant tribalism, suppressing
majoritarianism or even totalitarianism rather than enlightened democratic
consensus. If we take seriously the communitarian descriptive claim that
we are always bound by our social circumstances and traditional values, we
have to keep in mind that while the Western formulation of communitarian
thought is and must be committed to the promotion of the values of the
liberal tradition, this does not mean that other formulations of
communitarian thinking born in different cultural, social, and economic
contexts would (or should) end up with the same normative agenda. Quite
to the contrary, a communitarian movement born in a collectivist culture,
or even in a totalitarian political system, would turn out as an advocate of
very different "common values."[18] All in all, Western communitarian is universalistic and individualistic in its inner nature, while on the meta-level
communitarian thought still presents a form of particularism with a tendency towards cultural relativism.

VI. Conclusion

To conclude, I want to note that when we discuss communitarianism, we
should acknowledge how it works on two different levels (the descriptive
or methodological level and the prescriptive or normative level). Therefore, when we talk about the normative agenda of communitarianism in the
West, we should always start by taking the communitarian descriptive criticism of modern liberalism seriously. Taking into account our social ties
can remind us how social pressures always affect our moral development.
Further, it can help us to reconsider what is needed in order to build a

political order which is not only democratic in appearance, but also in all of its internal social practices. However, we should keep in mind that while in its Western formulation, communitarian thought is committed to individualistic and universalistic values and thus promotes moral autonomy, individual rights, equality, and tolerance, this is not case with a communitarian movement originating in different historical and social circumstances. Instead, communitarianism can easily be used to promote quite different views to morality; views that may end up being repressive and perhaps even immoral in themselves.

Sirkku Kristiina Hellsten, Department of Philosophy, University of Helsinki, Finland, SF-00014; The Ethics Center, University of South Florida, St. Petersburg, FL 33701; shellste@bayflash.stpt.usf.edu

NOTES

1. See Alasdair MacIntyre, *After Virtue*, 2nd ed. (Notre Dame: University of Notre Dame Press, 1984), idem, *Whose Justice? Which Rationality?* (Notre Dame: University of Notre Dame Press, 1988); Michael Sandel, *Liberalism and the Limits of Justice* (Cambridge: Cambridge University Press, 1982), idem, *Democracy's Discontent: America in Search for a Public Philosophy* (Cambridge, Mass.: Harvard University Press, 1996); Charles Taylor, *Hegel and Modern Society* (Cambridge: Cambridge University Press, 1979), idem, *Sources of the Self: The Making of the Modern Identity* (Cambridge: Cambridge University Press, 1989); and Michael Walzer, *Spheres of Justice* (New York: Basic Books, 1983), idem, *Interpretation and Social Criticism* (Cambridge, Mass.: Harvard University Press, 1987).

2. Michael Walzer, "The Communitarian Critique of Liberalism," *Political Theory* 18.1 (1990): 9–11.

3. In order to fulfill both of these tasks the Communitarian Network has turned from intellectual to social movement, which enforces the communitarian ideals and values. This Communitarian social movement is particularly active in the United States. Some of the communitarian core ideas such as the need to balance rights with responsibilities, however, has also gained some support elsewhere in Western Europe. Its normative agenda has, for instance, been supported by the British prime minister Tony Blair and other Labor Party politicians as well as by some members of the Green Party in Germany and by many social democratic parties in other continental and northern European countries; cf. The Communitarian Network, *The Responsive Communitarian Platform* (Washington D.C., 1997); see also *San Jose Mercury News*, 12 December 1992, 1G and *The Times*, 21 June 1997.

4. See Amitai Etzioni, *The Spirit of Community* (New York: Crown, 1993), idem, *The New Golden Rule* (New York: Basic Books, 1996), and idem, "Cross-Cultural Judgments: The Next Steps," *Journal of Social Philosophy* 28.3 (1997): 5–15. This communitarian network includes also such other political theorists as William Galston, Mary Ann Glendon, James Fishkin, and Robert Bellah, just to mention a few. However, not all of the theorists who promote communitarian ideas want to define themselves as communitarians; rather, they often formulate their views as alternative approaches to liberalism such as William Galston's perfectionist liberalism.

5. The moral standards of responsive community are to reflect the basic human needs of all its members. To the extent that these needs compete with one another, the community's standards reflect the relative priority accorded by members to some needs over others. See The Communitarian Network, op. cit., 4.

6. See G. W. F. Hegel, *The Elements of the Philosophy of Right*, ed. Allen W. Wood (Cambridge: Cambridge University Press, 1991), 189–98.

7. Etzioni, *New Golden Rule*, op. cit., 187f, and The Communitarian Network, op. cit., 5–10.

8. The communitarian platform declares that "while law does play a significant role not only in regulating society but also in indicating which values it holds dear, our first and foremost purpose is to affirm the moral commitments of parents, young persons, neighbors and citizen, to affirm the importance of the communities within which such commitments take place and are transmitted from one generation to the next" (The Communitarian Network, op. cit., 4).

9. Communitarians do not see humans as naturally egoistic like the liberal do, neither do they seem humans born with actual 'the will to do good', but rather with potential to good; cf. Etzioni 1996, 160-80.

10. See, for instance, Walzer, *Spheres of Justice*, op. cit., idem, *Interpretation and Social Criticism* op. cit.; and The Communitarian Network, op. cit. Welfare liberalism is theoretically most fully deliberated in John Rawls, *A Theory of Justice* (Oxford: Oxford University Press, 1971), and idem, *Political Liberalism* (New York: Columbia University Press, 1993).

11. Especially, since communitarians warn that bureaucratic welfare agencies and expansive government suffocates individuals' moral development and commercializes social relations, while simultaneously advocate wider social security coverage and universal social services traditionally related to the building of a welfare state (such as basic health care, education, child allowance, paid maternity leave, etc.); cf. Etzioni, *New Golden Rule*, op. cit., 51–57, 80–84, 145–52, and The Communitarian Network, op. cit., 9–16.

12. See for instance The Communitarian Network, op. cit., 4.

13. Political philosophy has traditionally focused on the relationship between the state and its citizens while moral philosophy has been usually more interested in the individual morality.

14. For instance, despite their focus on community in moral education they note that their goal is in treatment of one another with respect and recognition, not just before the law but also as moral agents; cf. The Communitarian Network, op. cit., 11; also Etzioni, "Cross-Cultural Judgements," op. cit., 5–15.

15. Walzer, "Communitarian Critique of Liberalism," op. cit., 6–23.

16. The Communitarian Network, op. cit., 3.

17. Communitarian democracy does not see that any traditions and traditional values should be promoted for their own sake, instead such traditions which conflict with the liberal values and undermine moral autonomy and individual rights should be rejected; see Etzioni, *New Golden Rule*, op. cit., 189–97, and idem, "Cross-Cultural Judgements," op. cit., 5–15.

18. On the different forms of communitarianism, see *Communitarianism and Individualism*, ed. Shlomo Avineri and Avner de-Shalit (Oxford: Oxford University Press, 1992). There are for instance earlier forms of communitarianism of Aristotle, St. Aquinas, Rousseau, and the later Burke, which emphasized the social and political nature of human beings. There are also clearly collectivist formulations of communitarianism (such as traditionalism and communalism) which are more typical to more collectivist, non-Western cultures, such as the African and Asian cultures. Even within the Western tradition the communitarian thought is formulated very differently in the different countries. For instance in Continental and Northern European countries the idea of social responsibility and solidarity is often built in the welfare state ideology, which is based on social liberalism—though maybe better defined as welfare liberalism. Also, many of the European countries are born as nation states and are more homogenous to start with. Thus, they tend to emphasize the importance of political consensus, where as the American communitarians with the pluralistic tradition rather speak about cross-cultural dialogue. Consequently, the European communitarians focus more clearly on the state as a moral and political agent while the American communitarians living in the multicultural society stress the role that smaller communities within a state have in our ethical development and education.

SOCIALITY, UNITY, OBJECTIVITY

Margaret Gilbert

Numerous social and political theorists have referred to social groups or societies as "unities." What makes a unity of a social group? I address this question with special reference to the theory of social groups proposed in my books *On Social Facts* and *Living Together: Rationality, Sociality and Obligation.* I argue that social groups of a central kind require an underlying "joint commitment." I explain what I mean by a "joint commitment" with care. If joint commitments in my sense underlie them, what kind of unity does this give social groups? In what sense or senses is it objective?

I. INTRODUCTION

It is commonly thought that the members of a social group are *unified* in an important way. If so, it would be helpful to have some characterization of their unity.

In my book *On Social Facts,* I argue that the paradigmatic *social* phenomena—including paradigmatic social groups—are what I call *plural subject* phenomena.[1] Here I address the question: insofar as social groups are plural subjects, what kind of unity do they have? In what sense, if any, is that unity objective? I first explain the nature of *plural subjects* in my technical sense. I briefly argue along the way for a plural subject account of a central social phenomenon: acting together.[2]

II. AN EXAMPLE

I start with a simple example. Anne and Ben are walking into town together—where this amounts to more than simply walking close to each other. What does such "walking together" amount to?

Is it simply a matter of Anne having the goal of walking into town close toBen, and Ben having the same goal? There is reason to reject this and other "shared personal goal" analyses which assume that what is central to walking together is that the parties have the same personal goal. These analyses seem unable to explain certain salient facts.

Suppose that Ben starts walking so fast that Anne cannot keep up with him. She will understand that he has failed to give her *something to which she has a right*: roughly, his best efforts to walk into town close to her. Relatedly, or so it seems, Anne understands that she has the right to say in a rebuking tone, "Hey, slow down!" In other words, she has the right to speak to Ben in a *commanding* manner, and to *rebuke* him as well.

Anne understands that *she has these rights by virtue of the fact that she and Ben are walking into town together*. That they are walking into town together *entails* that she has these rights. Ben has the corresponding rights in relation to Anne.

Suppose that Anne and Ben came to be walking into town together in the following way. Anne threatened Ben with something dire unless he walked into town with her, and Ben capitulated. One may want to say that in such circumstances Anne has *no moral right* to Ben's best efforts to walk alongside her. This would assume, perhaps, that she had no moral right to threaten Ben as she did. Whether or not it is true that she would then have no moral right, I suggest that Anne and Ben will still understand that each of them has a *right of some kind* to certain efforts of the other.

It is hard to see how a shared personal goal analysis can explain all this. That each of two people aims to walk into town in the other's company does not obviously give each one a right to the other's efforts.

Someone may argue that if there is *common knowledge* of the shared personal goal, it will be predictable that each will rely upon the other's expected efforts, and so each will have a moral right to these efforts. There is "common knowledge," in the relevant sense, between Anne and Ben that each has a particular personal goal if, roughly, the fact that each has that goal is entirely out in the open as far as the two of them are concerned.[3]

As it stands there is reason to doubt this argument. Even if one accepts it, it will be hard to sustain for cases involving coercion.[4]

What alternative is there to a shared personal goal analysis? People tend to walk somewhere together on the basis of an *agreement* to do so. But it seems that Anne and Ben could be walking into town together without what is literally speaking an agreement having taken place. Perhaps Ben sees Anne walking along, stops her, and asks where she is going. He says "I need to go there too! If we walk there together, the time will go more quickly!" "It will indeed!" Anne replies happily, and they set off side by side. They may in such a manner bring it about that they are walking into town together.

One might say that in this case they have *implicitly* agreed. But what precisely does that amount to? What, indeed, does an "explicit" *agreement* amount to? More to the point: What state of affairs is achieved by agreements, implicit agreements, and any other possible avenues to walking together that could explain how it involves the noted rights, rights of a kind that may persist in improperly coercive conditions?

III. JOINT COMMITMENT

My account of walking together invokes the *joint* acceptance of a goal. People *jointly accept a particular goal*, in my sense, when they are *jointly committed to accept that goal as a body*. I am not the only person to use the phrase 'joint commitment', and must make clear what I mean by it. It is the key term in my account of walking together, and, indeed, of paradigmatic social phenomena in general.[5]

I should first say something about *personal* commitments. I take it that if Anne makes a decision, she has made a personal commitment. *She* has committed *herself*. She may change her mind, of course. Her commitment is then at an end. She has, in effect, rescinded her commitment.

A *joint* commitment, as I understand it, is not a sum of personal commitments. The joint commitment of Anne and Ben does not have, as components, Anne's personal commitment and Ben's personal commitment. Rather, this joint commitment is the commitment *of Anne and Ben*. It is the result of *them* (Anne and Ben) committing *themselves* (Anne and Ben). Neither Anne nor Ben is in a position unilaterally to rescind their commitment. The commitment can be rescinded only by Anne and Ben together.

IV. THE FORMATION OF JOINT COMMITMENTS

How are joint commitments formed? In order that Anne and Ben become jointly committed it is clearly not enough for each of them to make a personal decision. Only a sum of personal commitments would emerge from that. What, then, is enough?

In general terms, Ben must make it clear to Anne that *he has done his part in creating the relevant joint commitment*, so that it remains only for her to do her part. Anne must do likewise. And these things must be common knowledge. These conditions are both necessary and sufficient for the creation of the relevant joint commitment.

I take it that everyday expressions of personal readiness *to do something with another person* are, in effect, expressions of personal readiness *to be jointly committed with that person to doing that thing together, jointly, or as a body*. In conditions of common knowledge, then, concordant expressions of this type suffice to create a joint commitment. "Doing something together with another person" is here construed broadly.

V. AN ACCOUNT OF WALKING TOGETHER

On my account, Anne and Ben are walking into town together only if they are jointly committed to accepting as a body the goal of their walking into town close to each other. There will, of course, be further mental and behavioral conditions also. Anne and Ben must be attempting to conform to their commitment and doing so with some degree of success. But the joint commitment is the core condition, presupposed by the others.

This joint commitment may come about in various ways. It may arise out of an agreement, as in the case where Anne says "Shall we walk into town together?" and Ben replies "Yes, run on" This case may also be described as follows: each expresses to the other personal readiness *to make a particular decision with the other*, in conditions of common knowledge. This creates a joint decision, in other words, a joint commitment to uphold as a body the decision in question.[6] In order to uphold that decision they must jointly accept the goal of walking into town together. Hence they are, at the same time, jointly committed to accepting that goal as a body.

Consider now the case in which Ben says "I need to go there too! If we walk there together the time will go more quickly!" and Anne replies "It will indeed!" Here we may not want to speak of a joint decision. Ben nonetheless makes clear his readiness to walk into town with Anne, and she responds similarly. Thus, each clearly expresses a personal readiness to participate in joint acceptance of the goal of walking into town together. Thus they create a joint commitment to accept that goal as a body.

VI. JOINT COMMITMENT, RIGHTS, AND OBLIGATIONS

An important merit of this account is that it neatly solves the problem of the rights inherent in walking into town together. In doing so, it appeals to an important source of rights that has gone unrecognized among contemporary theorists of rights. That source is joint commitment. I cannot go into this matter at length here, although I must say something about it.

It can be argued that rights—and obligations—*inhere in joint commitments as such.* That there is a joint commitment *entails* that the parties to it have rights of just the sort that are involved, intuitively, in walking into town together. One way of putting this argument is simple. A joint commitment is precisely the *joint* commitment of the parties to it. Each is therefore *answerable to the others* for failures to conform. Each has, accordingly, the standing to rebuke the others for such failures.

It is entirely natural to use the language of rights here: each has a right to the conformity of each of the others, a right *against* each of the others to his (or her) conformity. Correspondingly, we can use the language of *obligations*: each has an obligation to conform, an obligation correlative with the right to conformity that each has, hence an obligation that can be described not just as an obligation to do something but as an obligation towards another person or other people.

Once a joint commitment is in place, these inherent rights and obligations are there. This is so even if one party was improperly coerced into entering the joint commitment, for it is so purely by virtue of the nature of joint commitment. And it seems perfectly possible for someone to be ready to enter a joint commitment when improperly coerced. If the only way I can avoid disaster is to walk into town with you, I am likely to be ready to do so, whether or not you are, unconscionably, responsible for my having to make this choice.

I am of course not arguing in favor of improper coercion: I am saying that it is possible to create *joint commitments* and their *inherent* rights even when improper coercion is present. Given that this is so, it helps to explain a puzzling feature of a case considered earlier, the apparent presence of some kind of right in improperly coercive circumstances.

We may well need to distinguish between radically different kinds of rights and obligations. Perhaps those attached to joint commitments should not be called *moral* rights and obligations. Nonetheless, if there are joint commitments there are *real* rights and obligations of this kind.

VII. Plural Subjects

I say that there is a "plural subject" just in case two or more people are jointly committed in some way. If these people are jointly committed to accepting a given goal as a body, then they form the plural subject of such acceptance. And so on. I have argued in *On Social Facts* and elsewhere that many important social phenomena including group languages, collective belief and collective emotions are plural subject phenomena, along with joint decisions or agreements, and acting together.[7]

VIII. THE UNITY OF SOCIAL GROUPS AS PLURAL SUBJECTS

Those who act together have commonly been taken to constitute social groups, albeit sometimes small and transient ones. What sort of *unity* does this suggest for social groups? A shared personal goal analysis does not obviously endow those acting together with an important kind of unity. Of course they have something important in common. At a minimum, in a two person case, each personally espouses the goal that the other personally espouses.

Compare this, though, with the plural subject account with its requirement that those who are acting together be jointly committed. They could be referred to, with evident aptness, as possessing a "common will" or a "unified will," using terminology of a kind that was more popular in the past. Ben's joint commitment with Anne is a single indivisible commitment. The presence of this commitment is what justifies one in thinking of Anne and Ben as together constituting the subject of an action, or a *unit of agency.*

That those who constitute plural subjects are unified in a salient and striking way is, I suggest, supportive of a plural subject account of social groups in general. Some may use the phrase "social group" in a broad sense that does not warrant a plural subject analysis. It can then be argued that plural subjects are an important subclass of the so-called social groups.

IX. PLURAL SUBJECTS, UNITY, OBJECTIVITY

There is a well-known if somewhat ill-defined debate in the philosophy of social science between "individualism" and "holism." The fact that "holism" is so-called suggests that the question of unity is central.

Individualists may deny that a social group is a "genuine whole" or "real unity." In support of this, they may say that the unity of a social group is, at best, *all in the mind.* It is merely "subjectively real" not "objectively real." That is, no distinction can be made between the group members all believing that they are unified in the relevant way and their actually being so unified. The holist may deny these claims.

Consider, in this connection, John Searle's account of acting together—or the following version of it.[8] According to Searle, what is crucial to walking together, for example, is that each of the participants thinks "We are walking together." There is, evidently, a purported reference here to other people, and, Searle suggests, one who thinks "We are walking together" takes it that each of the relevant others also thinks "We are walking together."[9] If all of the relevant people do think this, and act accordingly in light of it, we have a case of walking together.

Given this picture, one might want to say that the unity of a social group—as exemplified in walking together—is "all in the mind." It is not all in *one* mind, of course, but it is a matter of the relevant persons all thinking that they constitute with the others a subject of action or unit of agency, while presupposing that the others so think. One creates a case of walking together by putting the right thought in the heads of the parties and setting each one to act in light of what he thinks (and assumes).

Compare this with the plural subject account of walking together. The parties must be jointly committed to accepting the relevant goal as a body. This requires that each one makes it clear to the others, in conditions of common knowledge, that he or she is ready to be jointly committed to accepting the relevant goal. As each understands, they are jointly committed when and only when this requirement is satisfied.

The unity of a plural subject is the unity of joint commitment. This is, indeed, a *humanly created* unity, but it requires more than the mere concurrence of isolated minds. It involves something "in the minds," but it involves more than that.

Perhaps Anne dreamt that she had expressed to Ben her readiness to walk into town with him, and that Ben had done likewise. Ben had the same dream. Later, confusing dream with reality, each thinks they jointly accept the goal of walking into town together. But they do not. It is true that there is a genuine readiness on each one's part to walk into town with the other. This readiness has not, however, been expressed to the other, in conditions of common knowledge. Thus no joint commitment to uphold the goal of walking into town together has been created.

There is, then, plenty of room for a distinction between the parties all *believing* there to be a joint commitment, and there really being a joint commitment. I conclude that plural subjecthood involves an important kind of unity that is *more than subjectively real.* Insofar as social groups are plural subjects, they may reasonably be deemed "objective units."[10]

Margaret Gilbert, Department of Philosophy, University of Connecticut, Storrs, CT 06269; gilbert@uconnvm.uconn.edu

NOTES

1. M. Gilbert, *On Social Facts* (Princeton: Princeton University Press, 1989); see also several of the essays in M. Gilbert, *Living Together: Rationality, Sociality, and Obligation* (Lanham, Md.: Rowman and Littlefield, 1996).

2. Cf. Gilbert, *On Social Facts*, op. cit., chap. 4; and idem, *Living Together*, op. cit., chap. 6.

3. The first published discussion of "common knowledge" in roughly this sense is D. Lewis, *Convention: A Philosophic Study* (Cambridge, Mass.: Harvard University Press, 1969). See also S. Schiffer, *Meaning* (Oxford: Oxford University Press, 1972), and, for some further discussion, Gilbert, *On Social Facts*, op. cit.

4. One reason for doubting the argument as it stands is that I may not be morally responsible for your reliance on my expected behavior. The conditions under which such moral responsibility arises may be fairly restrictive: they may require what is tantamount to a promise to behave in the relevant way.

5. For a recent, fuller discussion of joint commitment in my sense see Gilbert, *Living Together*, op. cit., Introduction.

6. I have argued in various places that everyday agreements may be understood as joint decisions. See, in particular, M. Gilbert "Agreements, Coercion, and Obligation," *Ethics* 103.4 (1993); also idem., "Is an Agreement an Exchange of Promises?" *Journal of Philosophy* 90.12 (1993), both in Gilbert, *Living Together*, op. cit.

7. Some of the relevant discussions can be found in Gilbert, *Living Together*, op. cit. See also M. Gilbert, Sociality and Reponsibility (Lanham, Md.: Rowman and Littlefield, 2000).

8. See Searle's discussion of "collective intentionality" in J. Searle, "Collective Intentions and Actions," *Intentions in Communication*, ed. P. Cohen, J. Morgan, and M. Pollack (Cambridge, Mass.: MIT Press, 1995), 401–15, and, more briefly, in his *The Construction of Social Reality* (New York: Free Press, 1995), 23–26.

9. See Searle, "Collective Intentions and Actions," op. cit., 407f. A similar view is to be found in W. Sellars, "Imperatives, Intentions, and the Logic of 'Ought'," *Morality and the Language of Conduct*, ed. G. Nakhnikian and H. N. Castaneda (Detroit: Wayne State University Press, 1963).

10. Thanks to David Lloyd-Thomas for comments on a late version of this paper, and to Keya Maitra and Kit Fine for related discussions.

COLLECTIVE ACCEPTANCE AND SOCIAL REALITY

Raimo Tuomela

Many social properties and notions are collectively made. Two collectively created aspects of the social world have been emphasized in recent literature. The first is that of the *performative* character of many social things (entities, properties). The second is the *reflexive* nature of many social concepts. The present account adds to this list a third feature, the collective availability or "for-groupness" of collective social items. It is a precise account of social notions and social facts in terms of collective appearance. The collective acceptance account has ontological implications in that it accepts mind-independent, group-dependent, and simply mind-dependent social facts.

I. THE COLLECTIVE ACCEPTANCE MODEL OF COLLECTIVE SOCIALITY

Many social and collective properties and notions are man-made. When people act on such notions a part of the social world becomes man-made. There are two important features of sociality and the collective creation of some central aspects of the social world that have previously been emphasized in the literature—by such authors as Barnes, Bloor, Kusch, and Searle.[1] The first feature is that of the *performative* character of many social notions. The second is the *reflexive* nature of many social concepts. My account adds to this list a third feature, the collective availability or "*for-groupness*" of collective social items.

I will argue in this paper that sociality is created through collective acceptance. I have elsewhere created a "Collective Acceptance" account of sociality.[2] The first section of this paper is concerned with the presentation of this account. The second section discusses the philosophical content of the account in more detail. The third section applies the account to the problem of the ontology of the social world.

According to the Collective Acceptance account of (collective) sociality developed in Tuomela and Balzer,[3] certain entities get their collective social status by being collectively created. For example, almost any kind of physical entity—for instance, squirrel fur—can "in principle" become money through the members of the collective in question accepting it as money. As soon as they cease to collectively accept it as money and to mutually believe that it is money, squirrel fur loses its status and function as money.

We must distinguish between a) the collective creation of an idea, b) collectively holding and maintaining it, and finally c) collectively realizing it or carrying it out. Collective acceptance relates to a) and b) in the first place. I argue that collective social reasons, viz., reasons for which collective social actions in general are performed, are special kinds of "we-attitudes."[4] The we-attitudes (social reasons) that are needed for collective acceptance basically belong either to the intention-family or to the belief-family of attitudes. My account concentrates on intentional achievement actions, since all collective acceptance can be or could have been intentional. (Even if in actual life collective acceptance may be non-intentional, it could have been intentional; and this suffices for the present account resembling political contract theories in this respect.) Since intentional actions are based on intentions and beliefs, it suffices to deal with these notions. Intentions entail motivating wants in a broad pro-attitude sense, and in this respect the present account also presupposes underlying wants.

Consider collective action performed with some collective intentionality, viz., collective social action performed for the same shared social reason. For instance, in a group there might be a (weak) we-goal to oppose a recent tax increase(s); viz., this is the group members' goal and they believe that the others share this goal and believe that this is a mutual belief among them. Collective acceptance in this kind of situation can be construed as acceptance either in the sense of conative commitment to s (intention to make s true or to uphold s, as in our example) or doxastic commitment to s (the "acceptance" belief that s is true). Collective acceptance here is a) (weak) "we-acceptance," viz., each person who comes to accept s, believes that the others accept s, and also believes that there is a mutual belief about the participants' acceptance of s. If a collective commitment (we-mode commitment) to s is also involved, we get the minimal sense of accepting *for the group* (and the involved "we-mode" togetherness) which (intersubjectively) involves the group. Without the "we-mode" mutual belief there is not enough intersubjectivity and collective commitment for the applicability of the phrase 'for the group' and for saying that the participants are attempting to see to it collectively that the accepted content will become or—as the case may be—remain satisfied. Acceptance "for the group" with collective commitment can accordingly be viewed in the present context as coextensive with acceptance in the we-mode: "We accept that s is correctly assertable for us in our group-related activities" is truth-equivalent with "We accept s in the we-mode." We can also say that we-mode acceptance consists of collective acceptance for the group with collective commitment concerning what has been accepted. When accepting something for the group the participants are collectively committed to a rule system which in general requires that the members perform certain actions (e.g., inferences) and permits the performance of some other actions.

Stronger forms of collective acceptance "for the group" are b) norm-based, institutional acceptance and c) plan-based or agreement-based collective acceptance. An example of b) is the collective acceptance that driving when drunk is wrong and punishable, that anniversaries in a marriage ought to be celebrated, and perhaps also in some collective that squirrel fur counts as money. The last example is based on the social norm (the genesis of which we will not here try to give an account of) that everyone in the collective ought to treat squirrel fur as money. An example of plan-based or agreement-based collective acceptance is the group members' joint decision to elect a certain person as their leader. In general, acceptance for a group entails mutual belief in the acceptance, at least in "egalitarian" groups and in groups in which the normative structure of the group does not affect collective acceptance.

The following general thesis of sociality in a "performative" sense or of can now be proposed:

> Collective Acceptance Thesis (*CAT*): The sentence s is *collective-social* in a primary sense in a group G if and only if the following is true for group G: a) the members of group G collectively accept s, and b) they collectively accept s if and only if s is correctly assertable.[5]

In the analysans a) is the assumption of the categorical collective acceptance of s while clause b) is a partial characterization of the kind of collective acceptance that is needed here. In symbols,

> (*CAT**) s is collective-social in a primary sense in G iff Forgroup(CA(G,s) & (CA(G,s) $\leftrightarrow$ s)).

Here the 'operator' CA represents the collective acceptance of s by G for G. Forgroup(G,s) means that s is correctly assertable (or, as a special case, true) for the group G in question.[6] Acceptance for the group in general entails mutual belief concerning acceptance. CA must be a performative achievement-expressing notion and 'acceptance' is general enough to cover both the creation and upholding of s and has achievement conceptually built into it. That a sentence is correctly assertable for G means, roughly, that the group members are collectively committed (in the "we-mode") to the sentence and hence to treating it as correctly assertable (or true) in their various intellectual and practical activities in group contexts and when acting as group members.

Consider now briefly the notion of collective acceptance as characterized by (*CAT**): Forgroup(CA(G,s) ↔ s). First consider the implication from left to right:

Forgroup(CA(G,s) → s) (Performativity)

This is true simply on the basis of the notion of collective acceptance, which is an achievement notion relative to the group's "intentional horizon." What is accepted by the group is correctly assertable or true for the group members.

Next consider the converse implication:

Forgroup(s → CA(G,s)) (Reflexivity)

This gives a central and often emphasized "mark of the social." For s to be correctly assertable within G it must be collectively accepted in G. The truth of s for G makes reference to s itself within the sentence CA(G,s). This condition will be discussed in section 2.

We can say that a sentence is collective-social in a derived sense if it is not collective-social in the above primary sense but presupposes for its truth (for the group) that there are some relevant true (for the group) sentences which are collective-social in the primary sense. For instance, sentences using "power" or "wealth" are at least in some cases candidates for collective-social sentences in a derived sense. Latent or unilateral social influence are social features of the social world that would not—and correctly so—be cases of even derivatively collective-social features even when many agents would be concerned. The same holds for "naturally" social emotions such as envy (unless they are specifically about socially constructed things). Many shared we-attitudes also are not socially constructed (for instance shared we-fear is a "natural" social phenomenon).

(*CAT*) leads also to an account of social institutions in the broad sense. Due to limitations of space, let me just briefly consider the matter and present the following suggestion:

> (*SI*) A norm-entailing sentence s expresses a *social institution* in a primary sense in a collective G if and only if the members of G collectively accept s for G, and act accordingly; herethat collective acceptance for the group entails and is entailed by the correct assertability (or truth) of s.[7]

Social institutions in a derivative sense can be characterized analogously. In them the sentence s is collective-social in the derivative (rather than in the primary) sense. Norm-based social power-relations could be cited as example of social institutions in the derived sense.

My somewhat tentative thesis is that the family of intention concepts (including agreements and commitments) and acceptance beliefs (doxastic takings) are the basic attitudes needed to sustain (*CAT*), but a detailed defense is not possible here.

Searle's theory of the construction of social reality shares many features of my above account.[8] His basic formula for collective acceptance in the context of social institutions is "We accept that S has power (S does A)."[9] This is understood to be implicitly entailed by my central acceptance sentence "We collectively accept s" (or CA(G,s)), but what is explicitly accepted in the Collective Acceptance account is the sentence s, e.g., s = squirrel fur is money, and not the underlying powers, rights and duties, concerning the possessors of squirrel furs and other members of the group.

II. THE SCOPE OF COLLECTIVE ACCEPTANCE

What is the precise class of sentences s to which (*CAT*) is claimed to apply? Underlying the Collective Acceptance model is the general assumption that in each context of application one can distinguish between sentences whose obtaining or "truth" is entirely up to the members of the group (or up to their conceptual activities, especially to what they on metaphysical grounds *can* accept as true) and sentences whose truth is at least in part up to nature (as opposed to them), to the way the world is, and thus in part dependent on the causal processes occurring in the world "outside them." It is built into the nature of the equivalence in (*CAT*) that it is concerned with things which are up to the group members and are as "viewed" by them. Therefore, group members can collectively accept (for the group) the correct assertability or truth of some sentences, e.g., "Stars determine our fate," without making it to be the case that those sentences are true in the standard sense.

Generally speaking, social concepts and sentences are reflexive in the following sense. A collective-social sentence using a putatively social predicate (e.g., "money," "leader," or "marriage") does not apply to real things (such as certain pieces of paper or squirrel furs in the case of "money") unless collectively accepted and, so to speak, validated for that task. Let us consider money as an example. The predicate "money" does not refer to itself but to coins, dollar notes, squirrel furs, and so on. Reference here means that "money" correctly applies to those things. The loose talk about reflexivity in this context therefore should be understood as being about presupposition-stating sentences such as "Money is not money unless collectively accepted to be money." This is not a matter of what phrase to use but what the concept of money is. This concept is expressed by what the user of the predicate "money" in English is entitled to say and, especially, extralinguistically do (and what he may be obligated to do). The concept of money thus connects with some deontic powers and obligations collectively bestowed upon those who use the predicate 'money' and who belong to the collective in question. The discussed presupposition (viz., that money is not money unless collectively accepted to be money) is central precisely because of the following assumed fact: It is up to the members of the collective—and nobody else—to bestow those extralinguistic deontic powers upon its members. This contrasts with sentences involving only physical predicates like "tree" or "mass." In their case it is not up to the members of the collective to do more than stipulate how to use certain linguistic phrases and, e.g., what word to use for trees and heavy objects.

It can thus be said that the alleged reflexivity of collective and social concepts strictly speaking is not directly concerned with the entities that the concepts (predicates) apply to. Rather, we may say that a collective-social concept is conceptually reflexive or "self-conceptual" in the sense that it presupposes itself; and this can be explicated in terms of truth for the group as follows. When for a social predicate q a sentence q(a) is true for the group this presupposes the collective acceptance of a as q for the group members. Thus, if $q(x)$ expresses that x is an item of money and a stands for a squirrel fur, then the statement $q(a)$ can be true for the group only if squirrel furs are, in fact, collectively accepted as money or "made" money for the group members. A similar point can be made about, meanings of words, leaders, marriages, property rights, and so on.

III. ON THE ONTOLOGY OF THE SOCIAL WORLD

The Collective Acceptance account seems to say that the parts of the social world it applies to are collectively-socially formed and are therefore human constructions. Indeed, this is basically right, but needs qualifications. Some remarks on the matter will be made below.

One can argue that reality is criterially connected to causality in the sense that an entity cannot be real in an objective sense unless capable of occurring in singular causal mind-independent contexts (viz., in claims of the form C(f,f'), C standing for causation and f, f' being facts related to the entity in question). Here mind-independence is inquirer-independence, viz., independence of an inquirer's mind or, somewhat differently, the "ideally rational" scientific community's "mind" (attitudes, views). Roughly speaking, the mind-independence of causation here can be understood in the sense of causation in a world similar to ours but in which there are no inquirers with minds.[10] Note that our present criterion for a mind-independent—and objectively real—world "out there" allows that there are creatures possessing minds (e.g., intentions and beliefs) "out there."

In addition to the two "levels" of a) mind-independent reality out there and b) the (ideal) scientific community's view or, put differently, the standpoint of the ideal best-explaining theory, we must also deal with c) a group's (any group's, large or small) point of view. From a group's point of view the social institutions and other collectively constructed and upheld things in that group are "mind-dependent" in the sense of dependent on the group's acceptance and thus its attitudes. These things— dependent on the group's "mind"—can nevertheless be said to be "socially real"—in the group. That is, they are intersubjectively real and objective both in an ontic and, generally, also in an epistemic sense, and they belong to the group's posited "public space." Let me emphasize that, furthermore, the fact that a group has collectively accepted and created certain entities or features of the social world itself is an objective fact independent of an external inquirer's or best-explaining theory's point of view (criteria a) and b) being fulfilled).

Let me note that criterion a) of independence may be argued to amount to b), but one may still want to keep these criteria conceptually distinct. What is group-dependent and collectively mind-dependent in sense c) is mind-dependent also in the other two senses, whereas the converse fails.

From a group's point of view there can then be things which depend for their existence (creation, recreation, and maintenance) on fully or partly intentional group activities, depending thus on the underlying intentions and beliefs of the group members.[11] Note that the group members generally need to have right thoughts about e.g., money and school, etc., when they act, but they need not of course think that by so acting they contribute to the maintenance and renewal of the institutions involved. Note that there are social entities and features which are not group-dependent in the sense of the CA account. These include non-constructed things and states (such as presumably love and we-fear can be), which accordingly are mind-independent and objective in our full sense a).

Recall that our collective acceptance model presupposes the distinction between sentences whose truth (or, more generally, correct assertability) is entirely up to the group members (or indeed any human beings or beings capable of operating as the CA-account requires) collectively considered and sentences whose truth is at least in part up to the way the inquirer-independent world causally is. This assumption of course presupposes that sense can be made of the causal processes occurring in the world "out there." (A realist is in general disposed to accept this.) Thus, according to this view, group members can collectively accept (for the group) the truth or correct assertability of such sentences as "Stars cause our fate to be what it is" without making it the case that those sentences are true in the standard sense.

Using other well-known philosophical terminology, one might argue that (*CAT*) applies only to the entities and features belonging to the conceptual order (the order of justification) rather than to the causal order. While on the right track, this is not too clear, for (*CAT*) has ontic import (viz., connects with the mind-independent causal order) by giving the participating group members rights and duties in a sense having naturalistic content, their having rights and duties entailing their being (conditionally) disposed to act in certain specific ways.

While making a distinction between what is up to us collectively to achieve and what is up to nature is basically right, I think, considering the matter epistemologically, that it need not be assumed on *a priori* grounds. Here is a point which supports its *a posteriori* status. Assume that a group g collectively accepts, among other things, causal statements (e.g., that a bridge collapsed because of a heavy truck crossing it or that smoking causes cancer). Here we have embedded causality in a broader frame of collective acceptance by putting a non-social claim, viz., a claim about a non-social causal connection, in the same "acceptance-box" as, say, the statement about stars determining our fate (a merely social claim). In more general terms, the embedding here proceeds as follows. We start with a comprehensive system of causal relations including relations of a purely social nature as well as other relations. In this system we can delineate the social causal relations as those which satisfy our CA-model. Now a good epistemic procedure should be able to distinguish between those collectively accepted causal connections which are not mind-independent in the intended sense from those which are. I submit that the scientific method (perhaps already our current view of it) is able to do the job. Thus, for instance, by means of theorizing and testing the constructed theories we are led to a warranted rejection of the claim that stars determine our fate, or that "*similia similibus curantur*" (the central claim of homeopathy), or that smoking is not a causal factor of lung cancer (up to now the central claim of tobacco industry). This *a posteriori* method does (or tries to do) "from within" what the older metaphysical views do from an external point of view and in an *a priori* sense. Recall that the kind of epistemic objectivity under discussion can be achieved also with respect to group-dependent things, although relative to the assumed fact of collective acceptance and maintenance.

According to our Collective Acceptance account social institutions, *qua* some kind of collections of position-involving normative structures, can be causally effective ultimately only via the group members' minds and actions. This is because we need not assume that they ontically include other, more "holistic" elements, although the social institution concepts seem to be irreducible primitives. Social institutions can have and often have causal impact via the participants' (in collective acceptance) thoughts and thus subjectively (in the group members' beliefs) *qua* social institutions, or at least their central nervous systems (in non-intentional cases). The "internalized" rights and duties related to, e.g., institutional entities like money or institutional positions (e.g., teacher) can, accordingly, in this embedding involve causal connections independent also of the group members' minds.

In "non-normative" cases (cf. leader, esteem, status) based on collective acceptance in the sense of mutual acceptance belief (viz., the acceptance of something as true for the group) the analogous observation holds, for collective acceptance always is group-relative, viz., it relates the constructed and recreated things to the group (thus to the mental life of the group members; cf. Tom is our leader only in so far as he is accepted by us as our leader).

Physical social artifacts such as church buildings, cars, chairs, and books exist as causally effective entities. They can enter causal connections not only *qua* having suitable physical features but also, and in the present context in an important sense, *qua* being artifacts expressing normative or non-normative collective practices.[12]

Various unintended and unanticipated consequences (cf. the states of high inflation and unemployment, pollution of the environment) also belong to social artifacts broadly understood. It seems that they generally fall outside the scope of primary social things. Nevertheless, they are often if not in general are collective-social in the derived sense, being based on things social in the primary sense.

Finally, there are social properties and relations which can be regarded as real in a more naturalistic sense and which correctly fall outside the scope of the CA-model. For instance, Tom's being jealous of Jane is (normally) an example of such a non-constructed social fact. Another example is provided by some shared collective attitudes (or we-attitudes) in the "I-mode."[13] A concrete example would be our we-fear that a lion will attack us.

We have in effect seen that the question "Is the social world real?" is not a very clear question, because the answer crucially depends on what is meant by the social world and by something being real. Basically, 1) a realist can regard the social world as real and objective in the mind-independence sense, viz., the social world exists independently of an inquirer's mind or of the viewpoint of the inquirers' community. But 2) a part of the social world is dependent on group-acceptance, as emphasized. Yet this part of the world is ontically objective in the relative sense of being grounded (sometimes in a historically solid, permanent sense) in group acceptance. As a consequence, in order to be intelligible (in the sense of being correctly explainable) at least this part of the social world must be conceptualized as its inhabitants conceptualize it (squirrel fur may have been money for medieval Finns but not perhaps for others). Finally, 3) social and institutional artifacts such as cars, tables, and church buildings, *qua* physical entities are objectively real in sense 1) and *qua* social and institutional entities in sense 2) because of having been socially constructed and "embodying" the ideas created in the sense of the Collective Acceptance account.

Prof. Raimo Tuomela, Department of Philosophy, University of Helsinki, Helsinki, Finland SF–00014; raimo.tuomela@helsinki.fi

NOTES

1. B. Barnes, "Social Life as Bootstrapped Induction," *Sociology* 17 (1983): 524–45; D. Bloor, "Idealism and the Social Character of Meaning," (1996, photocopied); M. Kusch, "The Sociophilosophy of Folk Psychology," *Studies in History and Philosophy of Science* 28 (1997): 1–25; and J. Searle, *The Construction of Social Reality* (London: Allen Lane, 1995).

2. See R. Tuomela and W. Balzer, "Collective Acceptance and Collective Social Notions," *Synthese* 117 (1999): 175–205.

3. Ibid.

4. Cf. below and R. Tuomela, *The Importance of Us: A Philosophical Study of Basic Social Notions*, Stanford Series in Philosophy (Stanford: Stanford University Press, 1995), chap. 1; also, Tuomela and Bonnevier-Tuomela, "From Social Imitation to Teamwork," *Contemporary Action Theory*, Vol. II: *Social Action*, ed. G. Holmström-Hintikka and R. Tuomela (Dordrecht and Boston: Kluwer Academic Publishers, 1997), 1–48.

5. Tuomela and Balzer, op. cit., 1997.

6. See ibid. for discussion.

7. See ibid.

8. Searle, op. cit.

9. Ibid., 104, 111.

10. Cf. R. Tuomela, *Science, Action, and Reality* (Dordrecht, Boston and Lancaster: D. Reidel Publishing Company, 1985), chaps. 4–7 for a discussion of this from the point of view of scientific realism.

11. Cf. the "duality models" of A. Giddens, *The Constitution of Society* (Cambridge: Polity Press, 1984); and R. Bhaskar, *Reclaiming Reality: A Critical Introduction to Contemporary Philosophy* (London: Verso, 1989).

12. See R. Tuomela, "A Defense of Mental Causation," *Philosophical Studies* 90 (1998): 1–34, for *qua*-causation.

13. But not those in the "we-mode," in the sense of Tuomela, *The Importance of Us*, op. cit.

FREEDOM AND EQUALITY IN THE COMPARISON OF POLITICAL SYSTEMS

Wolfgang Balzer

The notions of freedom and equality in a group are precisely defined in terms of individual exertions of influence or power. Freedom is discussed in the version 'freedom from' influence rather than in the version 'freedom to do' what one wants. It is shown that at the ideal conceptual level complete freedom implies equality. Given the plausibility of the definitions this shows that political 'folk rhetorics' in which freedom and equality often are put in opposition are misled and misleading. Quantitative notions of 'more freedom' and 'more equality' are introduced and shown to be independent of each other. The bearing of these conceptual exercises on the comparison of political systems is discussed.

During the last 5000 years the competition and contest of large, human communities or political systems, of which modern states are the pressing example, often was decided by a simple, 'evolutionary' mechanism: war and force. However, the increasing destructive power of artifacts, which are developed with the help of scientific knowledge, seems to diminish the importance of this device—at least among communities with a somewhat rational leadership. For the mere use of modern techniques increases the risk of self-destruction even for that party which otherwise would be said to have won the 'contest'. In this situation it would be desirable to have other, less violent criteria to check whether some political system is better than another one. If we could compare the quality of political systems in a purely conceptual way the practical competition among systems could be reduced to attempts at enlightening the citizens of the respective other system.

Recent views of the quality of political systems focus on different aspects or dimensions expressed by terms like freedom, equality, solidarity, human rights, and welfare. The problem with such a multi-dimensional approach to the quality of political systems is that the different dimensions have not been analyzed in precise terms and have not been thoroughly compared with each other. There is no common knowledge about how the different aspects jointly affect the quality of a political system. While the effect of each single aspect ceteris paribus is quite clear, problems arise when two or more of them are varied simultaneously. In 'folk' political rhetorics it is a common topic that freedom and equality, as well as freedom and solidarity, compete with each other or even are incompatible. When these labels are used as characteristic for given political systems, we arrive at the usual rhetoric of political competition among states where, say, a 'free' state and a 'socialist' state (i.e., a state characterized by equality and/or solidarity) strive for domination. These prescientific opinions lead to the expectation that a scientific investigation will yield similar results.

I think that this expectation requires caution. In the the real-world examples the key terms usually are applied to states without much justification, and in a propagandistic vein. In order to overcome this unsatisfactory situation the basic notions have to be studied in more precise terms and compared with each other with respect to their contributing to the quality of political systems. My discussion here will move in this direction and present some results showing that the scientific study of these aspects or dimensions is promising. I concentrate here on the most important notions: freedom and equality.

As a background for my explications, I use a theory of social institutions combining a power centered view of social affairs in the spirit of, say, Machiavelli, and a systemic, formal model of such affairs.[1] This theory is intended to model comprehensive social institutions like political systems and states—among other things. (In the social sciences presently the game theoretic view seems to prevail when institutions are discussed. However, what are called 'institutions' in the game theoretic approach are not political systems, but more local and abstract things like 'promise', 'convention', and the like. Up to now game theoretic analysis has not been able to model and to explain one single political system of the kind I am discussing here.) According to my theory a social institution is given by four parts: a micro-system of individuals and their actions and social relations; a macro-system of social groups and their properties and relations, and two 'images' of these two systems: a set of 'micro-images', images of the micro-system which are internalized by the institution's members; and a 'macro-image' in which the macro-system is represented in some more objective way, for instance, by written laws, norms, myths, poems, pictures, and the like.

Concentrating on the macro- and micro-systems, one basic feature of this theory is that individuals are engaged in power relations. Each individual tries to exert power over other individuals (or to influence them). An individual power relation in which power is exerted is constituted by the two individuals involved plus one action performed by each of them. For instance, Peter may exert power over John by uttering the command "Go and get me some cigarettes" and by John's getting the cigarettes, where Peter's action is the utterance and John's action is to get the cigarettes. A second basic feature is that individual power relations can be used to characterize groups and a status relation among groups. Roughly, a group G has lower status than another group G' if many members of G' exert power over many members of G but not vice versa. Inside one group, on the other hand, the exertions of power are in equilibrium. The third important feature is that in a social institution the groups are ordered by the status relation such that they form a connected, transitive graph with a unique top-element. This top-element is the 'top-group', a group which has highest status and whose members therefore exert power over most members of the other groups.[2]

In a model of this theory, freedom and equality can be defined as follows. At the micro level, a model contains four kinds of objects: persons i, j, actions a, b, and points of time t, t'. Persons perform actions and exert power over each other. Moreover, they have intentions and causal beliefs. I use the expressions that person i at time t performs action a; that i by doing a exerts power over j so that j does b in the period from t' to t; that at time t, i intends that j should do a; and that, at t, i believes that action a partially causes action b. With these expressions, we can define the action space of person i at time t to consist of all actions which are possible for i at t. I say that j's action b at t is the aim of an exertion of power iff there is some person i, some earlier instant t' and some action a such that i by doing a exerts power over j so that j does b in the period t', t. With these two auxiliary definitions we can define that person j is free at t iff no action b in j's action space at t is the aim of an exertion of power. That is, no action b in j's action space is induced by some other person's exerting power on j and influencing j to do b. Actually, in the present context the restriction to actions from j's action space makes no difference. It can be proved that one might equivalently use arbitrary actions.

This definition of freedom exclusively in terms of individual exertions of power apparently is exposed to a well known criticism of behaviorist approaches to power.[3] It seems that important ways of exerting power in a less direct, 'structural' way are not covered, like for instance excluding an issue from the agenda, or hiding an exertion of power behind the obligations of one's own social position. Yet this impression is misleading. First, on the present account, the notion of action is not understood in the naive way of positively doing something. Actions form a 'space' of actions in which there is room for neutral behavior (doing nothing) and also for negative behavior (expressed by a negated proposition) to count as an action.[4] Second, in the context of a social institution, each exertion of power is directly linked to mental predicates of intention and causal beliefs, and indirectly linked to macro-features like social positions and norms. I cannot describe the details here but just note that in an institutional embedding an exertion of power—though at the surface described by a relation among actors and actions—may acquire the full status of social or institutional power which is required for a proper understanding of domination.[5] When embedded in a social institution, the present definition of freedom expresses much more than the merely behaviorist absence of tokens of influence.

Of the two basic versions of freedom (freedom 'from' influence and freedom 'to do' what one wants), the above definition covers the first notion. It is difficult to relate these two notions in precise terms because the domain of humans wants is so fuzzy. If we could distinguish, in a given state, the domain of materially possible actions which j could perform if nobody would exert power over him and the domain of actually possible actions obtained by removing from the first domain all those actions which are made impossible by other persons' exerting power over j then we might say that 'freedom to do' is constrained in two ways. First, it is constrained by the domain of materially possible actions. A person cannot perform materially impossible actions, whether she wants to do so or not. Additional to this first constraint, 'freedom to do' is further narrowed down by other persons' influences making materially possible actions impossible. Under this perspective, if the domains of material possibility depend on the level of welfare then the level of 'materially possible' freedom, i.e., freedom that would prevail in the presence of freedom from influence, is higher in states with a higher level of welfare. However, this distinction does not seem to be fruitful for in reality the 'material' level and the level of influence are heavily dependent on each other. For instance, a rise of the level of welfare usually is accompanied by increased suffering of exertions of power so that the overall freedom 'to do' of a person does not increase (or even decreases) when welfare does. Moreover, freedom 'to do' allows for ideal, individualistic realization of freedom: I simply cut down my wants in order to become completely free (as the Hegelian slave). This shows that freedom 'to do' is not well suited for discussions of essentially social matters like the comparison of political systems, and that freedom 'from' is the right notion to be used in such contexts.

Equality can be defined by distinguishing *external* and *internal* equality. Let us say that two persons i, j at t are externally equal iff they exert 'the same' power over third persons k, and are affected by third persons exerting power over them in 'the same' way. Clearly, 'the same' here must be interpreted somewhat liberally. I take it to mean that whenever i exerts power over some k by means of some action a then there is an action a' by which j exerts power over k, and vice versa with i and j interchanged, and that whenever some k exerts power over i by means of some action a then the same k also exerts power over j by some a' and vice versa with i and j interchanged. In a more fine grained analysis one would use action-types and require that a and a' be actions of the same type; i and j are internally equal at t iff each exertion of power of i over j is matched by one of j over i and vice versa. Finally, we can say that i and j are equal (at t) iff i and j are externally and internally equal at t. Note that this definition captures social equality as contrasted to physiological or other kinds of 'non-social' equality. Two persons may be equal in the sense defined but still widely differ, say, in strength, intelligence or wealth.

It is easily seen by counterexamples that one person may be free but not equal to another one, or may be equal to another one but not free. Also, it can be shown by way of example that even complete equality of all persons in a group may go together with the absence of freedom in that group. In the reverse direction there is a positive result. If all members of a group are free then they are equal, or, more briefly: total freedom implies equality. This result holds for the notion of 'freedom from', and may be expressed in still other terms as saying that equality is a necessary condition for freedom ('freedom from'). In the comparison of political systems these notions typically are used in a quantitative way allowing for 'more' and 'less'. The definitions just described can be modified and turned into comparative notions of more freedom and more equality being present in one group than in another group of about the same size. Problems in application then arise in mixed cases like that of an increase of equality together with a decrease of freedom. There is no commonly accepted way of combining different criteria in order to obtain a definite result.

The condition of 'more freedom' on this account is directly linked to the presence or absence of power relations. An increase of freedom by the above definition implies that less exertions of power are made: 'more freedom implies less exertion of power'. On the other hand, equality may vary without any change in the numbers of exertions of power, for instance, by mere 'redistribution' of such exertions in the population. Moreover, the quantitavie notions of freedom and equality are independent of each other. This can be shown by logical comparison, and by showing that under fixed, hypothetical conditions, a variation in one dimension is compatible with no variation in the other. For instance, if freedom increases the degree of equality may remain unchanged. In particular this shows that freedom and equality—even if both are defined in terms of power—yield different criteria for the ranking of political systems. The fact that both these notions can be defined in terms of power does not imply that the comparison of political systems in these two dimensions can be 'reduced' to one, more basic criterion formulated in terms of exertions of power.

Wolfgang Balzer, Institut für Philosophie, Universität München, München, D-80539 Germany; balzer@lrz.uni-muenchen.de

NOTES

1. W. Balzer, "A Basic Model of Social Institutions," *Journal of Mathematical Sociology* 16 (1990), 1–29; and idem., *Soziale Institutionen* (Berlin: de Gruyter, 1993).

2. See Balzer, "A Basic Model," op. cit., for details.

3. See S. Lukes, *Power: A Radical View* (London, 1974).

4. See Balzer, *Soziale Institutionen*, op. cit., chap. 6.

5. Compare the definition in ibid., chap. 12.

LOVE, HONOR, AND RESENTMENT

Daniel O. Dahlstrom

For much of contemporary ethical theory, the universalizability of the motive of a contemplated action forms a necessary part of the basis of the action's moral character, legitimacy, or worth. Considering the possibility of resentment springing from the performance of an action also serves as a means of determining the morality of an action. However, considerations of universalizability and resentment are plainly inconsistent with the performance of some unselfish moral actions. I argue that the sphere of the moral adequacy of considerations of universalizability and resentment is limited. I profile key elements of "conformist" or "consensus-driven" ethical thinking modelled on Nagel's ethical theory. Then, I elaborate the measure of validity of the profiled ethical thinking as well as its limitation, suggesting that its proper domain is located in an ethics of honor, delimited by an ethics of love and friendship.

For a certain broad strand of contemporary ethical theory, the universalizability of the motive of a contemplated action forms, if not the basis, then at least a necessary part of the basis of the action's moral character, legitimacy, or, worth. In addition, at least for some proponents of this sort of ethical thinking (here dubbed "conformist" or "consensus-driven" ethics), consideration of the possibility of resentment springing from the performance or non-performance of an action serves as a means of further determining or specifying the moral correctness of the action. An action is thus said to be moral only to the extent that the motive for the action is universalizable and incapable of incurring resentment from an impersonal point of view. Yet considerations of universalizability and resentment are plainly inconsistent with the performance of some unselfish moral actions (paradigmatically, certain actions based on love or friendship). For this reason, it is argued in the following paper, the sphere of the moral adequacy of considerations of universalizability and resentment is limited. In the first part of the following paper, key elements of the aforementioned "conformist" or "consensus-driven" ethical thinking are profiled. For purposes of economical exposition, the profile is modelled on Thomas Nagel's ethical theory. In addition to the obvious reasons—its influence, its forthright statement of the necessity of a system of impersonal, neutral values, and its appeal to considerations of the possibility of incurring resentment—Nagel's ethical theory warrants particular scrutiny precisely because it attempts to accommodate some non-conformist, non-universalizable values within a moral viewpoint. The second part of the paper elaborates the measure of validity of the profiled ethical thinking as well as its limitations by suggesting that its proper domain is located in an ethics of honor, delimited by an ethics of love and friendship.

I

A "conformist" or "consensus-driven" ethics affirms the possibility and moral necessity of acting from a universal, impersonal point of view. Two assumptions, elaborated on the next few pages, underlie this equation of the moral point of view with a rational, natural one: (a) the assumption of a specific sort of dichotomy and hierarchy in the constitution of moral motivation and (b) the assumption that the moral point of view can be specified through considerations of resentment.

A. The Conformist Dichotomy and Hierarchy

The first mark of conformist or consensus-driven ethics is the assumption of a sharp distinction between so-called moral and subjective points of view (between "reasons" and "desires" or between "agent-neutral values" and "agent-relative values") and an ethical order of motivation according to which reason has the upper hand, mastering desires or "agent-relative" values as well as the feelings, passions, and emotions associated with those values. According to this assumption, actions are moral only when they are motivated by rational considerations independent of desires and emotions. This presupposition does not entail the claim that it is possible for a person to act without desires that are specific to his or her subjective condition and personal nature. However, an action motivated only in this manner would lack moral character or value. If, for some reason, a person finds it necessary to speak of moral desires or emotions, then the latter must be desires that—like respect, the "pineal gland" of Kant's moral philosophy—emerge from purely rational considerations. For the moral character of an action is supposed to reside solely in the sort of rational motivation that, it is argued, follows from the agent's consideration of the universal character of his or her situation or, in other words, from consideration of his or her position insofar as it could be occupied by anyone. That is to say, the action must be regarded by the agent in a way that abstracts from the personal perspective (desires, wishes, demands, and so forth) of the agent. On this assumption, it is necessary for a genuinely moral agent to understand his or her fellow beings as equals, in effect, to understand himself or herself as well as others from an "impersonal" standpoint. Since only a purely practical reason or, more precisely, a reason independent of personal desires and partial viewpoints can procure the requisite understanding, ethics of this stripe presupposes the indicated dichotomy and hierarchy.[1]

Presuppositions of this sort are readily apparent in Thomas Nagel's ethical writings. In *The Possibility of Altruism* he insists that a moral action must be motivated by a rational reflection on objective reasons, i.e., reasons not exclusively "mine" or "hers" or "yours."[2] If it be insisted that every action proceeds from a desire, then there are, according to Nagel, moral desires, based upon such reasons.[3] For this sort of motivation, the "recognition of the reality of other persons" is required, a recognition that ensues only if one adopts an "impersonal standpoint," conceiving oneself "as just one person among others."[4] Taking up the requisite neutral standpoint (the moral equivalent of shifting from the first to the third person[5]) amounts to embracing "objective reasons" for the existence of a certain state of affairs, that is to say, reasons that are valid, not simply for this or that person, but for every person.[6] Moral action, in other words, supposes that the agent regard herself as no different from others or, equivalently, regard herself in terms of those essential features that she shares with others.[7]

Without denying that a person always acts from a subjective standpoint, Nagel maintains that for every subjective reason there is a corresponding objective reason.[8] Moreover, the "motivational content" of the objective reason always overreaches that of the subjective reason.[9] Accordingly, only the appeal to an objective reason secures the congruence of subjective and objective standpoints.[10] The price paid by acting only on subjective reasons is a certain alienation or "dissociation" from oneself, as Nagel dubs it.[11] If a person acts in this manner, she distances herself from the idea that she is only one person among others, an idea that accurately captures a certain part of herself. This idea is intimately linked with the possibility of justifying an action. For a motive for acting can only be morally justified, Nagel claims, before the impersonal, neutral tribunal of reason.

While Nagel eventually calls into question the trenchancy of arguments in *The Possibility of Altruism*, he continues to uphold the necessity of an "impersonal" or "objective" standpoint for ethics.[12] By identifying a reason to act that does not depend upon any particular (subjective) point of view, one gains access to the appropriate moral standpoint: "the view from nowhere."[13] This "neutral" standpoint is supposed to mirror the objectively valuable consequences of an action, "considering the world as a whole."[14] Since the desired standpoint encompasses the particular perspectives of many individuals and their experiences of values within those perspectives, that universal standpoint by no means lacks content.[15]

That universal, impersonal standpoint is itself, Nagel acknowledges, merely a formal condition of the possibility of moral action, presupposing a substantive (material) theory of values.[16] In subsequent works he makes, by his own account, a sketchy and problematic attempt to address the question of what relative values—in contrast to purely egoistic values—can be objectified as neutral values.[17] Nevertheless, while the requisite values can be determined only on the basis of the objectification of certain subjective reasons, Nagel claims in *The Possibility of Altruism* that, as far as the morality of an action is concerned, the objective reasons must override subjective reasons.[18]

In contrast to his earlier position in *The Possibility of Altruism*, Nagel comes to accept the possibility of subjective ("agent-relative" or "personal") values, for which there are no "agent-neutral" or "impersonal" counterparts.[19] In *The View From Nowhere* Nagel accordingly employs the term "objective" in a new, wider sense; "objectivity" is no longer equivalent to "impersonal." Both neutral and relative reasons may be "objective" (according to the new use of the term) as long as they can be understood outside the perspective of the person possessing them. Objectively considered, for example, someone might have a good—although not necessarily a moral—reason to learn to play the violin. Such a reason is not at odds with the moral perspective; it may even be objectively valuable. Nevertheless, it cannot be universalized; its value is not neutral. In other words, x may not demand of others that they further x's learning of the violin.[20]

More importantly, by countenancing the possibility of the irreducibility of agent-relative values, Nagel acknowledges "certain discrepancies between what can be valued from an objective standpoint and what can be seen to have value from a less objective standpoint."[21] Nagel identifies three types of these relative values which—prima facie at least—cannot be universalized: autonomous values, like learning the violin, that emerge from the specific goals of the individual agent; obligatory values, such as parents' obligations to their children that stem from close relationships; and deontological values, like telling the truth, that stem from others' claims upon us. Reasons of autonomy are, as already noted, generally too idiosyncratic and personal to be subsumed under a neutral reason (though there are, Nagel argues, some "very general human goods"—pleasure and pain, freedom, life's necessities and universal opportunities—that, while they are objects of personal preferences, can be seen as having impersonal value).[22] The same holds for the deontological values, the personal demands made upon us by others to behave in a certain away (quite apart from whether they actually want us to have to behave so). Both sorts of values constitute possible reasons for action that "cannot be accommodated within a purely neutral system."[23] (Nagel is confident, on the other hand, that obligatory values might be so accommodated.) As a consequence of this development in his theory, Nagel concedes a legitimate role to the "dissocation" that had been the focus of criticism in his early work.[24] The question of the relation between such relative values and neutral ones becomes, in his eyes, "the central question of ethical theory."[25]

The acknowledgment of the objectivity of these agent-relative values adds a rich complexity to Nagel's ethical theory.[26] Deontological values in particular constitute a kind of limiting case and dilemma for his theory, as he himself acknowledges. If there be such values that cannot be derived from universalizable interests or from the general consequences (for oneself and others) in objectively determinate situations, they constitute limits to what one is permitted to do to others, even if such limits be contrary to or at least not subsumable under the "impersonal" standpoint or general consequences. (Consider the lie that, if told and believed, would be generally beneficial.) Whether someone who experiences the motivational pull of a deontological value or reason of autonomy should identify with the impersonal will presents "a genuine philosophical dilemma," rooted in human nature, from which Nagel infers that "a fully agent-neutral morality is not a plausible human goal."[27] While a purely "impersonal" morality must reject both autonomous reasons and deontological limitations, the latter are, Nagel concludes, "among the sources of morality."[28]

For the purposes of the present discussion, however, what is important is Nagel's continued insistence, despite this turn in his theory, upon the indispensability of the "impersonal" standpoint for both ethics and ethical progress.[29] He suggests that the harmonization of personal and impersonal claims will alter the personal components in the direction of "an internalization of moral objectivity."[30] In the penultimate chapter of

The View From Nowhere Nagel wrestles with the question of the relation between "living right and living well," namely, the demands of a moral life and those of a good life. He agrees that they cannot be fully reconciled and that the preponderance of reasons is on the side of morality and yet—for reasons that echo his early remarks about "dissociation"—he also rejects Bernard Williams' claim that impersonal morality is alienating.[31] According to Nagel, there are objective reasons, available from the impersonal standpoint of morality itself, why the impersonal standpoint must be tolerant of differences in human nature and, thus, essentially self-limiting.[32] In effect, from the same objective and impersonal point of view that generates morality's neutral values, it is clear that claims as to what we should do must take into account what we can do. Nevertheless, despite the purported rationality of this plea for excuses, Nagel concludes that "insofar as reasons are universal, the repeated application of impersonal standards seems to yield the most integrated set of requirements that can be hoped for, taking into account reasons derived from all pespectives."[33]

Nagel is honestly vague about the import of this conclusion. It seems, however, clearly to continue to give the impersonal standpoint the upper hand in forming whatever degree of integration of values is likely. Some indication of what this integration might mean can be gathered from the reason Nagel gives for neglecting so-called obligatory values—those reasons for acting, it bears recalling, that stem "from the special obligations we have toward those to whom we are closely related."[34] These values are not separately examined because, he informs us, he is less confident (than in the case of autonomous and deontological values) that they are able to withstand an "agent-neutral" justification.[35] Apparently, parents' obligations towards children or that of spouses or friends to one another are duties that—in contrast to reasons of autonomy or deontological reasons—can only be morally justified from a universal, neutral standpoint.

B. The Conformist Resentment

This attitude toward obligatory values appears to confirm Nagel's continued embrace of the initial assumption of conformist ethics that has been profiled: a moral action must be motivated by purely rational considerations that are clearly distinguishable from and superordinate to all other considerations. At the same time, Nagel's struggle with the question of the relation between living well and living rightly demonstrates his own recognition that much more remains to be said in regard to both the specification and justification of this criterion. The second assumption animating conformist ethics addresses both of these concerns at once. Let us begin with the question of justification of the aforesaid criterion. Why should a person act in this manner or, more precisely, why should a person be motivated to act in this manner? How is it possible to justify an action that amounts to helping a neighbor in need when it appears to be in fact against the agent's best interest? Conformist ethics responds to this question not only by insisting that the impersonal viewpoint is somehow intrinsic to the agent, but also by considering whether the neighbor would have reason to resent the agent if the latter did not lend a hand (or whether, should roles be reversed, the agent would have reason to resent others for not helping). This manner of justification of the aforesaid criterion also amounts to an interpretation of the morality of an action. The morality of an action consists in its being motivated not merely by the agent's consideration of the action from an impersonal or universal point of view, but also from the agent's consideration of the likelihood of others' resentment of the performance or nonperformance of the action. Indeed, the latter consideration provides a means of specifying the allegedly universal or rational standpoint of morality and demonstrates the nature of the efficaciousness of that standpoint as a source of motivation.

Nagel brings up the theme of resentment as a means of "intuitively representing" the rational altruism on which he initially stakes his ethical theory.[36] "How would you like it if someone did that to you?" is a clearly effective plaint when the person to whom it is addressed believes that her action could put her on the receiving end of such an action or when her sympathy might be elicited by the question. Yet, according to Nagel, even when these possibilities do not exist, the question remains efficacious because it alerts the offending party to reasons, the validity of which does not depend upon a particular person, situation, or point of view. Thus, a person can ascertain the morality of her motivation by questioning whether others have reason to resent her if she acts on that motive or, equivalently, whether she would have reason to resent someone who acts on that motive.

This appeal to considerations of the possibility of resentment is closely tied to the first assumption of conformist ethics, the assumption, namely, that genuinely moral motivation is constituted by a distinctive dichotomy and hierarchy. Thus, Nagel emphasizes that the added advantage of such considerations lies in the fact that, far from resting on feelings, it is a genuine argument, the conclusion of which is a judgment. In this way resentment is, from Nagel's moral point of view, more valuable than sympathy. Only the action motivated by considerations of the possibility of resentment has moral worth since such considerations alone correspond to the judgment that can be inferred from the universal standpoint of reason. As Nagel puts it: "The essential fact is that you would not only dislike it if someone else treated you in that way; you would resent it."[37]

Nor is this appeal to resentment confined to Nagel's early work. In *The Last Word* he asks his reader to consider whether, viewing the matter objectively, she could actually believe that it is unimportant whether she died of thirst or not and that her inclination to believe otherwise is only the false objectification of her love for herself. "One could really ask the same question," he adds, "about anybody else's dying of thirst, but concentrating on your own case stimulates the imagination, which is why the fundamental moral argument takes the form, 'How would you like it if someone did that to you?'"[38] The implication is patent; if one would hold a grudge against someone who so acts, then the act would be morally reprehensible. Nagel adds that it is "very difficult" to give a coherent egoistic answer to the question of the content of the reasons for an action.[39] Once again appeal is made to considerations of resentment as though such considerations represented the very antithesis of egoism and secured the non-self-centered standpoint demanded, on Nagel's view, by morality.

II

There are considerable problems with each of the assumptions of the conformist ethical position just profiled. The first assumption seems plainly counterintuitive inasmuch as it excludes some unselfish acts, notably, acts based upon friendship or love, from the realm of moral actions. Suppose that A is in need and B is a friend of A. It is impossible for B to be indifferent to A's situation or, more precisely, to the prospect that A's need is filled. If B then acts out of friendship, conscious of no other motive than the desire that A's need be filled, B's action would seem clearly to be unselfish and yet, according to the first assumption of conformist ethics, it would necessarily be deemed other than moral.

Both the dichotomy and the hierarchy assumed by conformist ethics are problematic on other grounds as well; not least, the supposition of the superiority, in moral understanding and efficacy, of an indifferent or neutral reason. Such neutrality is the very antithesis of the sympathetic reason that is not obligatory but unquestioningly expected and granted in matters of love and friendship. Moreover, far from being a hindrance to the claims of reason, partiality and affection in such cases constitute a necessary condition for an objective understanding of what is good for the parties involved in the situation. Why should acts of love and friendship be considered less than moral (though, to be sure, not immoral) as, indeed, they must from the impartial standpoint of conformist or consensus-driven ethics? If such acts constitute instead the very paradigm of a moral life, then the impartial standpoint is itself less than moral. These ruminations are admittedly question-begging since what counts as "moral" is precisely what is at issue. Nevertheless, given a prima facie cultural identification of deeds of love and friendship with moral actions or, more modestly put, given a long-standing and internalized tradition of finding fault or blameworthiness with violations of such bonds, then some more substantial reason than an alleged parallel with the objectivity of scientific thought must be advanced for placing them, not at the center, but at the periphery of considerations of criteria for living rightly.

Yet the alleged superiority of the impartial standpoint is itself not supposed without any further justification or explanation. The second assumption, as noted above, purportedly provides support and rationale for the criterion for moral action that emerges from the first assumption. The agent's consideration of whether it would be possible for others to resent his or her action is, on the second assumption, crucial for understanding the action from the allegedly moral point of view and for being motivated by this understanding.

In certain respects, however, this second assumption is the most egregious assumption of conformist ethics. In typically unselfish actions based upon love or friendship, the good of the beloved or the friend overrides all other values or reasons for acting. The act cannot properly be labelled an act of friendship if the motivation for the act is the result of having weighed the possibility of resentment—be it the agent's resentment of the other or others' resentment of the agent. Questions such as: "Would she hold a grudge against me if I behaved in this manner?" or "How would you like it, if I did the same thing to you that you are doing to me?" betray the attitude of someone who views his or her own interests as uppermost and expects others to do likewise. If one acts on the basis of such a consideration of the possibility of resentment, then the motivation for the action is plainly not unselfish and it is not clear why it should be deemed moral. It is also far from evident how such motivation is to be reconciled with the sort of motivation that is supposed to stem from consideration of a so-called "neutral" or "objective" (or even "intersubjective") standpoint—unless, of course, it is presumed from the outset that a community of like-minded egoists, incapable of friendship, occupies that standpoint.

Insofar as interpretations of certain non-egoistic actions appeal to resentment as a motive for such actions, the interpretation is inconsistent with the basic sense of such actions. In the case of an action motivated by friendship, a person acts unselfishly, but out of love, not out of resentment; that is to say, the well-being of the friend is the basis and purpose of such an unselfish action. For the ethical theory profiled on the previous pages, however, the decisive consideration is not the question: "What is the best thing that I can do for the sake of my fellow human beings?" but rather the questions: "Would others resent me if I act a certain way? Would

I resent others if they acted a certain way? How would I react to my neighbor if he or she were to do to me what I now intend to do to him or her (or vice versa)?" It is difficult, moreover, to see how such appeals to resentment do not present an egocentric predicament. For the answer to the question whether others would resent my action seems to depend in large measure upon the answer to the question whether I would resent others for acting in an analogous manner. In the final analysis, the moral agent would have to ask herself whether she would like to stand in the place of her fellow man in the wake of her action in order to determine whether her fellow man would like to be in this position. Insofar as one (with Nagel) combines the moral standpoint with the universal (neutral) standpoint, the moral agent is, to be sure, called upon to distance herself from her specific standpoint as well as from the thicket of feelings bound up with that standpoint. Yet she must, to the same extent, leave out of consideration the individual situation of her fellow man and friend—something quite unthinkable for a friend.

What underlies conformist or consensus-driven ethics? Why is the attempt made to interpret the moral nature and establish the moral value of unselfish actions in so clearly self-centered a phenomenon as resentment? Why might one be prepared to portray the richly differentiated colors of human relationships with the neutral shades of an impersonal ethical standpoint? Even if one is not ready to subscribe to the assumptions of conformist ethics, does it not indicate the indispensable and even sublime merits of a neutral, universal standpoint—at least as an ideal criterion and goal of certain actions?

These questions are, in my view, thoroughly appropriate and appropriately challenging (not least for the positions advanced in this paper) and I have no adequate answers to them. Yet, by way of conclusion, I would like to suggest that the key to solving these difficulties might be found in a closer consideration of the status of resentment in specific sorts of human relationships.

Resentment comes about when a person values herself to a certain extent and expects to be treated or respected by others in corresponding fashion. If a person felt that she had not been adequately respected by others, then she would typically think that she had cause to resent them. She may, of course, be mistaken; the resentment may be unreasonable. The resentment would be reasonable and fitting, it seems, to the degree that the person has and shows an appropriate estimation of herself and others. The basis for resentment in such cases is a specific concept of honor that consists in a certain kind and measure of reciprocal recognition of worth or dignity. Thus, a person extends honor (respect, tribute) to another only insofar as the other extends it to her. To honor and be honored reciprocally in this manner are, above all, liberal values in the political-economic sense of the expression. Although they are not the values underlying unselfish acts of friendship, these values are decisive for the determination of justice among fellow citizens or negotiating parties. Coercion may even be necessary, where property and security are concerned, to enforce actions reflecting these values. In any case, this sort of honor, demanding reciprocal recognition as it does, underlies and warrants the possibility and necessity of considerations of resentment to which conformist or consensus-driven ethical theories appeal.

One can, of course, honor another human being without loving him or her. The honor presupposed and extended in reciprocal recognition demands a price and the person who is "honorable" in this sense never lets completely out of sight what she has to gain from the recognition. Such is not the case, however, in a genuine friendship. If a person loves her friend, then she does not demand love or recognition as payment. The first thought of a lover or friend is not what she has to gain, but rather what is in the best interest of the beloved or befriended. If moral theory takes its bearings preeminently from the sort of standard of honor just proposed, then a conformist or consensus-driven interpretation of the morality of unselfish actions, with its insistence upon a neutral standpoint, becomes quite compelling. If, on the other hand, the highest moral value is accorded to unselfish acts of love and friendship, then such an interpretation is bound to appear as nothing short of an ethical swindle or perversion.

Daniel O. Dahlstrom, Department of Philosophy, Boston University, Boston, MA 02215; dahlstro@bu.edu

NOTES

1. We may ask ourselves what it would be like to be in another person's position or to be in his or her shoes; playing upon this image, we might say that the kind of ethical understanding profiled here supposes that there is a universal shoe size or one size for all moral agents.

2. Thomas Nagel, *The Possibility of Altruism* (Oxford: Clarendon Press, 1970), 3, 5f, 15f, 87f, 121–124, 144 (hereafter PA); for Nagel's acknowledgment of similarities with Kant's moral theory, cf. PA 11–14.

3. PA 81.

4. PA 3, 83f, 88, 100–102, 107, 124.

5. PA 104–109.

6. PA 90–97. A reason for striving to bring about a specific state of affairs is objective only if that state of affairs is objectively valuable or, in other words, only if the desirability of that state of affairs does not depend upon the subjective standpoint of any particular person who may happen to strive for it; cf. PA 100, 107.

7. PA 100: "To recognize others fully as persons requires a conception of oneself as identical with a particular, impersonally specifiable inhabitant of the world, among others of a similar nature."

8. Nagel assumes that one can always extract the rational part of the value of an action, a part independent of the interest of the agent; PA 90: "In any situation in which there is reason for one person to promote some end, we must be able to discover an end which there is reason for anyone to promote, should he be in a position to do so." Cf. PA 96: "Whenever one acts for a reason, I maintain, it must be possible to regard oneself as acting for an objective reason, and promoting an objectively valuable end." Cf. also Thomas Nagel, *The View From Nowhere* (Oxford: Oxford University Press, 1986), (hereafter VFN), 169f.

9. PA 94f, 102f, 114f.

10. PA 116–119.

11. PA 106–108, 116, 118f; cf. also VFN 198 where, contesting Williams' claim that impersonal morality requires self-alienation, Nagel observes that "universalistic moralities are supposed, after all, to answer to something very important in us. They are not imposed from outside, but reflect our own disposition to view ourselves, and our need to accept ourselves, from outside."

12. VFN 139, 159, 170.

13. VFN 141: "The method is to begin with the reasons that appear to obtain from my own point of view and those of other individuals, and ask what the best perspectiveless account of those reasons is." VFN 151: "The task of ethical theory is to develop and compare conceptions of how to live, which can be understood and considered from no particular perspective, and therefore from many perspectives insofar as we can abstract from their particularity." Cf. VFN 155; Thomas Nagel, *The Last Word* (Oxford: Oxford University Press, 1997), 120f (hereafter LW).

14. VFN 162f: "That is the essence of traditional forms of consequentialism: the only reason for anyone to do anything is that it would be better in itself, considering the world as a whole"—also von einem neutralen Standpunkt; cf. VFN 164f.

15. VFN 146f. The contrary position is "objective nihilism." Cf. LW 119–122.

16. PA 88, 97, 123f.

17. LW 124; VFN 161, 171f, 198. In *The Last Word*, Nagel sketches the different attempts of utilitarianism and contractualism to interpret the concept of objective values; cf. LW 122.

18. PA 124; VFN 155: "In deciding what to do, for example, we should not reach a result different from what we could decide objectively that that person should do . . . ."; cf. also VFN 146f; cf. LW 123: "The problem is to give more specific content to the idea that persons have value not just for themselves but in themselves—and therefore for everyone." The fact that ethical theories as diverse as utilitarianism and contractualism presuppose the moral standpoint articulated by Nagel provides, he submits, further corroboration of the correctness of that articulation; cf. LW 124.

19. If a reason or value can be formulated without essentially referring to the person possessing it, then it is "agent-neutral"; otherwise the value is "agent-relative." Cf. VFN 149, 152f, 155, 159, 170, 189. However, see also VFN 155: "We should be able to view our lives from outside without extreme dissocation . . . ."

20 VFN 167–171.

21. VFN 166.

22. VFN 171f.

23. VFN 163; cf. VFN 189f.

24. VFN 172: "Each person has reasons stemming from the perspective of his own life which, though they can be publicly recognized, do not in general provide reasons for others and do not correspond to reasons that the interests of others provide for him . . . . A certain objective distance from his own aims is unavoidable; there will be some dissociation of the two standpoints with respect to his individual concerns." Cf. VFN 166–175.

25. VFN 159.

26. VFN 180–185; Nagel posits but does not answer the question whether the so-called "deontological" values should be countenanced, though he seems to doubt the validity of deontological limitations of the moral point of view.

27. VFN 185, 189f. Cf. VFN 155: "In particular it is not easy to follow the objectifying impulse without distorting individual life and personal relations."

28. VFN 185, 165.

29. Cf. VFN 185–188: "Moral Progress"; this approach to ethics is also alive and well in The Last Word where Nagel equates impersonal values with "other-regarding" or "nonegoistic" values and construes relative values as "egoistic" ones; cf. LW 120–122.

30. VFN 187; quite advisedly, Nagel speaks of the internalization of moral objectivity, not moral neutrality.

31. VFN 195, 198–201.

32. VFN 201–203.

33. VFN 204.

34. VFN 165.

35. VFN 165: "I have less confidence here than with regard to the other two categories that in ordinary thought they resist agent-neutral justification."

36. PA 82; cf. Korsgaard, "The Reasons We Can Share: An Attack on the Distinction between Agent-Relative and Agent-Neutral Values," *Altruism*, ed. Ellen Frankel Paul, Fred. D. Miller, Jr., and Jeffrey Paul (Cambridge: Cambridge University Press, 1993), 27: "According to Nagel, I should see that I would not merely dislike this, I would also resent it, and my resentment carries with it the thought that my tormentor would have a reason to stop."

37. PA 82f; cf. 145: "When they are wronged, people suddenly understand objective reasons, for they require such concepts to express their resentment. That is why the primary form of moral argument is a request to imagine oneself in the situation of another person."

38. LW 122: Freilich läßt sich dieser komplexe Satz unterschiedlich deuten; d.h. meine Interpretation mag der Absicht Nagels nicht genau entsprechen.

39. LW 122.

A WESTERN PERSPECTIVE ON THE PROBLEM OF VIOLENCE

Robert L. Holmes

The following sketches a constellation of views constituting the implicit philosophy of violence that one finds in much of the Western world. While I believe that much of this philosophy is deeply flawed, I shall, in a sense, be setting forth the case for violence because any hope of a nonviolent and peaceful world order must begin with a deeper understanding of violence and its attractiveness. After exploring various arguments for violence, I conclude that once we probe beneath the surface, it is clear that most of those who deplore violence do not oppose all violence, only that of which they disapprove, and that social manipulation backed by violence in the end seems to most people to be justified.

People need to be able to explain what is going on around them and to have settled expectations about the future. Individuals are normally able to do this for themselves in the ordinary course of living. But societies do so as well in the course of evolving, most notably when they have a dominant religion or ideology, for these provide value-laden perspectives defined partly by reference to friends and enemies. They also come replete with convictions about how one may properly behave. These perspectives almost invariably contain at least an implicit philosophy of violence.

My concern at present is not with what enters into the formation of such perspectives. Suffice it to say that in a country like America, television, film, politics, and religion are among the chief influences. My concern, rather, is to sketch out a constellation of views that constitute the implicit philosophy of violence that one finds in much of the Western world. For the most part I will not attempt to evaluate this philosophy, though I believe that much of it is deeply flawed. Rather, I shall set it forth in the belief that if there is to be any hope of a nonviolent and peaceful world order, there must first be a deeper understanding of violence than we now have. And a part of that understanding must begin with an appreciation of the attractiveness of violence. So I shall, in a sense, be setting forth the case for violence, but doing so only because of the importance I attach to meeting the challenge it presents. But actually meeting that challenge will not be part of my present project.

I

The roots of the willingness to use violence no doubt grow out of an instinctive desire for security. Security has almost universally been taken to justify any means necessary to ensure it. These at one time included measures to provide protection against wild animals. Eventually the fostering of security extended to the control and use of animals. The book of *Genesis* gives humankind dominion over them, and such dominion has largely prevailed worldwide. Beyond this, with the development of science the control and use of nature itself eventually came to be one of those means. As John Dewey says, the scientific attitude "marks a revolution in the whole spirit of life, in the entire attitude taken toward whatever is found in existence . . . . [N]ature as it already exists ceases to be something which must be accepted and submitted to, endured or enjoyed, just as it is. It is now something to be modified, to be intentionally controlled."[1] But security requires protection not only against wild animals and hunger and cold and the depredations of nature, it requires protection against other humans as well. Here the quest for security has led to the organized and institutionalized violence of warfare.

The quest for security has almost universally been taken to justify violence. There are exceptions to this. Notable among them is Taoism in ancient China, Jainism in India, early Buddhism in India and China, possibly the Essenes within Judaism, and the early followers of Jesus within Christianity. Christianity represents the only major Western movement with a commitment to nonviolence at its core. Not that Jesus is known to have spoken directly about violence and war. He did not. But what he did say clearly implies their renunciation, and so his message was generally understood by early Christians. Not until Constantine in the fourth century did Christianity become the handmaiden of the state. And not until the fifth century was Christianity's transformation from its nonviolent beginnings complete, when Augustine provided a justification of war from a Christian perspective. This justification has been cited by practically all subsequent just war theorist in the West, religious and secular. When Nietzsche characterized Christianity as a slave morality that disavowed self-assertion and power, he was criticizing a Christianity that, as practiced, had long since ceased to exist, except in a few small sects.

These exceptions to the justifications of violence suffice to highlight deep-rooted differences between violence and nonviolence. These may be viewed as components in two broader competing philosophies, which Arthur Koestler has characterized as the outlooks of the "Yogi" and the "Commissar." The Yogi symbolizes change from within, the Commissar change from without. The former emphasizes self-discipline, personal purification, and means over ends. It looks more to spiritual development than to consequences. Most importantly, it involves a commitment to nonviolence. The Commissar, on the other hand, represents social regulation, ends over means. Its characteristic mode of calculation is utilitarian. And it is prepared to use force and violence when necessary. This willingness is one of its distinctive features.

We can see the Yogi and the Commissar reflected respectively in Gandhi and Lenin. Marx emphasized the need to free the individual from alienation. He allowed at least the possibility that revolution might in some places come about without violence. Lenin, however, brought the ideal of the Commissar to fruition in the commitment to change through social engineering, manipulation, and force. The implementation of this commitment fell to Stalin, the technician of forced collectivization and terror. The cost, of course, was horrendous. Millions died in the implementation of the scheme. Millions more were ground down under the weight of totalitarian rule. But the social good that beckoned on the horizon was a noble one. It was that of an egalitarian society, free of want. The effort to realize the greatest good was a grand experiment, unrivaled in scale by any the world has ever seen. But its failure was also a stupendous one. It marks one of the defining moments in history.

Gandhi, of course, was less purely a Yogi than Lenin was a Commissar. An idealist, to be sure, he was also a pragmatist. He sought social change through direct action. It is just that, for Gandhi, social action had to be rooted in nonviolence to be of lasting effect. Whereas the Leninist-Stalinist enterprise in the Soviet Union was far more a calculated experiment than the product of historical laws that Marxists would like it to have been, Gandhi expressly regarded his work as a deliberately undertaken experiment. It was an experiment in truth, he said. As such, it had decided success in helping free India of British colonial rule. But unlike that of the Soviet Union, Gandhi's experiment is a continuing one. It is one stage in an ongoing process, the outcome of which remains to be determined.

The Soviet Union, of course, represented a clear case of the embodiment of the outlook of the Commissar throughout an entire society. But there are no comparable cases of the attitude of the Yogi being embodied in an entire society of any size, and certainly not in a modern nation-state.

The interesting question, for our purposes, is how to understand the United States, for rightly or wrongly, it is often taken to epitomize contemporary Western values. On the one hand, with its materialism, militarism, and marriage to high technology, it obviously does not even begin to approximate the ideal of the Yogi. But when one sets its liberalism, democracy, and regard for personal liberties against the totalitarianism of the Soviet Union, it does not fully reflect the values of the Commissar either. Nonetheless, I was to suggest that in the end the United States—as well as other large industrial societies—embodies the outlook of the Commissar as decisively as did the Soviet Union. To see this requires considering the role of fear and force in the maintenance of society and the conduct of foreign relations.

To regulate behavior through fear and force is to control it from without. It is to compel people to do certain things and to refrain from others by the threat of what you will do if they do not comply. Where that fails, the compulsion takes the form of a direct and deliberate infliction of sanctions. These include pain, suffering, and sometimes death. The system of nuclear deterrence is a paradigm. According to its logic, you instill such fear of the consequences of an attack upon you that your adversary refrains. When he does the same with you, the resultant "balance of terror" supposedly immunizes both of you against attack, hence prevents nuclear war. When this thinking is extended to include conventional deterrence as well, practically the whole of a national security system based upon military power falls within its scope.

The same thinking operates in the attempt to maintain law and order within society. Indeed, the terms 'law and order' themselves imply regulation from without, the imposition of constraints. Hobbes, whose influence permeates Western thinking about the nature of the state, spoke specifically of the terror needed to govern society. One needs, he believed, to instill fear to maintain social order. Where nuclear deterrence is the paradigm of the use of fear and force in foreign relations, capital punishment is the paradigm here, and it is carried-out with increasing frequency in America since resumption of the death penalty in the mid-1970s. For less serious crimes the stakes are less high, but the principle is the same. It is to deter people from committing crimes by the threat of what will happen to them if they do. The whole judicial and legal system, backed by specialists in law enforcement, institutionalizes this thinking domestically. The government, Pentagon, strategists, and armed forces institutionalize it in foreign affairs.

Any society that relies ultimately in this way upon fear and force is beholden to the Commissar, whatever its government and socioeconomic system. It is also beholden regardless of the liberty it otherwise affords its citizens. Thus there are more similarities than differences between America and the former Soviet Union when the two are viewed in this light. They differed in the relations between the individual and the state, in that the United States enjoys considerable freedom, whereas the Soviet Union was brutally repressive. But in their attempts to maintain national security they both relied overwhelmingly upon fear and force. As measured by the organization of modern states (as opposed to the ideals and values contained in their ideologies), there is no contest between the Yogi and the Commissar. The Commissar stands astride us all, whatever other differences there may be among us.

II

At a time when violence is deplored by social and political leaders, it is important to appreciate the case for violence. For people implicitly distinguish between "good violence" and "bad violence."

Everyone knows what bad violence is. Domestically, It is that of muggers, murderers, rapists, wife-beaters—that of criminals generally. Internationally, it is that of tyrants, terrorists, and aggressors. Basically bad violence is that of which we disapprove, good violence that of which we approve. Good violence is also that which is used to try to prevent bad violence. The typical thinking here is simple. It is that considering how bad violence is, we must take drastic measures to counter it. These include using violence ourselves when necessary. In personal affairs the clearest case is self-defense.[2] Whatever else, people say, we all have a right to do whatever is necessary (possibly excepting the killing of innocent persons) to defend our own lives. Thus there is an understandable tendency on the part of those who want to justify violence to represent their acts as self-defense, even if there was no assault against them underway at the time. In domestic affairs, this is becoming a common defense of wives who kill abusive husbands, sometimes while they are sleeping. In international affairs, Israel's 1967 attack upon Egypt (after the latter blocked the Gulf of Aqaba) was alleged to be self-defense, even though Israel initiated the fighting.

If we are individually justified in using violence in our own defense, it would seem we have a right to authorize others to use it on our behalf. It takes only a small step to conclude that the police are justified in using violence when necessary, because they are, after all, authorized by us to do for us what we are entitled to do for ourselves. It is but a further step from this to justify waging war. For war, it is widely believed, is justified when necessary for national defense. This, for most, is a preeminent just cause. And just cause is the central condition in the Just War Theory, which provides the model for war's justification. Those in the armed forces are performing on our behalf every bit as much as the police. World War II stands as a paradigm. There the evil was unmistakable. The stakes were enormous. However great the cost, it is believed, victory over Fascism was imperative. Had Hitler prevailed the world might for generations have been under the rule of a ruthless and vicious totalitarian regime. If ever there was a just war, this was it. The sacrifice Americans made in defense of themselves and others testified to the best in American character. That sacrifice is properly remembered with the reverence it deserves.

Even where aggressive force has not been used, according to this way of thinking, self-defense still justifies going to war. As just noted, many believe that Israel was justified in going to war after Egypt closed off the Gulf of Aqaba. And even where self-defense is not at issue, many believe that war can serve valuable functions. Many see Egypt's 1973 war against Israel as redeeming Egypt after its humiliating 1967 defeat, thus making possible the Sadat initiative that resulted in a peace accord between Israel and Egypt. The war, by all accounts, was aggressive. But for all for its bloodshed, it nonetheless, according to this thinking, helped create the conditions for peace. Some people attribute the same role to the Palestinian *Intifada*. Although it was not a war, it was an uprising (albeit a largely nonviolent one) without which the 1993 peace agreement between Israel and the PLO likely would not have come about. Early just war theorists thought it did not really matter who initiated a conflict. What was important was the justice of the cause and whether it was ultimately undertaken in the interests of peace. That way of thinking, generally in eclipse through much of the twentieth century, began regaining favor towards the end of the century.

There is one more extension of this reasoning. If the police and military may justifiably use violence in defense of those from whom they have authorization, the military may do so on behalf of those who may be equally in need of defending, but who for various reasons (such as that they live in another jurisdiction) cannot give such authorization. If I may use violence to defend my own life, why may I not do so to defend yours? And if a nation may defend itself, why may it not defend another nation? And if it may do so to defend another nation, why may it not do so to defend people within that nation, with or without the consent of their government if they are under threat, either from others or from their own government itself? The fact that they are subject to a different government requires superceding the claims of national sovereignty. To use force within a country against the will of its government is to violate the traditional conception of sovereignty. The case here is for humanitarian intervention. The idea of humanitarian intervention is gaining acceptance in international affairs, particularly in light of crises such as those in Somalia, Bosnia, Haiti, Rwanda, and Kosovo. It presents a challenge to the UN Charter, which authorizes the unilateral resort to force only in the case of self-defense, and then only until such time as the Security council has acted.

III

Beyond these expressly moral attempts to justify violence in Western thought, two others merit special note. These see violence as not always bad, and as needing to be opposed. They see it as performing important positive functions. The first of these imputes to violence an important biological function. Seeing that nature is marked with conflict and struggle, the claim is that this is a biological necessity, and that in human affairs it is the way to progress. Through some sleight of hand, this is made to appear to be true of states as well. Thus in the words of Friedrich von Bernhardi in the early years of the twentieth century:

> By self-assertion alone can the State maintain the conditions for its citizens, and insure them the legal protection which each man is entitled to claim from it. This duty of self-assertion is by no means satisfied by the mere repulse of hostile attacks; it includes the obligation to the whole body of the nation embraced by the State .... From a given moment [strong States] require a continual expansion of their frontiers, they require new territory for the accommodation of their surplus population. Since almost every part of the globe is inhabited, new territory must, as a rule, be obtained at the cost of its possessors—that is to say, by conquest, which thus becomes a law of necessity.[3]

This was very much in the spirit of Treitschke in the nineteenth century, and came to be an important element in the Nazi ideology, and in Hitler's thinking in particular. War, as painful and destructive as it is, came to be seen as the engine by which the best that is in humankind could be made to flourish. Once the biological orientation is in place, it is easy to apply such thinking to domestic as well as international affairs. Hannah Arendt warned of the dangers of such thinking:

> Nothing, in my opinion, could be theoretically more dangerous than the tradition of organic thought in political matters by which power and

violence are interpreted in biological terms . . . . The organic metaphors with which our entire present discussion of these matters . . . is permeated—the notion of a "sick society," of which riots are symptoms, as fever is a symptom of disease—can only promote violence in the end. Thus the debate between those who propose violent means to restore "law and order" and those who propose nonviolent reforms begins to sound ominously like a discussion between two physicians who debate the relative advantages of surgical as opposed to medical treatment of their patient. The sicker the patient is supposed to be, the more likely that the surgeon will have the last word.[4]

What Arendt calls "organic thought" leads readily into a second justification of violence. This involves what we might call the "medicalization" of violence. It is becoming common in the closing years of the twentieth century. Thus we hear with increasing frequency in domestic affairs of the epidemic of violence, and in international affairs of the virus of terrorism or of surgical precision in bombing. And the "treatment" in this medicalized way of thinking about violence extends to psychological disorders as well.

Jean-Paul Sartre, in his preface to Frantz Fanon's *The Wretched of the Earth*, writes of the resistance against French colonial rule in Algeria:

There is one duty to be done, one end to achieve: to thrust out colonialism by *every* means in their power. The more farseeing among us will be, in the last resort ready to admit this duty and this end; but we cannot help seeing in this ordeal by force the altogether inhuman means that these less-than-men make use of to win the concession of a charter of humanity. Accord it to them at once, then, and let them endeavor by peaceful undertakings to deserve it. Our worthiest souls contain racial prejudice.

They would do well to read Fanon; for he shows clearly that this irrepressible violence is neither sound and fury, nor the resurrection of savage instincts, nor even the effect of resentment: it is man recreating himself. I think we understood this truth at one time, but we have forgotten it—that no gentleness can efface the marks of violence; only violence itself can destroy them. The native cures himself of colonial neurosis by thrusting out the settler through force of arms.[5]

On Sartre's view there is a good to be achieved by violence. It is measured not merely by the formal liberation of a people, which could be achieved by the cessation of colonial rule and the departure of the colonizers. It can be achieved only by a psychological process that destroys the "colonial neurosis" and restores the humanity of the oppressed.[6]

There is a hard word in all of this, too, for advocates of nonviolence. In an obvious allusion to Albert Camus' pacifistic essay, "Neither Victims Nor Executioners." Sartre adds later:

A fine sight they are too, the believers in nonviolence, saying that they are neither executioners nor victims. Very well then; if you're not victims when the government which you've voted for, when the army in which your younger brothers are serving without hesitation or remorse have undertaken race murder, you are, without a shadow of doubt, executioners . . . . Try to understand this at any rate: if violence began this very evening and if exploitation and oppression had never existed on earth, perhaps the slogans of nonviolence might end the quarrel. But if the whole regime, even your nonviolent ideas, are conditioned by a thousand-year old oppression, your passivity serves only to place you in the ranks of the oppressor.[7]

According to Sartre, violence may have the therapeutic function of humanitarian restoration. To oppose violence in those cases signifies complicity in the dehumanization of the oppressed. This claim would hold against those who refuse to use violence in many other contexts as well. Indeed, wherever violence is thought to be justified on any of the preceding grounds (such as self-defense or humanitarian intervention), refusal to use it in those cases would make one liable to the accusation of complicity in the wrong the violence is deemed necessary to remedy. Such reasoning surfaced in the early 1990s regarding opposition to military intervention by the U.S. in Somalia. It was argued that if America refused to intervene militarily, that would make Americans responsible for the starvation of thousands of Somalis. Later, with regard to the former Yugoslavia, it was argued that refusal to intervene would make Americans complicit in the ongoing atrocities there.

This argument carries particular force for those concerned about the Third World. More advanced nations often conspire with oppressive regimes to preserve conditions of profitability for their companies with commercial interests within those countries. In these cases, the conditions of stability—of "law and order," if you will—often perpetuate injustice. The status quo is maintained by a privileged elite backed by a strong military, often trained and equipped by outside powers. In these circumstances it's those who initiate force who will invariably be seen—and seen correctly—to be disturbing the peace. For they will be fighting against injustice and the injustice will be integral to the status quo. Even pervasive and cruel oppression is compatible with peace if peace is understood merely as the absence of war. Oppressive regimes can then represent themselves as defenders of the peace. And they will be right. In these cases, if one opposes violence and nothing more, one stands as Sartre says, on the side of the oppressors. To oppose violence is to preserve the status quo. And it's unconscionable to preserve the status quo when it is the status quo that needs to be changed.

We come here to the last piece in the case for violence. It seeks to warrant violence without sanctifying it with a moral justification. The contention is that violence is sometimes "necessitated."

Augustine said that when one takes up the sword in a just cause, it is necessity at work, not one's own will. On the face of it this would seem to absolve just warriors of responsibility for the violence they do. What such "necessity" is remains unexplicated, however—other, of course, than as the violence thought necessary to remedy the wrong in question. This way of viewing violence has worked its way deep into our thinking. We commonly find world leaders saying when they go to war or resort to force, that "we have no choice . . ." or that "we are forced to . . . ." The idea has been encapsulated in the notion of military necessity. Here it stands for measures necessary to attain the ends of war—sometimes with the qualification that the means must be consistent with the laws of war. The paradoxical nature of this approach to violence is evident in this feminist account, very much Sartrean in character:

> Yet simply to condemn violence in a situation of oppression also supports the status quo and makes the goal of human freedom nothing but an idealist and ineffectual dream. Those who work to end oppression must therefore adhere to an ethics in which acts of violence are clearly condemned; at the same time, these reformers and revolutionaries must recognize that oppressive societies and the violence of others sometimes place individuals in impossible situations where violence cannot be avoided. Acting against the oppression may of necessity involve violence; but not acting against the oppression affirms, collaborates with, and even reinforces the oppression and its violence.[8]

This preserves at the intellectual level the divided thinking of society as a whole. People think of themselves as opposed to violence. They are outspoken against it. But when pressed they'll say that sometimes violence is necessary. And they unquestioningly support massive expenditures to devise weapons of destruction and to train young men and women in their use. Here the necessity derives not from the fact that violence is the only means that will be effective against evil. Necessity as conceived here might obtain even when that is not the case. The idea is that there are some situations in which one cannot avoid doing violence.

IV

Two conclusions emerge here. The first is that, once we probe beneath the surface, it is clear that most of those who deplore violence do not oppose all violence, only that of which they disapprove. Violence, on their view, is sometimes necessary and justified. When extremists resort to violence they use means that are accepted by most of society. This constitutes a common ground between them and others. It also creates a common ground between extremists and their opponents—usually the government or those who wield power. However loudly people condemn violence, they approve its use on their behalf by the police and military. Most individuals and groups (whether governmental, religious, or terrorist) are willing, when they deem it necessary, to kill to achieve their ends—or, at any rate, to see others kill on their behalf. They differ only over the circumstances in which they think it is justified to do this and for what purposes.

This means, as I have said, that the common outlook—indeed, the virtually universal outlook—is in this respect essentially that of the Commissar. In the end, according to this reasoning, one must be prepared to maintain the status quo, or to initiate constructive change from without. Liberals and conservative will disagree whether that should be through social engineering, and if so, to what degree. But they agree, in effect—though they rarely think of themselves as expressly holding this—that it should be through manipulation of fear and force.

The second and possibly more important conclusion is that this manipulation of fear and force backed by violence in the end seems to most people to be justified. We can count on the reasonableness and cooperativeness of people up to a point, they say, but human nature being what it is, there comes a point beyond which we have to threaten force and be prepared to use it. This is what holds together the very fabric of society. It is what allows peace-loving people to live under conditions of stability and order. It allows democracy and a free economy to flourish. And so long as the use of fear and force is carefully monitored and accompanied by safeguards against abuse, it is regrettably but realistically the foundation of the social values we cherish. Not only are fear and force woven into the fabric of society, they are also necessary to protect the country from external threats as well. Here again there are risks. We are all aware of examples of the military being used for evil ends. But again, the military of a free and democratic people is different. It may be misused—as, in the view of many, it was in Vietnam. But one of the strengths of democracy is that such abuses can be argued in public debate and harmful tendencies brought to light and corrected.

On this view, nonviolence is a nice ideal, and may even have some limited role in a new world order. But realistically, order depends upon fear and force. Violence and the threat of violence are here to say. The place to focus time and energy is upon the elimination of bad violence; seeing to it that criminals learn that crime does not pay and that the greatest goods of civilized, democratic life are open to them only if they are respectful of the rights of others. Internationally, the focus must be upon seeing to it that potential aggressors, and perhaps those who abuse their own citizens, learn that a civilized world will no longer tolerate *their* use of fear and force in the oppression of peoples.

There is a powerful case here for violence. If it is sound, one might suppose, it means that the prospect of a nonviolent world order is naive at best, and at worse subversive of the very conditions of civilized life. It is a case that even many pacifists at least tacitly accept. They, like everyone else, enjoy the security they do, and the capacity to promote pacifistic ideals, because others, like the police and the military, undertake the hard and dangerous work of trying to hold in check the threats to what is good and decent in the world. If we benefit from their efforts, the argument goes, how can we with consistency, much less with moral or intellectual integrity, argue for dismantling the institutions through which they work? Unless one has an answer to this, it is best to step aside and let people with an equally humane but more realistic vision go about the hard word of working in a practical way for peace and justice.

This is the challenge of violence for the twenty-first century. It is one that draws in various ways upon a multilayered philosophy of violence that has deep roots in widely accepted ways of thinking. The one thing that is certain is that there is virtually no chance of achieving a nonviolent world without radical changes in our thinking, and radical restructuring of society.

Robert L. Holmes, Department of Philosophy, University of Rochester, Rochester, NY 14627; hlms@mail.rochester.edu

Notes

1. John Dewey, *The Quest for Certainty: A Study of the Relation of Knowledge and Action* (New York: Capricorn Books, G. P. Putnam's Sons, 1960), 100.

2. Self-defense may not be the clearest case for some of the justifiable use of violence. For some, the defense of their children is the clearest case. With or without a rationale, many would instinctively do whatever is necessary to protect their children. This represents an area that merits further study on its own. I owe this point to Julia Bartkowiak.

3. Friedrich von Bernhardi, *Germany and the Next War* (New York: Longmans, Green, and Company, 1914), 21.

4. Hannah Arendt, *On Violence* (London: Allen Lane, The Penguin Press, 1969), 75.

5. Jean-Paul Sartre, preface to *The Wretched of the Earth*, Frantz Fanon (New York: Grove Press, Inc., 1963), 21.

6. In similar fashion, it has been reported that the Indian nuclear tests in 1998 had the effect of countering the "emasculation" of Indian males by the British attitudes under colonial rule; cf. *Christian Science Monitor*, 4 June 1998.

7. Sartre, op. cit., 25.

8. Linda A. Bell, *Rethinking Ethics in the Midst of Violence* (Lanham, Md.: Rowman and Littlefield, 1993), 193.

POLITICS AND ANTI-POLITICS

Newton Garver

Three very different things present themselves under the title "politics," even when we restrict the domain of politics to civic concerns. One is the highly partisan activity that begins with the distinction between friends and enemies and culminates in wars or elections. Another is legislation, litigation, and diplomacy, often making use of conciliatory negotiation with adversaries (no longer "enemies" but honorable fellows). The third is civic action aimed at limiting, circumventing, or constraining the role of the first two. I call the first kind "zero-sum politics," the second "integrative politics," and the third "anti-politics," anti-politics having affinities with what Pettit calls anti-power. My aim is to distinguish the three by sketching their salient differences. The important point, as Wittgenstein said, is that these language-games are played. Clarity about their differences can enhance both our understanding of public affairs and the quality of public discourse.

I. INTRODUCTION

There are three very different things that present themselves under the title "politics," even when we restrict the domain of politics to matters of state or to civic concerns. The word refers primarily to what affects or determines control of the use of state powers in general and the state's monopoly of the legitimate use of force in particular. Within this very broad domain there are at least three different kinds of endeavor, no two of which can in any easy way be performed by the same person or persons at the same time. One kind is the highly partisan activity that begins with the distinction between friends and enemies and culminates in various sorts of showdowns, sometime elections, sometimes war of ethnic cleansing. Another kind is legislation, administration, litigation, and diplomacy, undertaken in the shadow of state power and often making use of conciliatory negotiation with other parties (who are no longer "enemies" but are now honorable adversaries). The third kind is civic action aimed at limiting or circumventing or constraining the role of first two.

The contrast between the first two kinds of politics can be illustrated by current rhetoric. When Tom Daschle became Minority Leader of the U.S. Senate in January of 1995, he remarked in his initial interview that he thought the American people wanted Congress to "put politics aside and get down to the business of government," using the words "politics" and "government" in such a way that there is a strong semantic contrast between the two. The sentiment has been widely echoed on various occasions by the media and by other politicians. One ought to be struck by public figures dichotomizing politics and government in this manner. In the second sense indicated above government just *is* the business of politics. It is clear that two concepts that contrast cannot be the same two concepts as two concepts one of which includes the other, so we must be dealing with at least two significantly different conceptions of politics.

The third sort of "politics" is activity undertaken by groups with no state power in order to limit or focus state power or to promote civic activity that flourishes outside the apparatus of the state. One manifestation of this sort of "politics" is anarchism, but one should bear in mind that neither Gandhi nor Martin Luther King was politically active in either of the first two senses. Other examples of political activity which do not fit either of the first two rubrics are the Bill of Rights, Human Rights Watch, Habitat for Humanity, the humanitarian work of the American Friends Service Committee (AFSC),[1] and NGOs active at the United Nations.

Although the three sorts of political activity are clearly distinct, there are no established labels to distinguish them. I am not comfortable with labels in philosophy, and there are reasons not to be satisfied with the labels I shall use. Nonetheless I shall call the first of these three sorts of endeavor or "zero-sum politics" or "partisan politics," the second "integrative politics,"[2] and the third "anti-politics" or "alternative politics." The labels are merely a matter of convenience. To distinguish the three sorts of activity by sketching their salient differences is my main task in this paper. I shall associate the first with Machiavelli and Carl Schmitt, the second with Jürgen Habermas and John Rawls, and the third with Thomas Jefferson and Jimmy Carter.[3]

II. Zero-Sum Politics

While political "realism" has had many advocates in this century, Carl Schmitt is one of the most profound and illuminating. Two essential features of the political, according to Schmitt, are that politics begins with a distinction between friends and enemies and that politics has to do with the exercise of powers of the state. Schmitt has stronger conceptions of "friend" and "foe" than we ordinarily employ. Schmitt's foes are locked in dire struggle, not just opposed in philosophy or legislative strategy. In Hegelian terms, our foes belong to a different moral community and therefore cannot engage in genuine dialogue with us.

That foes are not just adversaries helps to appreciate how zero-sum politics generates partisan intolerance. Since zero-sum politics begins with the distinction between friends and foes, anyone who argues against using the friend/foe opposition, or who insists that it is possible to enter into genuine dialogue with any human being, is undermining politics. It is on this basis that Schmitt argues that liberalism is not political at all, but the negation of politics.[4] Since integrative politics involves aspects of liberalism, he would no doubt also argue that integrative politics is a negation of politics, as would be the kind of moral universalism that subordinates partisan loyalties to moral principles or moral virtues. Beginning with the friend/foe opposition results in a clear conception of politics as inherently partisan and focused on domination and control, and in a sharp dichotomy between politics and negotiation or accommodation. This clarity is helpful for illuminating the close connection between politics and war and for dispelling illusions about politics always being a means to social harmony. Schmitt's conception of politics as essentially partisan brilliantly illuminates why politics has acquired a bad name in our liberal culture, and why there are many popular confusions about politics and politicians.[5] I shall therefore consider Schmitt's main point to be that politics, beginning with a distinction between friends and enemies in some sense or other, is thoroughly and essentially partisan.

Schmitt knew the work of Clausewitz, and it is useful to note the continuity between the two.[6] Clausewitz said, famously, that war is a continuation of politics by other means. This remark is generally understood, rightly, to insist on a measure of pragmatic rationality in military action, via specific well-defined goals. One can see Schmitt's conception of the political already contained in Clausewitz's remark, if one asks what sort of thing politics must be if it can be continued by war. The sort of politics exemplified in democratic elections cannot be continued by war: war by the losing party, or against the losing party, would not be a continuation of the electoral politics but a destruction of the electoral system and of the conditions that makes such politics possible. The kind of politics that might be continued by war is just the sort of politics Schmitt describes, involving loyal friends opposed to implacable foes and pertaining to matters of state.

Zero-sum politics is typically fueled by ideology.[7] Personal rationalizations also play a role in public affairs, and even in politics, as when a politician or administrator admits to having forgotten, or been too busy, or even being drunk. As John Ladd has pointed out, however, the rationalizations lying behind collective violence have an intractability that is qualitatively different from that of personal rationalization.[8] It is therefore, Ladd argues forcefully, a common fallacy of political thought to treat collective violence as a collection of acts of individual violence, or to treat ideology as a form of personal rationalization. Ideology gives collective violence its special vehemence and intransigence because of ways in which it differs from psychological bases of violence, such as anger, or inadvertence, or carelessness. One of the differentiating characteristics is that regret and apology make little sense for a collectivity.[9] Another is that, whereas the psychological factors make individual violence seem irrational, ideology gives the collective violence a veneer of rationality. One of the special merits of Ladd's discussion is his identification of five typical components or "premises" of an ideological framework, based on a bifurcation between the "Chosen Group" and the "Other Group" that is equivalent to Schmitt's distinction between friend and foe.[10]

Ideological politics regularly makes pawns of its participants, because its ideologically generated "necessities" leave them "no choice," as Saddam Hussein left President Bush "no choice" in 1991.

III. INTEGRATIVE POLITICS

The hallmarks of integrative politics are respect and civility towards one's adversaries and recognition of the legitimacy of the interests of all parties. There is, therefore, no dichotomy between friends and foes, and no one is excluded from serious dialogue. Dialogue is the essence of politics in this second sense, casting off the subordination to decisive action to which it is ignominiously assigned by Machiavelli and Schmitt. Liberalism is reinstated to a place of honor in integrative politics, and Habermas and Rawls, modern followers of the cosmopolitanism of Kant, are among its contemporary philosophical proponents.

Jimmy Carter has been an effective public practitioner of integrative politics. The most prominent instance during his presidency was the negotiation of the Camp David accords between Israel and Egypt. Begin and Sadat were unable to remain civil when meeting face to face, so President

Carter (with help from Roger Fisher of the Harvard Negotiation Project) created the "single-text" technique of negotiation, assuming authorship of the text that he presented for comments alternately to each of the principals. Although Begin and Sadat began as "foes" in Schmitt's sense, Carter insisted on civility and on the legitimacy of each party, and it was on this basis that agreement was achieved. The incident marks a landmark in the history of alternatives to traditional power politics; it served as the model for President Clinton's initiatives during the meetings with Netanyahu and Arafat at the Wye Conference Center in October of 1998.

In 1995 Carter again placed integrative politics on a highly visible stage, once in Haiti and once in North Korea. In both cases President Clinton had arrived at an impasse, where he could do nothing other than issue ultimatums and make threats—which is war talk rather than dialogue. In both cases Carter made a visit that stressed civility and geniality, Mrs. Carter being especially prominent in the visit to Haiti. Humanizing the contact in this way reestablished the legitimacy of the adversaries, reopened dialogue, and led to agreements that avoided the threatened violence. There was military force in the picture, especially in the case of Haiti, but force was not used and the achievements were genuinely integrative rather than purely Machiavellian.[11]

More generally, much of the work of Congress is a matter of integrative politics rather than politics in Schmitt's sense. One feature of the legislative process is the formal civility required by parliamentary procedure, which contrasts with the rhetoric of electoral politics and which is naturally often accompanied by respect for the interests of adversaries. Negotiation therefore takes the place of bluster.[12] In Congressional deliberations there is rarely any question raised whether the interests of the tobacco farmers of North Carolina, the sugar beet farmers of Utah, or the apple farmers of Washington should be respected by the full House and Senate. Solutions are sought which integrate various interests in the final legislation, particularly in budget bills.

Administrative law and procedure is another area of government where integrative politics has an established and respected place. It is now common practice for details of administrative rules to be drawn up by means of negotiation that includes all interested parties, who then formally agree not to sue to block implementation of rules whose formulation they have endorsed in the negotiation.

The combination of these administrative practices and the legislative process sketched in the preceding paragraph shows clearly that there is much of government that proceeds in a manner very different from that of partisan politics, even in instances where there are substantial special interests involved. Government that proceeds by negotiated consensus is very different from the process involved in attempting to achieve or maintain political office. The advantages of integrative politics are obvious, and it is a mark of a statesman like Carter to be able to turn zero-sum issues into consensus issues. The distinction between these two dimensions of government, gives substance to Senator Daschle's distinction, and is of importance for the quality of public life.

Nonetheless, integrative politics can never completely replace partisan politics, except perhaps in a Platonic utopia where elections have been eliminated. Three points deserve special notice in this connection. One is that negotiation often takes place in the shadow of bellicose threats. Thus the Carters' trip to Haiti took place as Clinton was preparing to send in the Marines, and negotiated administrative regulations are crafted with the knowledge that failure means prolonged litigation. Another point is that we have no model, except in small private groups or hereditary institutions, for determining high political office by means of negotiated consensus. The third point, perhaps the most important of all, is that there is no guarantee that negotiated consensus will result in *just* outcomes. Negotiation aims at mutual accommodation rather than at justice, which, in turn, rarely aims at being accommodating.

IV. ANTI-POLITICS

Broad social movements challenge our conception of politics. On the one hand they take up matters that normally fall within the domain of politics, such as self-determination, civil rights, and women's rights. The impetus from the social movements then often—perhaps ideally—carries over into legislation, as in the case of the Voting Rights Bill. The movement itself, however, remains outside the political process and operates independently of its rules. Neither Gandhi nor King participated in politics—not electoral or legislative or administrative politics. Their role needs to be *contrasted* with that of politicians. The difference stems largely from the fact that movements lack defined roles and offices. Even though politics is not confined to matters of state power, it does pertain primarily to matters where power and authority is institutionally defined. Social movements are anti-political, or a kind of alternative politics, because they thrive outside the institutional frameworks for determining and distributing formal power and authority in society.

When I speak of anti-politics or alternative politics, I refer to civic activities outside of either partisan or integrative politics.[13] The central thought behind anti-politics is that government needs to be limited. One side of this thought is that there are things that governors and governments should not do, which leads to constitutional limitations, balances of powers, and rotation of officeholders. Another side is that there are things that government cannot effectively do, which leads to social movements and to voluntary and not-for-profit organizations. Jefferson, as well as such thinkers as Tolstoy, Bakunin, and Thoreau, deserves recognition as a proponent of the first side, not only for his role in formulating the Bill of Rights but also for his comments on the arrogance of government administrators (at the time of Shays's rebellion, for instance) and his views on the importance of occasional revolutions in a healthy society. Volunteerism has found many advocates in recent years, but the role Jimmy Carter has played in Habitat for Humanity stands as an especially good example of alternative politics and a thoughtful symbol of things that government cannot do.

As examples of anti-politics and alternative politics, I include the whole range of actions and organizations that attempt to limit or constrain or expand the domain of politics, or to influence political action by limiting the power of certain political offices, or to respond to social needs normally within the domain of politics. Human rights organizations, such as the American Civil Liberties Union (ACLU) and Human Rights Watch (HRW), and service groups, such as the American Friends Service Committee (AFSC) and Habitat for Humanity, are good examples of anti-politics in action. With respect to the international issues that come before the United Nations, the so-called non-governmental organizations (NGOs) play an analogous role. Neither domestically nor internationally do these organizations seek office or political power, and they rarely threaten the tenure of anyone holding political office. The service groups circumvent politics by responding to public needs. The rights groups attempt to limit the powers and actions of politicians to acts that conform to principles of human rights—ACLU through litigation and HRW through carefully researched studies that are given wide publicity.

The methods of groups such as the ACLU can be tough and pugnacious,[14] but they are not political. They aim only to limit the powers of legislators and office-holders, not to gain office or governmental power. The action they take, the tools they use, and the issues they address are all in the public domain and generally concern actions of public officers— but all that does not suffice to make ACLU a political organization. HRW, on the other hand, is concerned with some of the same rights, but treats them as human rather than civil rights, the principal difference being that human rights belong to each person whatever constitutional and positive law may say, whereas civil rights are enjoyed because of what the laws of a particular country say. The significance of this difference is that human rights do not involve judicial interpretation or enforcement, and so the methods of the ACLU are inappropriate. HRW has therefore devised methods of research and publicity, putting well-documented reports in the hands of members of the U.S. Congress and other opinion makers. A political realist might think such methods futile. Regimes that wish to do business with the rest of the world, however, need to be more accommodating to world opinion than do military dictators, and therefore HRW has had significant success, providing an alternative to both politics and litigation in matters of high public interest.

A service organization such as Habitat for Humanity, whose volunteers help low-income people build sound housing for themselves, illustrates another sort of alternative politics. Public policy with respect to housing is often a matter of contentious political dispute. The work of Habitat falls outside all such disputes, but its work responds to the conditions that give rise to them. It builds houses for people who lack adequate housing, it does so at a cost far below the market costs or the costs at which the government could provide housing, and it builds the houses to standards that far exceed the minimum codes. By operating in this way Habitat frees people from dependency on government, and thus from the uncertainties of both partisan and integrative politics.

What I am speaking of here is related to what Philip Pettit discusses in his helpful essay, "Freedom as Antipower." The difference between the two concepts is that antipower (like power itself) is a potential whereas anti-politics (like politics) is an activity. Pettit writes, "As a care for freedom as noninterference goes with a concern to maximize the range of uninterfered-with choice, so a care for freedom as antipower goes with a concern to maximize the range over which undominated choice is enjoyed,"[15] where domination (or subjugation) is the *power* to interfere with impunity and at will, even if there is no *actual* interference. Pettit sees antipower as promoted by "the introduction of protective, regulatory, and empowering institutions."[16] Much of what Pettit discusses requires formal state initiative, but he explicitly notes that "institutions that promote antipower are by no means restricted to the more or less legal instruments whereby the state operates; they also include various instruments of civil society."[17] One might therefore say that the various forms of anti-politics are activities designed to increase antipower, and thereby to increase freedom as antipower.

V. CONCLUSION

Three distinct sorts of activity have been delineated, each having distinctive merits and limitations. No general comparative evaluation has been made, and none may be possible. The important point is, as Wittgenstein said in another connection, that these language-games are played. Clarity about their differences can enhance both our understanding of public affairs and the quality of public discourse.

Politics is too often construed as zero-sum politics, and however inescapable, it plays too large a role in our lives. Our lives would be richer and more robust if more conflicts were redefined as variable-sum rather than zero-sum situations and if pugnacity were more often replaced by civility. This is, in large part, what Pettit has in mind when he advocates freedom as antipower, that is, as a condition opposed to subjugation rather than to interference. We need to study and promote structures and strategies that do these things. Integrative politics and anti-politics offer alternatives to the tedious and impoverishing pugnacity of intensely partisan politics and upbeat ways out of the exasperation generated by trying, as fundamentalists are wont to do, to solve the problem by another zero-sum political effort.

Newton Garver, Department of Philosophy, State University of New York at Buffalo, Buffalo, NY 14260; garver@acsu.buffalo.edu

NOTES

1. I refer to the work for which the AFSC and the British FSC were awarded the Nobel Peace Prize in 1947. Recent work of the AFSC has become more political in a partisan sense, based on a criticism of the humanitarian work as "mere band-aids" and an emphasis on economic justice over harmony and simple humanitarian needs.

2. I borrow the term 'integrative' from Dean G. Pruitt, *Negotiating Behavior* (New York: Academic Press, 1981), who speaks of negotiation as aiming at integrative solutions to conflict.

3. Jefferson's role in the formulation and adoption of the Bill of Rights, and especially of parallel documents in Virginia, distinguish him as the only U.S. President better known for limiting the powers of the presidency than for exercising and stretching them. See Garry Wills, *Inventing America: Jefferson's Declaration of Independence* (Garden City, N.J.: Doubleday, 1978); and Newton Garver, *Jesus, Jefferson, and the Task of Friends* (Wallingford: Pendle Hill, 1983) for further details and discussion. See also Jimmy Carter, *Negotiation, the Alternative to Hostility* (Macon, Ga.: Mercer University Press, 1984); Jürgen Habermas, *Between Facts and Norms: Contributions to a Discourse Theory of Law and Democracy*, trans. William Rehg (Cambridge, Mass.: MIT Press, 1996); and John Rawls, *Political Liberalism* (New York: Columbia University Press, 1993).

4. "But the question is whether a specific political idea can be derived from the pure and consequential concept of individualistic liberalism. This is to be denied." Carl Schmitt, *The Concept of the Political*, trans. George Schwab (Chicago: University of Chicago Press, 1996), 70–71.

5. I find the limitation of politics to matters of state rather narrow: whatever its theoretical merits, it does not conform to our current usage. Matters of state are indeed the prime domain of political behavior, but they are not the only one. Politics in the workplace and the academy, pertaining to theories and practices as well as to budgets, is a very real phenomenon, and one which is equally focused on control and domination. There seems nothing metaphorical about university politics or departmental politics, in the zero-sum sense. I also find the strong conceptions of "friend" and "foe" too strident and contentious, as is their consequence that liberalism is not politics at all. However provocative, this way of speaking fails even more conspicuously to conform to current usage. Both these contentious points, furthermore, obscure the merits of Schmitt's concept of the political.

6. Schmitt seems to agree. He writes: "War is for him [Clausewitz] a 'mere instrument of politics'. This cannot be denied, but its meaning for understanding the essence of politics is thereby still not exhausted. To be precise, war, for Clausewitz, is not merely one of many instruments, but the *ultima ratio* of the friend-enemy grouping. War has its own grammar (i.e., special military-technical laws), but politics remains its brain. It does not have its own logic. This can only be derived from the friend-enemy concept . . ." (Schmitt, op. cit., 34n). Cf. Carl von Clausewitz, *The Art of War* (Princeton: Princeton University Press, 1976).

7. Schmitt overlooks this historical/sociological truth. His oversight makes John Ladd's "The Idea of Collective Violence," *Justice, Law and Violence*, ed. James B. Brady and Newton Garver (Philadelphia: Temple University Press, 1991), a critical complement to Schmitt's for an understanding of zero-sum politics.

8. Ladd, op. cit., 16–21.

9. Such apologies do sometimes occur, but it took over 50 years for an entirely different Japanese government, in an entirely reconstituted Japanese society, to apologize for using Korean women as sex slaves during their internment in the Second World War. Such apologies occur too rarely for one to know what to make of them. In the "truth and reconciliation" commissions in South Africa and Latin America, it is individuals rather than collectivities who have apologized.

10. Ladd, op. cit., 39–41

11. The disdain and belittling with which much of the press commented about Carter's intervention in these cases can teach us a great deal about the role of the media in promoting partisan politics.

12. There is a good account of this process in Roger Fisher and William Ury, *Getting to Yes* (Boston: Houghton Mifflin, 1981).

13. If one were to accept Schmitt's conception of the political, integrative politics would be included as a form of anti-politics. I have set this challenging alternative aside, in order to delineate what I see as three distinctly different sorts of civic activity. In another context the alternative conceptualization would deserve much fuller treatment.

14. There are certainly problems about litigation, for whatever end. Litigiousness is a form of pugnacity just as much as violence is, and threatening someone with a lawsuit can be a form of harassment and a means of coercion. Attorneys, for example, frequently advise clients not to talk with the other party directly, and they sometimes refuse to represent clients who do so. Such practice effectively eliminates personal conciliatory action. Yet neither the law itself nor legal practice in general is inherently pugnacious. Law, however formal and unfriendly it sometimes feels, provides a way to resolve conflicts without fighting.

15. Philip Pettit, "Freedom as Antipower," *Ethics* 106 (1996): 592. Cf. idem, *Republicanism: A Theory of Freedom and Government* (New York: Oxford University Press, 1997).

16. Pettit, "Freedom as Antipower," op. cit., 590.

17. Ibid., 592.

AESTHETICISM, OR AESTHETIC APPROACH, IN ARENDT AND HEIDEGGER ON POLITICS

Michael Halberstam

Hannah Arendt's aesthetic approach to politics is regarded as frequently reflecting the anti-political substitution of nonpolitical concerns for political ones characteristic of the German tradition from Schiller to Heidegger and beyond. Arendt's relationship to this tradition can be understood as squarely calling into question her central claim to have rehabilitated the political. This paper examines the relationship between Arendt's and Heidegger's political thought in light of the distinction between an aestheticism and an aesthetic approach. Two issues are at stake: can such a distinction help distance Arendt's aesthetic approach from those elements we find so troubling in Heidegger's thinking and his relation to politics? Can this help us to recuperate a certain aspect of German political thought which is reflected in Arendt's work?

In his recent book on Hannah Arendt and her relationship to Martin Heidegger, Dana Villa thematizes what he calls Hannah Arendt's aesthetic approach, defends this reading of Arendt in the face of contemporary misreadings and misappropriations of Arendt's political philosophy, and makes an argument for the validity of the aesthetic approach as affording us a new and profound access to the political phenomena of action on their own terms.[1] Why this central thrust of Arendt's philosophy has both been misunderstood and repressed in recent appropriations of her work in favor of a neo-Aristotelian or neo-neo-Kantian reading of Arendt is because of the highly charged question it forces upon us: What relationship does Arendt's political philosophy have to that German tradition of political philosophy we might understand, with Chytry, as the ideal of the aesthetic state?[2] The strong criticism of Arendt by thinkers well conversant with post-Kantian German thought and its anti-liberal anatomy has to be understood as placing Arendt squarely into this camp.[3] Arendt's indebtedness to Heidegger—so well established by Villa—only supports such critics, who see themselves as inveighing against an anti-political, irrationalist, and metaphysical approach to politics that set the stage for the horrors of National Socialism.[4]

On behalf of Arendt, Villa insists that she "offers us a unique vision of an aesthetic politics, one built on a rejection of the antipolitical in Nietzsche, one keenly aware of the deformities inherent in the aestheticization of politics performed by the German philosophical tradition from Schiller to Heidegger."[5] Villa invites further reflection on what is meant by an aestheticization of politics. In this paper I hope to contribute some thoughts towards a distinction between aestheticism and an aesthetic approach—a distinction implicit in Villa's discussion of Arendt and Nietzsche.[6] Can such a distinction help distance Arendt's aesthetic approach from what we find so troubling in Heidegger's thinking on politics? Can it help us recuperate a certain aspect of the German tradition of political thought which is reflected in Arendt's work?

Nietzsche's famous remark in the *Birth of Tragedy* that "it is only as an *aesthetic phenomenon* that existence and the world are eternally *justified*,"[7] counts as the quintessential expression of aestheticism. Not history as the world's final court of appeal, but aesthetic representation and experience. In other words, Nietzsche challenges Hegel's claim that "art no longer counts for us as the highest manner in which truth obtains existence for itself."[8] Aestheticism makes aesthetic experience or the work of art the final court of appeal and thereby displaces all other valuations or truths.[9]

An aesthetic approach, as against aestheticism, can be said to aim at an openess to experience, at the reestablishment of a relationship between thought and reality, or "thought and event."[10] An attention to that which presents itself on the level of sensibility prior to its subsumption under concepts of the understanding, as the ground upon which all thought finally rests, is common to all proponents of the aesthetic approach. Even Kant comes close to suggesting, in the introduction to the third *Critique*, that every empirical concept originates with an aesthetic reflective judgment that wrests from experience a unity of sense thereby providing the basis for the analytic unity of any given empirical concept. In other words, that way of looking, that standpoint we take up in the aesthetic experience, is also the standpoint that reveals to us the sensible structure of appearances, that is, that side of appearances that is always already overlaid by and taken up within the conceptual articulation of appearances by the understanding. The aesthetic approach therefore flatly denies Hegel's basic claim put forward in §20 of the *Encyclopaedia*, that we cannot mean anything apart from what can be taken up in language, and therefore by the universal.[11] Hegel's rationalism severs thought from sensible experience, privileging a standpoint that undercuts self-understandings, going so far as to reject the idea of a particular, unique self altogether. An aesthetic approach seeks to reunite thought and experience in a different key by preserving that openness to experience on the level of sensibility which engages my particular standpoint and which all genuine thought is taken to be dependent upon for its persistent reinvigoration.

Both Heidegger and Arendt share this aspiration. According to Arendt, however, Heidegger fails in his openness to experience. This indictment is profound indeed. It suggests nothing less than the failure of Heidegger's thinking.

The promise of an aesthetic approach to politics is evident in Heidegger's "Origin of the Work of Art," and his *Introduction to Metaphysics*. The *polis* is here understood as a work of truth: "Unconcealment occurs only when it is achieved by work:[12] the work of the word in poetry, the work of stone in temple and statue, the work of the work in thought, the work of the *polis* as the historical place in which all this is grounded and preserved."[13] Heidegger here echoes Aristotle's claim in Book VI of the *Nichomachaean Ethics* that "the virtue of a thing is relative to its proper work," referring to his distinction between the contemplative and the calculative intellect.[14] But for Heidegger, as he tells us in the "Origin of the Work of Art," the work or creative product is first of all to be understood as a *work of art*.

Aristotle's distinction of work into different types yields context specific criteria for evaluation, just as the distinction of virtue into different practices yields local or regional criteria. Politics, which is a matter of practical reason, is further distinguished by Aristotle into legislative and executive spheres:

> Political wisdom and practical wisdom are the same state of mind, but their essence is not the same. Of the wisdom concerned with the city, the practical wisdom which plays a controlling part is legislative wisdom, while that which is related to this as particulars to their universal is known by the general name 'political wisdom'; this has to do with action and deliberation, for a decree is a thing to be carried out in the form of an individual act.[15]

While critical of Aristotle in other respects, Arendt follows this impulse on the part of Aristotle to preserve distinct spheres with their distinct activities. Her distinctions between labor, work, and action in *The Human Condition* are intended to preserve local criteria and to prevent an unhinging of one human activity through the privileging of another as one uniquely suited for the realization of human essence: "The modern reversal [of the *Vita Activa* and the *Vita Contemplativa*]," charges Arendt, "shares with the traditional hierarchy the assumption that the same central human preoccupation must prevail in all activities of men, since without one comprehensive principle no order could be established."[16] Heidegger develops the structure of work from an understanding of the work of art. Heidegger's narrowing of work to the work-being of the work of art unhinges regional criteria by privileging a single structure of experience.

Heidegger's "Origin of the Work of Art" can be read as a direct attempt to take on Plato's condemnation of poetry and the imitative arts in Book X of *The Republic*. It is significant that Heidegger engages with Plato about the status of poetry in relation to politics. His challenge to Plato in the last book of *The Republic* has to be taken as an attempt to unravel Plato's entire argument. We might recall here that the stage for Plato's discussion of poetry in Book X is set by his answer in Book IX to the main challenge to any conception of justice raised at the beginning of *The Republic*, that is, that might makes right, that justice is the advantage of the stronger. And it is precisely this position, that political action is first of all a violent, creative self-assertion, which Heidegger ends up affirming in the *Introduction to Metaphysics*.[17]

In Book X Plato argues that the imitative artist presents himself as a creator of all things. The imitative artist is one "who makes everything that each one of the manual artistans makes separately. For this same manual artisan is not only able to make all implements but also makes everything that grows naturally from the earth, and he produces all animals—the others and himself too—and, in addition to that, produces earth and heaven and gods and everything in heaven and everything in Hades under the earth."[18] But the creation of the imitative artist is an illusion, a play of mirrors and reflections capturing only the way a use-thing or a piece of equipment looks—this being his expertise—rather than the way in which it works. The very claim "[he] knows all the crafts and everything else that single men severally know," (598d) disqualifies the imitative artist from genuine knowledge in Plato's eyes. The truth is that he who does know how to produce use things is "compelled to listen to the man who knows how to use them." (601c) For example, the maker of bridles has to listen to the horseman. Imitative artists "don't lay hold of the truth; rather, as we were just now saying, the painter will make what seems to be a shoe to those who understand as little about shoemaking as he understands, but who observe only colors and shapes." (601a)

Heidegger takes on Plato and inverts his hierarchy. The work of art is falsely understood when taken as a thing with something extra added on—where things are "comprehended with the help of the Being of equipment (the matter-form structure)."[19] It is quite the reverse for Heidegger: the equipmental quality of equipment is grasped in its general essence by bringing ourselves before the work of art. In his conversation with Plato, Heidegger goes so far as to draw on the very same craft example:

> The equipmental quality of equipment was discovered. But how? Not by a description and explanation of a pair of shoes actually present; not by a report about the process of making shoes; and also not by the observation of the actual use of shoes occurring here and there; but only by bringing ourselves before Van Gogh's painting. This painting spoke. In the nearness of the work we were suddenly somewhere else than we usually tend to be. The artwork lets us know what shoes are in truth.[20]

For Heidegger, it is not the painting that "draws a likeness from something actual and transposes it into a product of artistic—production . . . it is, on the contrary the reproduction of the thing's general essence."[21] The great work of art takes the place of the Platonic Ideal for Heidegger. This ideal is like a god who founds a world.[22] Heidegger contradicts Plato: the great artist does create heaven and earth and everything in between ("[the work of art] does not only reveal the being of what is; at the same time it establishes a world"[23]).

The world-establishing power of art is developed in Heidegger's example of the Greek temple:

> A building, a Greek temple, portrays nothing. It simply stands there in the middle of the rock-cleft valley. The bulding encloses the figure of the god, and in this concealment lets it stand out into the holy precinct through the open portico. By means of the temple, the god is present in the temple. This presence of the god is itself an extension an delimitation of the precint as a holy precinct. The temple and its precinct, however, do not fade away into the indefinite. It is the temple work that first fits together and at the same time gathers around itself the unity of those paths and relations in which birth and death, disaster and blessing, victory and disgrace, endurance and decline acquire the shape of destiny for human being. The all-governing expanse of this open relational context is the world of this historical people. Only from and in this expanse does the nation first return to itself for the fulfillment of its vocation [*Bestimmung*].[24]

We might grant for the sake of argument that the work of art makes the world visible, but how does it establish a world? As Karsten Harries remarks, there is a false concreteness to Heidegger's example:

> Which temple is he speaking about? The temple work is said to first open up the world of the Greek people. But how can this be? Does the building of any particular temple not presuppose the Greek world? Perhaps we should say rather that each temple re-presents and lights up this world in its own unique way by transporting those who visit it into the presence of a divinity, be it Zeus or Athena, Aphrodite or Apollo.[25]

Heidegger's claim, as it is presented here clearly does not stand. To the extent that the artist can be said to set up a world, as Baumgarten suggests he does in his foundational, eighteenth-century work on aesthetics (*Aesthetica*), this world has to be distinguished from the real one. It is this distinction between *Schein* (Illusion) and *Erscheinung* (Phenomenon or Appearance) that is deliberately elided by Heidegger.[26] The clarity and concreteness of the aesthetic idea that is presented in the work of art depends upon the establishment of a perspective, on the fact that something has been put into a frame. If we understand this, we can also appreciate the force of Heidegger's temple example. As Harries puts it,

> setting itself apart from its context, the temple brackets that context in a manner that must be understood exclusively and inclusively. As a seemingly self-sufficient presence the temple draws our attention, pushing its setting at a distance. Thus distanced, the setting is, so to speak, put in a frame. Framed it is re-presented. The temple thus lets us look again not just at itself, at its form and materials, but at its site.[27]

Though the work of art can make a claim on me to assume a given standpoint, to accept a frame, the work of art as such cannot force me to adopt this particular perspective as my own. In its profoundly monological character, Heidegger's interpretation of the peasant shoes, for example, recommends just such an elision of the act of framing:

> From Van Gogh's painting we cannot even tell where these shoes stand . . . . And yet. From the dark opening of the worn insides of the shoes the toilsome tread of the worker stares forth. In the stiffly rugged heaviness of the shoes there is the accumulated tenacity of her slow trudge through the far-spreading and ever-uniform furrows of the field swept by a raw wind. On the leather lie the dampness and richness of the soil. Under the soles stretches the loneliness of the field-path as evening falls. In the shoes vibrates the silent call of the earth . . . .[28]

However, as Meyer-Shapiro suggests: why peasant shoes? The shoes Van Gogh painted were, most likely, those of a worker in the city. As Derrida suggests: even if peasant shoes, why the shoes of a female peasant?[29]

Heidegger's aesthetic approach closes in on itself. "The work," writes Heidegger, "belongs, as work, uniquely within the realm that is opened up by itself."[30]

In the *Myth of the State*, Ernst Cassirer acknowledges the puzzlement Plato's attack on poetry creates for the modern reader. "No modern writer would ever think of inserting his objections to poetry and art into a work dealing with politics."[31] But Plato, he argues, cannot be understood as attacking poetry as such. In *The Republic* he

> . . . thinks as a lawgiver who estimates and judges the social and educational values of art . . . . What is combated and rejected by Plato is not poetry in itself, but the myth-making function . . . . Plato admits no mystical ecstasy by which the human soul can reach an immediate union with God. The highest aim, the knowledge of the idea of the Good, cannot be attained in this way. It needs a careful preparation and a slow methodical ascent. The end cannot be reached by one leap.[32]

What does Heidegger demand of the work of art? "It would not be extravagant," suggests David Haliburton, "to compare the general tenor of poetic thinking with the thinking of *mythical Dasein*."[33] It is the mythical function of poetry, the capacity to afford a symbolic synthesis of the real and thereby to restore individual Dasein to its place in a common historical world that Heidegger demands of art.

> In at least one important respect, *mana* relates to the thing in much the same way as art does. As Heidegger demonstrates in the "Origin of the Work of Art," the work possesses a thingly character . . . yet it is more than a thing. So, too, *mana* is a thing and more than a thing: "Things endowed with *mana* present themselves as having a power and destiny which enable them to be detached from their thingly context . . . and to pack within themselves the full sense of world as, e.g., sacred stones, trees, bread, etc." (Heidegger, 'Ernst Cassirer's Mythical Thought').[34]

Hannah Arendt's awareness of the deformities inherent in the aestheticization of politics are evident in a well-known footnote in "What is Existenz Philosophy?" (1947) in which Arendt condemns Heidegger for his not so latent romanticism. Heidegger's "entire mode of behavior [during the third Reich] has such exact parallels in German Romanticism that one can hardly believe them to result from the sheer coincidence of a purely personal failure of character. Heidegger is really (let us hope) the last Romantic—an immensely talented Friedrich Schlegel or Adam Mueller, as it were, whose complete lack of responsibility is attributable to a spiritual playfulness that stems in part from delusions of genius and in part from despair."[35] Arendt suggests that Heidegger recommends to us a standpoint and a mood that shares a great deal with the romantic poet's retreat from a disenchanted world from "within the walls of cities" into "inviolate retirement, subject . . . to conscience only," from there to experience in moments of ecstatic rapture the deeper unity between self and world. If we understand the space of freedom as the locus of the true self—a rather basic assumption for us moderns, even for those who would deny freedom altogether, for to deny freedom is also to deny the existence of a self—then Heidegger's attempt to link freedom to the ecstatic revelation of being in "On the Essence of Truth"[36] suggests just the kind of transfiguration of the commonplace and recuperation of the world through the quivering oneness between mind and nature that Wordsworth refers to as the "high argument" of Romanticism. The role of the poet, Heidegger writes in "Hölderlin and the Essence of Poetry," is "Des Vaters Stral, ihn selbst, mit eigner Hand/Zu fassen und dem Volk ins Lied Gehüllt die himmlische Gaabe zu reichen."[37]

Heidegger both wants to accord the work of art its autonomy, as well as the culturally privileged status of opening up "the Being of Beings."[38] Yet such openess is understood by Heidegger in terms of the private ecstatic revelation of beings, which fundamentally breaks with what is intersubjectively given. Where Heidegger relies on the modern narrowing of the aesthetic to the realm of art and then seeks to impose its criteria onto the realm of politics, Arendt harks back to a broader conception of the aesthetic as the realm of taste. But such a broadening of aesthetics also disenfranchises the privileged status of art in its capacity to set up a world. Taste understood as *bon sense* indeed discloses the world to us "insofar as it is a common world."[39] But it can do so only because it is constituted by an activity which inherently takes common sense or shared understandings into account. Taste is exercised through judgment. "Taste, insofar, as it, like any other judgment, appeals to common sense, is the very opposite of 'private feeling'."[40] In her well-known discussion of judgment, Arendt draws on Kant's third *Critique* and enlists it for her understanding of the political. "That the capacity to judge is a specifically political ability in exactly the sense denoted by Kant, namely, the ability to see things not only from one's own point of view but in the perspective of all those who happen to be present; even that judgment may be one of the fundamental abilities of man as a political being insofar as it enables him to orient himself in the public realm in the common world—these are insights that are virtually as old as articulated political experience."[41]

Where Heidegger privileges the origin and creation of the work of art, Arendt privileges the moment of reception, which is fundamentally intersubjective. "Even Cicero's *cultura anima*," she argues, "is suggestive of something like taste, and generally, sensitivity to beauty, not in those who fabricate beautiful things, that is, in the artists, themselves, but in the spectators."[42] It is the reception of the work of art—not its work-being—that primarily contributes to its world constituting power.[43] And this reception finds its limits within the political, understood here in its broadest sense as the care and responsibility for the common. The work of art finds its limits within an already established public realm that it depends upon for its power to persuade. (To recognize this is not to assert an arbitrary censorship, but to appreciate that responsibility is not a category altogether irrelevant to aesthetic judgment and controversy.)

In "The Crisis in Culture," Arendt does suggest that "culture must somehow take as its starting point the phenomenon of art."[44] But for Arendt, the work of art does not ground or unify a culture. It does not provide an aesthetic ideal that compels and founds a historical group, but it figures the promise of agreement in matters of taste. Arendt's emphasis on the aesthetic, therefore, rejects both Plato's theoretical grounding of the *polis* in a transcendent truth, as well as Heidegger's grounding of the political in an immanent aesthetic truth. Judgments of taste do not compel but seek to persuade. The specific validity of judgment is found in the potential agreement of others.

An aesthetic distance or framing does indeed play a crucial role for Arendt in establishing an openess to experience. "In order to become aware of appearances we must first be free to establish a certain distance between ourselves and the object . . . . This distance cannot arise unless we are in a position to forget ourselves, the cares and interests and urges of our lives, so that we will not seize what we admire, but let it be as it is, in its appearance."[45] But this openness to experience is established by the closely related capacity for *enlarged thought*, the capacity to take into account the standpoint of others. "Judging," according to Arendt, "is one, if not the most important activity in which this sharing-the-world-with-others comes to pass."[46]

It is such a notion of judgment that is fundamentally missing both in Heidegger's earlier and later philosophy. Heidegger can conceive of judgment either only as opinion/doxa or as an objectively valid, correct statement. It is the latter identification of truth and judgment as objectively valid that he regards as a disfigurement of an originary openness to reality that has to precede the judgment that posits this truth.[47] As Harries suggests, Heidegger's understanding of the constitution of *Dasein* moves from *Entschlossenheit* as self-assertion to *Ent-Schlossenheit* as letting be or giving oneself over.[48] What Heidegger fails to appreciate is the activity of judging in Arendt's sense, viz. the capacity for taking the standpoint of others into account, without thereby taking their standpoint as mine.[49] On being challenged by Jaspers in a letter in 1949 to enter into a dialogue,

Heidegger responds as follows: "What you say about monologues is fitting. But much would already be gained simply by allowing monologues to be what they are. It almost appears to me that they are not yet; they are not yet strong enough."[50] Villa's emphasis on the singular importance of Arendt's conception of action is worth recalling here. One might ask whether such an emphasis does not also narrow Arendt's conception of political experience unduly. In "The Crisis of Culture," and also in her later work, Arendt regards judging as the quintessential political activity. In the *Human Condition*, Arendt advances a phenomenology of forgiving and promising in her discussion of the public realm. These are all actions, to be sure. But are they to be understood according to the model of the Greek *agon*?

Michael Halberstam, Department of Philosophy, University of South Carolina, Columbia, SC 29208-0001; mhalberstam@wesleyan.edu

NOTES

1. Dana Villa, *Arendt and Heidegger: The Fate of the Political*. (Princeton: Princeton University Press, 1996). The conception of *praxis* or action is the centerpiece of Arendt's political philosophy. "Following Aristotle," writes Villa, "Arendt passionately asserts that the essence of politics is *action*. Laws and institutions which to the liberal mind are the stuff of politics, for Arendt supply the framework for action" (4). Having conceded this much to those, like Jürgen Habermas, who want to credit Arendt for her "systematic renewal of the Aristotelian conception of *praxis*," (3) Villa's book sets out to rescue Arendt from the standard readings, which place her work squarely within a tradition she radically rejects. Arendt is far from being a neo-Aristotelian. As Villa rightly shows, her theory of political judgment is not concerned with reviving an Aristotelian conception of *phronesis* or practical reason. Nor is she content to think of action as measured by its end or telos, as Aristotle finally does. Arendt's return to Aristotle is intended to overcome the way in which Aristotle has figured the Western conception of action and politics. "Arendt's notion of action," writes Villa, "refers us less to Aristotle than it does to another overcomer of the tradition: her teacher, Martin Heidegger."

2. Josef Chytry, *The Aesthetic State: A Quest in Modern German Thought* (Berkeley: University of California Press, 1989), xi:

> Starting shortly after the middle of the eighteenth century, a number of original thinkers from the German-speaking lands created a paradigm drawn from their impressions of a distant historical reality, ancient Athens, added to it a new mode of thought, modern dialectics, and at times even gave a new obeisance to the ancient Greek deity Dionysos, to materialize their longings for an ideal. The influence of these forces, extending

over the next two centuries, came to permeate modern German consciousness, deifying the concept and activity of art, reviving the Platonic (and Sanskrit) vision of the cosmos as play and aesthetic creation, and projecting a way of life and labor that would honor not the commodity but the aesthetic product. It was an ideal that gave birth to classical Weimar culture; commanded the loyalty of the most powerful and influential line of formal German speculation, from Hegel through Marx to Heidegger; inspired that most German of artists, Richard Wagner, to give birth to the major European project in the religion of art, Bayreuth; triggered the boldly experimental thinking of the founder of modernism, Friedrich Nietzsche; and, finally, inspired the contemporary Marxist radicalism of Herbert Marcuse.

3. Walter Z. Lacquer calls Arendt an aesthete, "qui n'aime que les trains qui partent." And Berlin is equally dismissive. See *Conversations With Isaiah Berlin*, ed. Ramin Johanbegloo (London: Peter Halban, 1992), 82–83: ". . . she produces no arguments, no evidence of serious philosophical or historical thought. It is all a stream of metaphysical associations." Cited by Benhabib, *The Reluctant Modernism of Hannah Arendt* (Thousand Oaks: Sage Publications, 1996).

4. Terry Eagleton writes, for example, that "the wholesale aestheticization of society had found its grotesque apotheosis for a brief moment in fascism, with its panoply of myths, symbols, and orgiastic spectacles . . . ." Eagleton, *The Ideology of the Aesthetic* (Oxford: Basil Blackwell, 1990). See also Chytry, op. cit.

5. Dana Villa, "Beyond Good and Evil: Arendt, Nietzsche, and the Aestheticization of Political Action," *Political Theory* 20.2 (1992): 276.

6. Ibid., 299: "Arendtian aestheticism, an aestheticism predicated on a love of the world and which admires great action because it possesses a beauty that illuminates the world, is critically different from Nietzschean aestheticism, the aestheticism of the *artist.*"

7. Friedrich Nietzsche, *The Birth of Tragedy* (New York: Vintage, 1967), 52.

8. See Heidegger's challenge to Hegel's remark in "The Origin of the Work of Art," in *Basic Writings* (New York: HarperCollings, 1993), 205 (hereafter OWA).

9. In the moral realm, aestheticism displaces the claim of morality by the aspiration to live one's life as if it were a work of art. In the political realm, aestheticism displaces principles of justice by the demand that the state be ordered in accordance with an aesthetic ideal. In the realm of science, understood here in its broadest sense as *Wissenschaft*, aestheticism displaces the claim of rational and objective understanding with the claim of the interesting. In each instance, however, the judgment that such displacement is illegitimate depends upon an ability to identify the claims of morality, the claims of justice, and the claims of reason, independently of their aesthetic appearance. This is precisely what Nietzsche denies in *The Birth of Tragedy*, and in *Beyond Good and Evil.*

10. See "What is Existenz Philosophy?" and "Concern for Politics in Recent European Philosophy," in Arendt, *Essays in Understanding: 1930–1954* (New York: Harcourt Brace Jovanovich, 1992).

11. "Indem die Sprache nur Allgemeines ausdrückt, so kann ich nicht sagen, was ich nur meine. Und das *Unsagbare,* Gefühl, Empfindung, ist nicht das Vortrefflichste, Wahrste, sondern das Unbedeutendste, Unwahrste. Wenn ich sage: das *Einzelne, dieses* Einzelne, Hier, Jetzt, so sind dies alles Allgemeinheiten; *Alles* und *Jedes* ist ein Einzelnes, Dieses, auch wenn es sinnlich ist, Hier, Jetzt. Ebenso wenn ich sage: Ich, meine ich Mich als diesen alle Anderen ausschließenden, aber was ich sage, Ich, ist eben jeder: ich, der alle anderen von sich ausschließt." G. W. F. Hegel, *Enzyklopädie der philosophischen Wissenschaften im Grundrisse, 1830. Erster Teil: Die Wissenschaft der Logik* (Frankfurt: Suhrkamp, 1986), 74.

12. See, for example, Alexander Schwan, *Politische Philosophie im Denken Martin Heideggers.* (Köln und Opladen: Westdeutscher Verlag, 1965), 15. Schwann's is perhaps still the most useful treatment of Heidegger's political philosophy.

13. Martin Heidegger, *An Introduction to Metaphysics* (New Haven: Yale University Press, 1987), 191 (hereafter IM).

14. 1139a18.

15. EN 1141b24–27.

16. Hannah Arendt, *The Human Condition* (Chicago: Chicago University Press, 1958), 17.

17. IM 152f. See especially Karsten Harries, "Heidegger as a Political Thinker" in *Heidegger and Modern Philosophy*, ed. Michael Murray (New Haven: Yale University Press, 1978), 317f. Harries is substantially in agreement with Schwan.

18. Plato, *The Republic*, trans. Allan Bloom, (New York: Basic Books, 1991), 596c.

19. OWA, 155.

20. Ibid., 161.

21. Ibid., 162.

22. The original German is most striking here: "es ist ein Werk, das den Gott selbst anwesen läßt und so der Gott selbst *ist*." See M. Heidegger, "Der Ursprung des Kunstwerkes," in *Holzwege* (Frankfurt am Main: V. Klostermann, 1980), 39.

23. Karsten Harries, "Modern Art and the Essence of the Modern," review of *Philosophische Analysen zur Kunst der Gegenwart*, by Walter Biemel, *Man and World* 4:2 (1971): 207.

24. OWA, 167. The German reads "Bestimmung," which has a great variety of meanings, the most straightforward of which is "determination" pure and simple.

"Destiny" is another common rendering. "Vocation" is somewhat misleading, since it does not convey the threat of heteronomy which is, to my mind, implicit in this passage. Moreover the root of "Bestimmung," viz. "Stimmung," is the word for "mood." Here again, the passivity and lack of autonomy with regard to our own being-in-the-world is assocated by Heidegger in *Being and Time* with the way in which mood strikes us.

25. Karsten Harries, *The Ethical Function of Architecture* (Boston: MIT Press, 1996), 279.

26. OAW, 162.

27. Harries, *The Ethical Function of Architecture*, op. cit., 280.

28. OWA, 159.

29. It might be objected that the whole point of Heidegger's work analysis is to establish a common world. "Preserving the work does not reduce people to their private experiences, but brings them into affiliation with the truth happening in the work. Thus it grounds being for and with one another as the historical standing-out of human existence in relation to unconcealment." (OWA, 193). This aspiration is not denied here. The question is raised, however, whether it is theoretically possible according to the account Heidegger gives.

30. OWA, 167.

31. Ernst Cassirer, *The Myth of the State* (New Haven: Yale University Press, 1966), 67.

32. Cassirer, *The Myth of the State*, 66–7; also, 65: "The idea of the Good in its perfect beauty cannot be seen in a sudden rapture of the human mind. In order to see and understand it the philosopher must choose 'the longer way'." Perhaps Cassirer has Heidegger in mind here. For a similar indictment of the "leap" or "Ur-sprung" endorsed by Heidegger in "The Origin of the Work of Art," see Karl Jasper's letter to Heidegger dated August 17, 1949. *Briefwechsel. 1920-1963. Martin Heidegger; Karl Jaspers* (Frankfurt: Vittorio Klostermann; Mûchen: Piper, 1990), 182ff.

33. David Haliburton, *Poetic Thinking: An Approach to Heidegger* (Chicago: University of Chicago Press, 1981), 208.

34. Ibid.

35. Arendt, *Essays in Understanding*, op. cit., 187.

36. Heidegger, "On the Essence of Truth," in *Basic Works*, 125f:

> Freedom is not merely what common sense is content to let pass under this name: the caprice, turning up occasionally in our choosing, of inclining in this or that direction. Freedom is not mere absence of constraint with respect to what we can or cannot do. Nor is it on the other hand mere readiness for what is required and necessary (and so somehow a being).

> Prior to all this ('negative' and 'positive' freedom), freedom is engagement in the disclosure of beings as such. Disclosedness itself is conserved in ek-sistent engagement, through which the openess of the open region, i.e., the 'there' ['Da'], is what it is.

37. Martin Heidegger, "Hölderlin und das Wesen der Dichtung," *Holzwege*, op. cit., 44.

38. OWA, 165.

39. Hannah Arendt, "Crisis in Culture," *Between Past and Future* (New York: Viking, 1954/1968), 221.

40. Ibid., 222.

41. Ibid., 221.

42. Ibid., 213.

43. Ibid.

44. Ibid., 210.

45. Ibid.

46. Ibid., 221.

47. Heidegger, "On the Essence of Truth," op. cit., 118: "Both concepts of the essence of *veritas* have continually in view a conforming to . . . [*Sichrichten nach* . . .], and hence think truth as *correctness* [Richtigkeit]." Also, 122: ". . . what first makes correctness possible must with more original right be taken as the essence of truth." See also Heidegger, *Being and Time* (Albany: SUNY Press, 1996), sec. 44, "Dasein, Disclosedness, and Truth," 196–208.

48. Harries, "Heidegger as a Political Thinker," op. cit., 310:

> . . . what is to distinguish the readiness be resolved from a readiness to be seized? Resolved to be resolved, man is in a vulnerable position. He opens himself to attack and seizure, even if such seizure is what the individual has chosen for himself. Heidegger suggests this in those later works where *Entschlossenheit* (resolve) is said to be *Ent-schlossenheit:* the hyphen is to suggest that the resolved individual has unlocked and opened himself, ready to listen and to respond to what is.

49. See Alessandro Ferrara, "Judgment, Identity and Authenticity: A Reconstruction of Hannah Arendt's Interpretation of Kant." Paper presented at the Conference on Hannah Arendt: Twenty Years Later, Harvard University, March 1996, 22–23.

50. Heidegger to Jaspers, August 12, 1949, op. cit., 183: "Was Sie von den Monologen sagen trifft. Aber es wäre schon viel gewonnen, wenn die Monologe bleiben dürften, was sie sind. Mir scheint fast, sie *sind* es noch gar nicht; sie sind noch nicht stark genug dazu."

EDUCATING FOR PRACTICAL REASONING

Thomas Magnell

Some decisions can be made employing closed systems of practical reasoning. Other decisions require open systems of practical reasoning. These kinds of practical reasoning differ epistemically. Closed systems of practical reasoning can rely on thinking with a basis that is epistemically robust. Open systems of practical reasoning must also allow for thinking with a basis that is epistemically slight. In making moral and prudential decisions about what we are to make of our lives, we use open systems of practical reasoning that proceed by precept. Precepts are generalizations for use as premises in practical reasoning that may only be indirectly tied to empirical evidence. Intelligent selection of precepts may come from education in the arts and sciences. The twin towers of a liberal education offer the best hope for judgment in the practical reasoning that may help us to make the moral and prudential decisions that are our concern.

THREE BROAD TYPES OF REASONING

The idea of educating humanity deserves to be among our grand millennial thoughts, and central to it must be the notion of educating for practical reasoning—the type of reasoning employed in making moral and prudential decisions. Following Aristotle, we may categorize reasoning into three broad types, theoretical reasoning, productive reasoning, and practical reasoning, where the ends of the reasoning are theoretical knowledge, productive knowledge, and practical knowledge. In the roughest way, theoretical knowledge has to do with what we think of the world, productive knowledge with what we make, and practical knowledge with what we bring about through our actions. These types of knowledge are personified by the scientist, the poet, and the sage. I do not mean to slight others who might stand in as representatives, such as mathematicians and historians for theoretical knowledge, and musicians and painters for productive knowledge. But even keeping to a simple image, we may ask how formal education promotes the kind of reasoning employed in gaining each type of knowledge. For theoretical reasoning and perhaps even productive reasoning, there is a ready answer of sorts: formal education promotes theoretical and productive reasoning in courses designed to do so.

"So you want to be a scientist? Take a science course." No one would demure too much from that. "Oh, you want to be a poet? Take a poetry course." Even this does not sound completely silly. "Ah, you want to be a sage? Take a sagacity course." This does sound silly, and not only because the question itself is unusual. It might be nice to think that the response, "Take a philosophy course" would do, but any prospective sage who took this advice would likely be disappointed in a way that a prospective scientist or poet would not be for enrolling in a science or poetry course. Philosophy is not sagacity, though some philosophers are sages. Philosophy courses may certainly be good for a proto-sage, but so may all manner of other courses. Inasmuch as moral reasoning is a type of practical reasoning, ethics courses may have an edge over some others. But it would be dangerous to make too much of this, since much more than a course or two in ethics is needed to develop the kind of practical reasoning required even for moral reasoning.

SYSTEMATICALLY CLOSED AND SYSTEMATICALLY OPEN REASONING

None of this goes to show that practical reasoning cannot be taught or that courses in practical reasoning are uncommon. When we need to fix a faucet or a tooth, or when we need to draw up a contract, we call on plumbers, dentists, and lawyers. We go to them for their practical reasoning about faucets, teeth, and contracts. They are likely to have learned their trade or profession in vocational or professional schools that provide courses for particular types of practical reasoning. There is nothing especially ineffable about practical reasoning that makes it less easy to teach than theoretical or productive reasoning. Some practical reasoning is fairly easy to teach. What then separates practical reasoning used in making dental decisions and practical reasoning used in making moral decisions? The answer lies in the systematic differences in the two types of reasoning. Practical reasoning for dental decision-making is largely, as we may say, systematically closed. Moral decision-making, in contrast, employs practical reasoning which we may characterize as systematically open.

At an annual checkup, Carries Grant is found to have a cavity by Bitey Davis, D.D.S. What should Bitey do? Should she drill and fill, cap or crown, extract, or just leave it be for now? Her decision, if made well, will need to take several considerations into account. The size of the cavity, the condition of the root; Carries's age, general health, temperament; his responsibilities for the day, the week, the month; his wallet, his insurance plan—these are some of the relevant conditions for a decision. Often the preponderance of considerations may point the same way, making the decision an easy one. Sometimes, the considerations may diverge, making the decision more difficult.

I do not mean to minimize the potential difficulty in making a dental decision. But in only the most exceptional circumstances are the practical reasons involved likely to be anguishing to the dentist. Any anguish in this case is more likely to be heard from the mouth of Carries Grant than Bitey Davis. To reach the decision calls for judgment, practical reasoning for making evaluative assessments of the relevant considerations. What keeps the level of angst down for the dentist is that the relevant considerations are readily determinable, the weighting in making a decision relatively straightforward, and the probable consequences of alternative decisions knowable. All of this makes the practical reasoning pretty much systematically closed. When practical reasoning is systematically closed, it is possible, and sometimes even effective, to reach a decision by going through a checklist. The matters for consideration can be set down in advance; points can be assigned to them if a simple weighting is sought; alternative possible decisions can be outlined based on the number of points tabulated. Thus Bitey could work from a sort of score sheet for the dental considerations: with the recommendations zero to one, leave the tooth for the next visit; two to five, drill and fill; six to eight, cap or crown; and nine to ten, extract.

Plainly no good dentist would need such a score sheet. The decision tree should be second nature. A dentist who used something akin to a cheat sheet would not inspire confidence. But the point is that the elements of the decision procedure employed in the practical reasoning are enumerable and easy to tabulate. Indeed, they can be mechanized or programmed in an expert system without much ado. The more nearly closed a system of practical reasoning, the more it will share these features. Faucet fixing and plumbing work in general can be done by checklist. Much legal work also falls in this category and can be performed from a closed system of practical reasoning.

When judgments depend on a limited number of factors, it is possible to become familiar with all of the factors and their likely consequences in combination. Education for a closed system of practical reasoning can focus on acquiring such familiarity. What needs to be known can be largely specified in advance. The basis for decision then is epistemically robust. This is the case when it comes to faucets, teeth, or contracts, though to varying extents. The factors for fixing faucets may be more limited than the factors for working on teeth or for drawing up contracts. Systems of practical reasoning vary in size, those for dental and legal work being larger than that involved in plumbing. There is simply more to learn about teeth and contracts than about pipes. Also, unless a system of practical reasoning is completely closed, some of what needs to be known in advance may not be entirely specified in advance. Systems of practical reasoning form a spectrum, from the fully closed to the wide open. Simple card games involve fully closed systems of practical reasoning, which is why lessons in Go-Fish are not exactly demanding. The range of learning for dentistry is greater than the range of learning for plumbing. Still, in both cases, education can focus on attaining familiarity with a limited number of factors that regularly appear in dental work and plumbing. Education for closed systems of practical reasoning can take the form of training to promote expertise that is narrow in scope.

Moral and Prudential Decisions about Life Work

The situation is different when it comes to moral and prudential reasoning. As we grow up and become morally autonomous, we need to decide what to make of our lives. Do we develop our talents primarily for ourselves or also for others? Which talents do we develop? What sacrifices are we willing to make? Only in the most reflective moments do we keep to such generalities. But even in our day to day musings as we wait in a checkout line or wait to go online, we weigh our responsibilities to ourselves, our loved ones, our friends, and our colleagues; we consider our obligations to our employer, our community, our country, and even to the world as a whole; we consider how to budget our money and our time. All this might come under the heading of life work. Like all work, it may be done well or poorly. It may be done intelligently or haphazardly. But unlike narrow lines of work, whether on pipes, teeth, or contracts, decisions about life work inevitably demand judgments on matters that raise multiple considerations that can be difficult to see how to weigh, and this for several reasons.

People have multiple aims. It is fair to say that some individuals are more directed than others, though I have never known anyone so single minded to have but one aim in life. We may speak of a single, over-arching aim: the living of the good life. But while this aim, more nominal than real, may be put to use as a marker in normative theories, in practice it is likely to cover a multitude of sins. As it is, we seek knowledge, love, power, security, tranquility, excitement, material well being, spiritual fulfillment, and, as sociobiologists like to emphasize, heirs. Of course some of these aims may conflict and so require rethinking. But to the extent that they are compossible, they form a hierarchy of values that represents a complex structure of desires. Gaining insight into the hierarchy and understanding the structure, even in our own case, is hard. Indeed, it may be particularly hard in our own case.

In making decisions about life work, we must assess probable consequences of live alternatives—this after determining what our live alternatives are. The implicit comparisons that lie in assessments are hard to make under the best of circumstances. When the consequences of alternatives range years into the future, rational comparisons are all the more difficult. The comparisons must take into account the future desires of others as well as ourselves. Added to this is the difficulty that structures of desires are mutable. Structures of desires may change over the years so that what satisfies present desires may do little for an individual in the future or, at the extreme, produce loathing. Of course not all our desires or our orderings of them change. Basic desires for love and health, for instance, tend to be stable. But change even among basic desires is not uncommon. To some extent, the mutability of the structures of our desires is predictable. Perversely, desires for excitement in our youth tend to become attenuated over time until they are replaced by desires for security in old age. A more reasonable arrangement would be to start off favoring caution but allow it to give way to ever increasing abandon in our golden years.

Decisions about what to do in life, moral and prudential decisions about life work, call for assessments that are challenging for lack of robust evidentiary support. We face serious epistemic constraints against weighing the relevant considerations for choosing among possible alternatives in coming to rational decisions. We are in a very real sense behind a veil of ignorance, not a self-imposed veil to promote impartiality, but a natural veil that dims our vision. When it comes to making the judgments, it is hard to see and easy to make mistakes. The decisions cannot always be made in the same way that decisions can be made about faucets, teeth, or even contracts for which the epistemic basis is robust. Much of the time, the relevant factors cannot be simply toted up on a checklist that can be counted on to give the right alternative to act upon. The basis for decision is then epistemically slight. When it is, we must employ practical reasoning that is systematically open.

PRECEPTS AND EDUCATION IN THE ARTS AND SCIENCES

Practical reasoning that is systematically open must proceed by precept or exemplar. Here let us focus on precepts and leave exemplars for another occasion. By a precept I mean a generalization for use as a premise in practical reasoning that may only be indirectly tied to empirical evidence. Aphorisms, maxims, rubrics, adages, even philosophical observations may be taken as precepts. There is no single source for precepts. They may come from science, literature, poetry, religion, or even popular culture. Their source is not important, though finding sources for them is. Precepts may be universal generalizations or existential generalizations. They may take the form of imperatives. "Nature favors the prepared mind" may be taken as a precept. So may "The love of money is the root of all evil," "Hope lies eternal in the human breast," "Thou shalt not covet thy neighbor's ox," and "Character counts." Precepts may be more or less accurate, or useful in some contexts but not in others. That is a matter for empirical confirmation. Determining the appropriate range of application for a precept may be hard, but a precept that could not be given any empirical support would be useless or dangerous. Learning which precepts to live by is a matter of education.

Scientific education is particularly good for developing thought that is epistemically robust. It promotes a healthy respect for facts. It illustrates the importance of subjecting hypotheses to careful testing and prepares the mind for long chains of reasoning that are sometimes needed for such testing. Science shows the importance of quantifying, where possible, and of being cautious about what people think obvious. None of this is to suggest that the importance of scientific education lies only in its suitability for developing thought that is epistemically robust. It plainly has high inherent value as well as other instrumental value.

Education in the arts serves well to prepare the mind for thought that is epistemically slight. Where work in the arts is truth directed, as it is to some extent in the humanities, the observations, conclusions, and speculations are not always closely linked. Hypotheses are imaginatively entertained. Conclusions are advanced sometimes by leaps that allow for multiple paths of justification. Where work in the arts is not truth directed, as in music and the fine arts in general, it can provoke different patterns of thought that are drawn to aesthetic values. It gives expression to things that people seek and shun. It displays what fascinates and bores, and reveals connections among our preferences. In doing so, it offers insights into structures of desires.

Education in the arts and education in the sciences are complementary components of an education for practical reasoning. They are the twin towers of a liberal education, which is why institutions intended to promote liberal education were chartered as colleges of arts and sciences. No doubt there are many reasons to prize liberal education, despite doubts voiced from various quarters. A reason that deserves continued thought is that education in the arts and sciences serves to build what is all too often missing from discussions of practical reasoning—judgment. Because of the epistemic constraints we face in making moral and prudential decisions about what to make of our lives, we must employ an open system of practical reasoning. We need to be adept at making decisions from thinking with a basis that is epistemically slight as well as thinking that is epistemically robust. For this, we must rely in part on precepts. We need to select our precepts intelligently. Education in the arts and sciences is our best hope for doing so. We saw earlier how silly it would be to think we could take a course in sagacity as we might take a course in poetry or science. This does not mean, however, that sagacity cannot be a goal of education. If a course in poetry or science is not enough for wisdom, a course in poetry and a course in science, along with other courses comprising a well designed curriculum of a liberal education may nurture patterns of thought for judgment that leads to wisdom.

Thomas Magnell, Department of Philosophy, Drew University, Madison, NJ 07940; tmagnell@drew.edu

PAIDEIA AS THE SUBJECTIVE CONDITION FOR A SAGACIOUS IMPLEMENTATION OF HUMAN RIGHTS

Ioanna Kuçuradi

Two opposite tendencies characterize the intellectual and political developments in our world as a whole at the end of the twentieth century: on the one hand, we promote respect for human rights, i.e., for certain "universal" norms; on the other, we promote equal respect for all cultures, i.e., respect also for sets of parochial, "relative" norms, which are not only often discrepant among themselves, but often discrepant vis-à-vis human rights as well. In light of this, I argue that we need *paideia* for a sagacious implementation of human rights in the twenty-first century.

I

Two opposite tendencies characterize the intellectual and political developments in our world as a whole at the end of the twentieth century: on the one hand, we promote respect for human rights, i.e., for certain "universal" norms; on the other hand, we promote equal respect for all cultures, i.e., respect for sets of parochial, "relative" norms, which are not only often discrepant among themselves, but are also often discrepant vis-à-vis human rights.

In the political sphere, on the one hand, we create and promote the creation of supranational bodies and, on the other hand, we establish and promote the establishment of smaller and smaller independent states, sometimes of only one million citizens. Are we really aware of what we are doing?

Our age is called, by some, a post-modern age—one marked by a revolt against "reason" equated with so-called "western rationality";[1] and, by others, as the information age, characterized by daily invasions of information, i.e., invasions of second-hand knowledge—true, false, or manipulated knowledge, which we are mostly unable to verify. These waves of information, which most of us take for granted, drag us to and fro. Are we really aware toward what directions?

These and other such problematic developments nonetheless have an impact upon our conception of education, which (as "scientific" or "ideological" education) has shaped the minds of most of the decision makers of our present world, and is now (as "acculturation" or "post-modern education") shaping the minds of future decision makers—conceptions of education that are far from being *paideia*.

Thus, at the end of the century, many of us have started to feel the need to revise and change the prevailing conceptions of education. I hope that this Congress—the last World Congress of Philosophy in our century—*by focusing on paideia*, will play a significant role in such a change worldwide.

II

What kind of education could be called *paideia*? Or, what conception of education does the term *paideia* intend to express?

There might be, and in fact are, different conceptions of *paideia*. Allow me to present to you, how *I* conceive of *paideia* as philosophical education in the broad sense that also constitutes the necessary subjective condition for fighting against social injustice and for the implementation of human rights in general.

Paideia, as I conceive it, is education which does not aim at "acculturation," as many educators at present advocate, nor at its opposite, i.e., at a mere formal-methodological training, as some others favour; rather, *paideia* aims at helping the trainee—be he a child, an adolescent or a grown up—develop his own intellectual *and* ethical capacities *simultaneously* and to the maximum possible degree in each individual case.

By "training aiming at the development of one's *intellectual capacities*," I mean training that helps the trainee to develop the capacity to objectify, and get direct knowledge of, the "object" of the issue he deals with,[2] and the capacity to see this "object" with his own eyes, so that after such training he can manage to do it in everyday life without the help of a παιδαγωγός, on his own account. This is a training which shows the trainee where to look, and not what he will see.

The most promising way to achieve such an aim that *I* know (as a teacher of 38 years) is the Socratic method—a method which παιδεύει the trainee, i.e., "tortures" him in the way that Socrates "tortures" Meno in the

Meno, until he becomes able, so far as his natural capacities allow it, to see the "object" with which he deals.

This training can often lead the trainee to grasp problems, theoretical as well as practical, i.e., discrepancies between what he has been taught on a given issue and quite naturally believes to be the case, and what at a given moment he suddenly sees with his own eyes—a training that anyone can undergo at any age.

Such intellectual training of children and adolescents, if undergone without simultaneous ethical training, can lead some people to creativity, but not to the ethical consideration of what is happening around them.

By "training aiming at developing one's ethical capacities," I mean training that aims to help the trainee have an insight into the *human identity* of all human beings and thus awaken the sincere will to act so as—to use Kant's words—the other will "be treated as a goal, not as a means only,"[3] to which I wish to add "in the light of ethical *value knowledge*."

The most promising way to lead young people towards such an aim, that *I* know, is the teaching of *philosophical ethics* and the philosophical teaching of human rights,[4] both however based on a training in making right (or even wrong) evaluations of different kinds of objects of evaluation. This is a mode of evaluation, that I distinguish from those other modes that I call "value ascription" and "value imputation," that are mostly made in life and which do not—and cannot—lead to *the knowledge* of the value of a given object of evaluation.[5]

This is an intellectual training, which, in order to play its part in ethical training, has to start very early, i.e., before the ethical grab-bag of the trainee starts being filled with ethical errors or ethical crimes. Because ethical training is training in our ethical relation with ourselves, training for ethical freedom is the only training that can lead us to respect ourselves. As Kant put the matter, "if [the respect for ourselves in the consciousness of our freedom] is well established, so that a man fears nothing more than to find himself on self-examination to be worthless and contemptible in his own eyes, every good moral disposition can be grafted on this self-respect, for the consciousness of freedom is the best, indeed the only, guard that can keep ignoble and corrupting influences from bursting in upon our mind."[6] Only "well established" self-respect can ensure that one is at peace with himself.

III

As you have certainly noticed, so far I have given only a formal account of *paideia*, understood as the simultaneous development of the intellectual *and* ethical capacities of an individual, which is also the subjective condition of the possibility of abolishing social injustice and of implementing human rights in general. However, the exercise of such an education needs content: Different kinds of knowledge must be possessed by educators, as well as by those who are responsible for the protection of human rights at the national and international levels. Lack of such knowledge has led us in the second half of the twentieth century to anticipate and follow ways that have not only *not* secured a better protection of human rights, but also have created some of the global problems we are faced with at the turn of the century—among which are deepening social and global injustice. It has also led, among other things, to the inflation we observe at present in the number of human rights and to the promotion of discrepant norms that I mentioned previously.

Now, in connection with the issue of this plenary session—i.e., social justice and human rights—what might be the content of the knowledge to be used in the philosophical training of human rights? In other words: What are the objective conditions of the possibility of abolishing social injustice and for implementing human rights? So far as I can see, these main *objective conditions* are philosophical knowledge of human rights—e.g., what kind of norms human rights are, what kinds of rights and human rights there are, what each human right demands, and so forth—and knowledge of how it is possible to put such a norm in connection with the existing real conditions and deduce its implications in these conditions. Thus, the first question I shall try to answer briefly here is "what are human rights?"

So-called "human rights," i.e., rights which all human beings possess only because they are *human* beings and in which "all human beings are equal," constitute a part of the rights of the individual, i.e., his basic rights. A part of these basic rights demand the direct protection of certain human potentialities in individuals: e.g., the demand that "nobody" touch an individual for any reason while this individual is engaged in actualizing such a human potentiality. (All interdictory demands concerning the security of the individual and/or the so-called fundamental freedoms belong to this category of basic rights.) The other part is that of demands related to the general pre-conditions necessary to afford each individual the possibility *to develop* his potentialities. Rights such as the right to a standard of living adequate for one's health, the right to education, the right to work, and so forth, belong to this category. These are also rights that individuals possess for the sole reason that they are human beings, i.e., they are basic rights of the individual or human rights. But they differ from the rights of the first category in that they can be protected only indirectly, through other rights *given* to individuals by a state—by means of social and economic rights—and through public institutions founded, not always but mostly, by political decisions.

These given rights, i.e., the social and economic rights, are rights of the individual, but not basic rights—i.e., they are not rights in which all human beings are equal. They are limits drawn by the state: they delineate some areas within which the citizens of a given country may act as they like and they demand that no citizen transgress these limits. These are rights whose limits are—and must be—drawn differently today in different countries. However, they are rights in which all (concerned) citizens in each country are equal. (The determination of the minimum wage, or of the minimum number of years of work required for retirement are such rights.) Now, the way how the limits of these rights are drawn in a country determines whether they may protect or not protect, or even hinder the protection of, the basic rights to which they are related.

Social injustice appears as a question related to the connection between these two kinds of rights of the individual, the given rights and the indirectly protected basic rights; and it is a state of affairs having to do with (a) the way the limits of these given rights are delineated, i.e., with how social and economic relations are arranged by law in a given country, and also with the way the relevant laws are implemented; and consequently with (b) the establishment or non-establishment and the functioning of some public institutions in the existing conditions.

IV

The question of social injustice in its relation to basic rights, at the national level, can be treated from two different perspectives: that of the individual, and that of the state. The former affords us the possibility of grasping the nature of social injustice, the latter of understanding how social injustice originates today in many non-affluent or developing countries. Taken together, both make it possible to conceptualize, in a cognitively justifiable way, social justice (which is a principle and *not* a state of affairs as is social injustice).

So far as the individual is concerned, social injustice is the situation in which basic rights are not protected *for all* individuals concerned, in a given country, rather than being a state of affairs in which basic rights are not at all protected. In other words, it is a state of affairs in which the possibilities for the protection of rights in which all human beings are equal, but which can be protected only indirectly, are not equally afforded—that is, afforded *to the same degree*—to all citizens. From this point of view social injustice appears as an ethical question.

As far as the state is concerned, social injustice appears as a political fact, i.e., a fact related to the arrangement of social relations in the broad sense—the way they are established and the way they function; in other words, a fact related to the rights given or not given and the possibilities afforded to the citizens by the state.

When in a country some citizens live in air-conditioned villas or flats while others live in caves or mud-brick houses, there prevails social injustice. Wherever some children are taken to school in Cadillacs, while other children go through the garbage looking for something to eat, there prevails social injustice. Where some women can afford to buy three fur coats at once—because they like them equally and cannot decide for one against the other—while others, in order to survive, consent to be sold, there again we meet social injustice.

Social injustice arises first of all when governments, while drawing the limits of social and economic rights, do not take into consideration the connection existing between this kind of rights and indirectly protected basic rights; when, during the drawing of limits, factors other than the demand to protect the respective basic rights interfere—ignorance above all, and interests: personal, group, class interests, and so forth. Or, when laws determining the establishment and operation of social and economic relations (for example, tax-laws, the civil code, and other acts or laws of narrower scope) are enacted without taking into account the intimate connection existing between these kind of rights and indirectly protected basic rights, i.e., when the limits of social and economic rights are drawn without taking into account their *foreseeable* implications for the indirectly protected rights under the existing conditions of a country.

This is something we see in countries in which governments cannot or do not fulfil one of the main *raisons d'être* of the state as a human legal institution: The duty of arranging the relations among citizens. These are cases in which governments cannot or do not keep certain citizens from exploiting other citizens—and the state as well—and, consequently, cases in which they cannot or do not prevent some citizens from securing for themselves certain privileges while protecting mostly their personal interests, or, sometimes, their basic rights, at the expense of the basic rights of many other citizens.

From the point of view of the state, another cause of social injustice in developing countries is something that governments do not or cannot do: "distribute" *privations* equally among the citizens. This is a fact we observe especially in countries in which the resources available to the state are limited: though laws aiming to protect indirectly protected rights are in fact enacted, the non-existence of some other laws coupled with the lack of satisfactory institutions necessary for the operation of the former, makes it unthinkable for the state to afford equal protection of these rights to all citizens. Thus, certain basic rights of some citizens are "protected" more than the means available to a state allow, while rights of many others are not protected at all. (Some citizens, for example, can afford to buy three pots of an imported beauty-cream, while others cannot find heart medicine or, if they find it, cannot buy it because it is too expensive.)

It is usually claimed that social injustice is the result of the unequal distribution of what "exists." Yet, in many developing countries, either the state cannot dispose of what "exists," or what is at its disposal is not enough for the fulfillment, even to a minimum extent, of the basic rights of all its citizens at any one moment. Thus, from the point of view of the state, social injustice arises not because of the unequal distribution of what "exists," but because of the unequal "distribution" of privations. For social injustice at the national level has almost nothing to do with the degree of protection of the indirectly protected rights—i.e., with the dimensions of the limits of the given rights which protect their relative basic ones—but with a failure to afford the possibilities of equal protection of these rights to all citizens, whatever the degree of this equal protection may be.

In many developing countries today, social injustice exists because governments do not distribute what is at the disposal of the state *unequally* (i.e., in favour of the needy); that is, they do not distribute it in such a way that the basic rights of poor citizens can be protected to the minimum degree that human dignity necessitates.

This means, further, that social injustice emerges when governments do not fulfil another *raison d'être* of the state: when public administration is not capable of using (i.e., distributing) what belongs to the public so that the needs relative to the basic rights of all citizens may be fulfilled equally. Failure on this point is also caused by a lack of institutions aiming at the at the protection of basic rights.

Thus, considered from both perspectives, social injustice at the national level in many developing countries today is the state of affairs in which the rights given and the possibilities afforded to individuals by the state—the social (including the so-called cultural) and economic rights—either do not protect equally, or hinder the equal protection of, the indirectly protected basic rights of all citizens. In a country where, by the equal "distribution of privations," the rights of all citizens would be protected equally (albeit at a relatively low degree), there would be no question of social injustice at the national level; there we would raise only the problem of global injustice, on which I shall not dwell here.[7]

Starting from the above considerations related to social injustice as a state of affairs, we can now formulate *the principle* of social justice as the demand that the state, i.e., each government that comes to power, must afford uninterruptedly the equal protection of indirectly protected rights for all citizens, e.g., their rights to food, health, education, and so forth, rights that constitute the general preconditions for the development of certain human potentialities, which can be protected only indirectly. This means that laws regulating social and economic issues should be drafted by taking into account their foreseeable implications for the human rights of all citizens in the existing conditions of a country.

V

What I have presented here, is part of the knowledge with which those who possess the will to protect human rights, as well as the educators of human rights, must be equipped. However, this knowledge and other similar philosophical knowledge regarding human rights and their relation to other rights is not sufficient for their implementation, i.e., for deducing their *different* implications for action in different countries and regions of our world. The possibility of such a deduction presupposes one's being able to make right evaluations.

Now I will address the activity of right evaluation of a situation, which is a basic condition of implementing a human right in a given country at a given moment, and constitutes one crucial component of *paideia*.

How can we make a right evaluation of a situation without imputing value or ascribing value to it?

Put very briefly: A situation is not there; it does not stand before our eyes, like you and me. It becomes the special situation when it is put forth, that is, when we name it. This seems to be the main reason why one and the same situation is often presented as a few different ones.

Thus, the first step in the effort to evaluate a situation is *to put it forth*. This amounts to becoming aware of the relationship between various simultaneous events that are the outcome of the situation or its symptoms; it amounts to discovering, among other different causes, the *common cause* of certain independent events that happen at that moment. This makes it possible to diagnose and name the situation under consideration correctly—which not only has implications for finding the proper measures to be taken in order to change this situation, but also bears implications for the legal treatment of those involved in it.

The second step in such an evaluation is *to explain how the situation under consideration came about*. This amounts to becoming aware of the way a number of other (earlier) simultaneous events were entangled around a human group and the role played by each of these independent events in the creation of the existing situation. This makes it possible to find out what has to be done to change the situation, nevertheless in any direction or toward any purpose we might have.

These two sets of events—those which are the causes of a situation and those which are its outcome—should not be confused in any attempt to evaluate a situation. Such a confusion easily leads to the application of ready-made precepts for the implementation of human rights, as a result of which damage is done to human rights in the name of human rights.

Connecting this real, historical, unique situation with the knowledge of human rights constitutes another step in the right evaluation of a situation. This connection, made after a right explanation of the situation under consideration, not only helps us to become conscious of the consequences that the entanglement of events around a group bears for their life as human beings, but also makes it possible to find out what should or might be done in this concrete situation, and how, for the protection of human rights. The implementation of human rights depends on our capacity to make right evaluations of situations and to find out what should be done to cut successfully the knot created by the above mentioned entanglement of independent events in which that situation consists, i.e., what should be done *in the existing situation* for the protection of human rights.

If we possess the will to effectively implement human rights in the twenty-first century, if we are determined, as the Heads of State and Government stated in the Copenhagen Summit three years ago, to "eradicate poverty in the world, through decisive national and international action and cooperation, as an ethical, social, political and economic imperative of human kind"[8]—something that we were unable to do in the twentieth century—we need *paideia*, i.e., intellectual and ethical training, based on different kinds of *knowledge*. A considerable part of this training consists in the exercise in making right evaluations of situations, events, and other components of human reality, and it is among the *sine qua non* conditions of the possibility of implementing the same principles of human rights in the different existing conditions in *different* parts of our world.

We need *paideia* in order to sagaciously implement human rights in the twenty-first century.

Ioanna Kuçuradi, Department of Philosophy, Hacettepe University, Beytepe, Ankara, Turkey

NOTES

1. For this equation, see my "Modernity as a Concept and as a Project or 'Modernity', 'Modernization' and Beyond," *Cultures in Conflict or in Dialogue?* (Cairo, 1991), 81–97.

2. For this "objectification," see my "Knowledge and Its Object," *The Concept of Knowledge*, Boston Studies in the Philosophy of Science 170 (Dordrecht: Kluwer Academic Publishers, 1995), 97–101.

3. I. Kant, *Grundlegung zur Metaphysik der Sitten* (Ankara, 1995), 46.

4. For such a teaching of human rights, see my "The Philosophical Teaching of Human Rights: Teaching Human Rights as Philosophy Courses," *Teaching Philosophy in the Eve of the Twenty-First Century* (Ankara: International Federation of Philosophical Societies, 1998), 221–37.

5. For the main characteristics of this mode of evaluation, see my "From Revolt to Philosophy," *Philosophes critiques d'eux–mêmes/Philosophers on Their Own Work/Philosophische Selbstbetrachtungen 11* (Bern, 1984), 109–119; for a more detailed analysis my *Etik* (Ankara, 1996), 15–37, 82–99, 124–43, 149–64.

6. I. Kant, *Critique of Practical Reason*, trans. Lewis White Beck, (Indianapolis and New York: The Liberal Arts Press, Inc., 1956), 147.

7. For this point, see my "Goals and Traps in the Ways out of the Current Stalemate of Poverty," *Futures Beyond Poverty-Ways and Means out of the Current Stalemate* (Turku, Finland: World Futures Studies Federation, 1997), 88–99.

8. Draft Declaration of the Copenhagen Summit, Commitment 2.

PAIDEIA ET PHYSIS DANS LA CONCEPTION GRECQUE ANTIQUE

Pierre Aubenque

Ce discours va partir des livres VI and VII de la *République* de Platon pour montrer en quoi il gouverne encore notre projet d'éducation philosophique de l'humanité, mais aussi en quoi il n'est pas seul représentatif de la conception grecque antique, à l'intérieur de laquelle sont nés plusiers modèles concurrents, générateurs d'une alternative peut-être encore instructive pour la discussion actuelle.

I

Notre Congrès est placé sous le signe de la *Paideia*. Il n'est pas tellement courant aujourd'hui qu'un mot grec serve à exprimer, en la cristallisant, une problématique moderne, celle de l'éducation de l'humanité par et dans la philosophie.

Cette problématique, qui est en même temps l'indication d'une tâche à accomplir, à une origine historique précise, qui est le projet d'éducation des gardiens de la cité, tel qu'il est présenté dans les livres VI et VII de la *République* (*Politeia*) de Platon. Je voudrais partir de ce texte bien connu, pour montrer en quoi il gouverne encore notre projet d'éducation philosophique de l'humanité, mais aussi en quoi il n'est pas seul représentatif de la conception grecque antique, à l'intérieur de laquelle sont nés plusiers modèles concurrents, générateurs d'une alternative peut-être encore instructive pour la discussion actuelle.

Le livre VII de la *République* commence ainei (514 à 1): "Maintenant représente-toi notre nature (*physis*) selon qu'elle est caractérisée par l'éducation ou l'absence d'éducation (*paideias te peri kai apaideusias*)." Cette phrase introduit ce qu'il est convenu d'appeler l'allégorie de la caverne, où la non-éducation, l'inculture, est symbolisée par la situation des prisonniers de la caverne et où le processus d'éducation est symbolisé par la montée vers la lumière du jour, qui est elle-même une métaphore pour l'intellibilite' des Idées. Si l'on fait abstraction du contenu et que l'on s'intéresse à la procédure par laquelle l'homme d'abord inculte accède par l'education à la sagesseou du moins à la philosophie, on voit immédiatement que l'éducation (qui est à la fois l'acte d'éduquer et le résultat de cet acte, i.e., le fait d'être éduqué, la culture) est mise en rapport avec la nature (*physis*). Mais comment entendre ce rapport? Dans le texte d'où je suis parti, il semble que la nature soit en tant que telle un état neutre, indifférent à ce qu'on fait de lui: la nature peut dès lars soit être abandonnée à elle-même, laissée dans un état d'inculture, soit au contraire être façonnée par la *paideia*. Il y aurait donc deux natures de l'homme: une nature sauvage et une nature cultivée. Mais on ne peut pas dès lors ne pas se poser le problème suivant: comment la nature cultivée se greffe-t-elle sur la nature sauvage? S'agit-il d'une seconde nature, qui détruit la première en se substituant à elle? Ou s'agit-il au contraire du développement harmonieux de la première? Y a-t-il continuité ou discontinuité quand on passe d'une nature à l'autre?

La réponse de Platon n'est pas claire. La lettre même de l'allégorie platonicienne semble indiquer que l'éducation est un processus difficile parce qu'elle fait d'abord violence à la nature spontanée, c'est-à-dire aux désirs et à l'affectivité, de ceux qu'il s'agit d'éduquer. Les prisonniers se meuvent à l'aise dans le monde de ombres et l'inertie, la paresse, font qu'ils ne souhaitent pas le quitter. Il faut donc les d'etourner de la perception complaisante des seules choses sensibles pour tourner leur regard vers la lumière du jour, qui, au premier abord, les éblouit. Il y à de la violence, de la contrainte (*anankazoi*, 515 e), conséquence de quelque artifice (*diamechanesasthai*), dans cette conversion qui est la négation de l'attitude naturelle.

Mais, d'un autre côté, Platon refuse une conception selon laquelle la culture serait une violence faite à la nature. Si la culture était surajoutée artificiellement à une nature réfractaire, l'homme cultivé serait constamment déchiré entre la nature et la culture en lui. Platon admet donc que la nature doit être prédisposée à recevoir la culture. Mais toute nature n'est pas dans ce cas. Il y a de bonnes et de mauvaises natures. Avant d'éduquer les philosophes qui gouverneront la cité, il faut sélectionner les "natures philosophiques," les *philosophohoi physeis* (*Rép.*, VI, 485 a), c'est-à-dire les types d'hommes prédestinés par le hasard et la bonne naissance (*eugeneia*) à la philosophie. Mais on peut faire ici deux objections: 1) Ceux qui naissent avec un bon naturel n'ont pas besoin d'éducation. A cela Platon répond de façon incidente par un mot qui jouera un grand rôle dans la théorie adverse d'Aristote: même les bonnes natures peuvent et doivent être "perfectionnées" ou plutôt "parachevées" (*teleiotheisi*) par l'éducation (487 a). 2) La deuxième objection est que, s'il y a une dichotomie absolue des natures, l'education, qui est presque superflue pour les bonnes, est sans emploi pour sauver les autres de leur aveuglement congénital.[1] L'éducation perdrait ainsi sa vocation universelle, qui est de tirer vers le haut (*e-ducere, er-ziehen*) non seulement les plus doués, mais aussi et d'abord les autres.

Platon renonce pour ces raisons à une théorie des deux natures pour lui substituer celle d'une seule nature humaine, mais ambiguë, tiraillée entre les désirs sensibles qui la poussent vers le bas, et le désir de connaissance, qui l'élève vers la contemplation de l'être et du bien. Le dernier mot de la théorie platonicienne de la *paideia* rétablit la continuité, qui paraissait d'abord menacée, entre la nature et l'éducation. La *paideia* ne peut être un pur artéfact, comme certains (*tines*) prétendaient qu'elle l'était, et qui consisterait à placer, si l'on peut dire, une prothèse dans une âme malade. Ces "certains" prétendaient mettre la science dans l'ame où elle n'est pas "comme on mettrait la vue dans des yeux aveugles" (518 b). L'education, objecte Platon, ne peut se substituer à l'organe sain; elle ne peut qu'en présupposer l'existence: "Toute âme a inhérente en elle la faculté (*dynamis*) d'apprendre et un organe à cet effet" (518 b). L'éducation, dès lors, ne consiste pas à mettre la vue dans l'organe, puisqu'il la possède déjà; mais, comme il est mal tourné et regarde ailleurs qu'il ne faudrait, elle en ménage la "conversion" (518 d). Si cet organe ne remplit pas sa fonction naturelle, c'est qu'il est mal dirigé, tel un oeil qui, par habitude, par paresse ou même par complaisance, ne serait dirigé que vers l'obscurite. Il faut donc, par l'éducation, tourner l'organe de la vision vers la lumière qui est accordée à sa véritable essence. Ce n'est pas l'aliénation qui est anti-naturelle, mais l'aliénation de l'âme aveuglée à sa propre destination. L'éducation ne fait que rétablir, même si c'est pas la contrainte passagère de la conversion, la direction naturelle du regard et la vocation même de l'âme. L'éducation est une antiviolence: elle restaure, contre la violence de la déraison, la véritable natture rationnelle de l'homme.

Tous les commentateurs, de Hegel à W. Jaeger, ont reconnu que ce passage, outre qu'il exprimait la conviction propre de Platon, avait une visée polémique et qu'il était dirigé contre la conception sophistique de la *paideia*. Certes, les sophistes maintiennent en théorie le *to pos* grec du primat de la nature sur l'artifice: "L'enseignement, dit Protagoras, a besoin de la nature et de l'exercice" (fr. 3, Diels). L'homme ne saurait donc être éduqué que s'il y est naturellement prédisposé. Mais cette thèse paraît bien être contredite par la pratique des sophistes, qui se flattent de pouvoir enseigner n'importe quoi à n'importe qui, sous la, seule condition d'une rémunération adéquate. Les sophistes sont connus à Athènes pour le fait qu'ils font payer leurs leçons. Autrement dit, la condition pour accéder au savoir polymathique et polytechnique que les sophistes enseignent dans leurs écoles est purement sociale: l'éducation est un métier pour celui qui la dispense et une merchandise pour celui qui paie le prix du marché pour y accéder ou tenter dly accéder. Socrate et à sa suite Platon protesteront contre la réduction sophistique de la relation d'éducation à un pur rapport d'lextériorité.

Mais, d'autre part, il y à de la grandeur dans ce projet sophistique. Donner la vue à une âme aveugle, créer une seconde nature sur les ruines de la première, créer un *homo faber* et *sapiens* à partir d'une table rase ou en tout cas d'une nature défaillante et avare: ce rêve en quelque sorte prométhéen de la création par l'éducation d'un homme nouveau et l'idée corrélative d'un progrès irréversible de l'humanité par le développement des connaissances et des techniques semble avoir inspiré de fait un certain nombre de sophistes comme Hippias, Gorgias ou Antiphon et quelques philosophes. C'est ainsi que Démocrite attribue à l'enseignement le pouvoir démiurgique de façonner l'homme, de lui donner une forme, une figure (*rhysmos*). Mais alors l'enseignement fait concurrence à la nature, qui possède un pouvoir semblablement démiurique: "La nature et l'enseignement ont des fonctions semblables, car l'enseignement façonne l'homme et, en façonnant l'homme, il crée une nature *(metarhysmoi ton anthropon, metarhysmousa de physiopoiei)*"(fr. 33 Diels). Ce texte est l'origine historique de l'expression "seconde nature" pour désigner la culture. C'est la l'exaltation la plus haute de la *paideia*, si du moins on la considère comme une rupture avec la première nature

Mais le problème demeure du rapport entre ces deux natures. Comment la deuxième nature peut-elle s'articuler sur la première sans la détruire? Et pourquoi détruire la première, si elle est le cadre dans lequel nous sommes appelés à vivre et qui est en quelque sorte notre destin, *moira*, le lot qui nous est imparti? Les Grecs ne sont jamais allés—et c'est peut-être ce qui les distingue le plus fortement des Modernes—jusqu'à transgresser la nature. Cette transgression, dont ils ont pu avoir la tentation comme le montre le texte cité de Démocrite, est généralement associée à des expressions péjoratives: c'est l'*hybris*, la démesure, le refus de l'ordre naturel et le déi lancé aux dieux. C'est aussi le *nomos*, la loi, mais aussi la convention, qui, lorsque on l'oppose à la *physis* comme le font lea sophistes, comporte la connotation pejorative de l'artifice et de l'arbitraire.

II

S'il est un précepte de la sagesse grecque qui n'a jamais été véritablement mis en question par les Grecs, c'est qu'il faut "suivre la nature," *akolouthein te physei*. L'éducation ne peut donc créer en l'homme une surnature ni même une seconde nature qui, même si elle est meilleure que la première, demeure grevée du soupçon d'antinaturalité. On ne peut d'autre part renoncer à l'éducation sans maintenir l'homme dans la barbarie. Que faire alors? Entre l'utopie prémoderne de l'homme nouveau, du héros prométhéen, et la soumission paresseuse à la nature, il me semble que la sagesse grecque traditionnelle, reprise et théorétisée par Aristote, a trouvé une troisième voie, que je voudrais maintenant esquisser.

Si l'on considère les deux termes que nous avons jusqu'ici opposés, *physis* et *paideia*, on constate que, dans leur compréhension originaire, ils désignent deux processus qui ne sont pas nécessairement antithétiques. *Physis* est un concept dynamique, que la traduction latine par *natura* ne reflète pas adéquatement. *Physis* (de *phyesthai*) signifie originellement la croissance et, per extension, la croissance originelle et primordiale qu'est la naissance. Ce sens archaïque est présent explicitement chez certains Présocratiques comme Empédocle, chez celui-ci négativement pour dire qu'il n'y a pas de génération (*physis*) véritable, mais seulement des recompositions d'éléments, et en un sens positif par Héraclite. L'étymologie de *physis* sera rappelée par Platon et surtout Aristote.[2] De cette étymologie le concept philosophique de *physis* conserve l'idée d'un d'eveloppement spontané comportant une finalité, un *telos* immanent, qui est celui de l'auto-achèvement. L'être naturel est celui qui, selon la formule de Pindare, "devient ce qu'il est"[3] et dont on peut dire qu'il n'est vraiment "naturel" qu'au terme de ce proceesus d'auto-réalisation. La nature est à la fois au début et au terme du processus, ce qui fait dire que la *physis* comme genèse est un acheminement (*odos*) vers la *physis* en tant qu'accomplissement.[4] Par opposition à ce qui est adventice (*epitheton*), le caractère naturel d'une propriété, d'une capacité même apparemment acquise, est la garantie de son identification au sujet.[5]

Or qu'en est-il de la *paideia*? *Paideia* vient de *pais*, enfant, et désigne le procès par lequel l'enfant devient un homme, c'est-à-dire devient ce qu'il était déjà potentiellement, s'approprie sa propre nature. L'idée de maturation est commune aux deux termes grecs, avec en plus cette connotation normative, présente à la fois dans *physis* et dans *paideia*, que cette maturation doit être préservée de toute entrave, mais aussi de tout foisonnement qui ne soit pas contrôlé par la forme même du *telos* (foisonnement qui, dans l'ordre biologique, produirait des monstres).

Dans le cas de cet être naturel, mais aussi doué de parole et par là de raison, qu'est l'homme, la *paideia* est la forme proprement humaine, et devenue consciente grâce à la philosophie, de cette auto-régulation qu'exige, en vertu de son *telos*, le développement naturel.

Aristote a développé ce thème principalement à propos de l'art, de la *techne*. La technique a un rapport étroit avec l'éducation, d'une part parce que l'apprentissage des techniques est, comme nous l'avons vu à propos des sophistes, un élément important de l'éducation est elle-même une technique, dont les Grecs ont contribué à élaborer les régles sous le nom de "pédagogie." Au premier abord, la technique s'oppose à la nature pour une raison qu'Aristote indique au livre II de la *Physique*: l'être naturel est celui qui a en lui-même la cause de son propre mouvement; l'être artificiel est celui qui ne se meut pas de lui-même mais est mû de l'extérieur. Mais Aristote corrige aussitôt cette opposition, dans la mesure où la technique ne peut avoir d'autre finalité que d'imiter la nature: elle doit s'efforcer de reproduire par des moyens artificiels la spontanéité, l'automotion de la nature. Aristote donne aussi la raison de ce redoublement de la nature par la technique: "La technique exécute ce que la nature est impuissante à réaliser et, d'autre part, l'imite.[6] Cette phrase célèbre n'est compréhensible que si elle est lue dans l'unité de ses deux moments: la technique n'imite pas la nature dans son inachèvement, mais dans la finalité encore inaccomplie vers laquelle cet inachèvement même fait signe. Dans le *Protreptique* (fragment 11, Walzer), Aristote dit que la technique comble les lacunes de la nature, *to paralipomenon*, ce que la nature a laissé inachevé." Or il est caractéristique que la même idée soit expressément étendue à l'éducation: "Toute technique et toute éducation visent à remplir (*anapleroun*) ce qu'il reste à accomplir dans la nature."[7] Et Aristote redit la même chose à propos de l'éducation morale, de la formation des vertus, qui sont des "habitudes" que l'éducation doit nous inculquer: "Ce n'est ni par nature ni contrairement à la nature que naissent en nous les vertus, mais elles adviennent à des êtres qui, comme nous, sont capables par nature de les recevoir et qui sont parachevés par l'habitude."[8]

Il y a là, je crois, une philosdphie profonde des rapports de la culture (terme dans lequel nous pouvons désormais englober la technique) et de la nature. La nature est bonne, parce qu'elle a un *telos*, qui est l'auto-réalisation non seulement d'elle-même en général, mais aussi de chacun des êtres qui la constituent. Elle est, en vertu même de son caractére tél'eologique, inachevée; il y à toujours en elle une part de potentiality. Or la potentialité est toujours ambivalente, car aussi longtemps qu'elle n'est pas réalisée, elle est potentialité des contradictoires: elle peut se réaliser ou ne pas se réaliser. Dans le cas des êtres animés et raisonnables, cette puissance des contradictoires se spécifie en "puissance des contraires":[9] la nature peut bien ou mal se réaliser. Si le bien est la fin de la nature, son instauration, singulièrement chez les être animés toujours capables du contraire, est précaire et fragile. Cette idée d'une fragilité fondamentale de ce qui est bon dans son principe, mais reste toujours en deçà de son propre *telos*, a été fort bien dégagée par Martha Nussbaum dans son beau livre sur *The Fragility of Goodness*.[10] L'homme en tant qu'être naturel participe de cette fragilité; elle est encore renforcée chez lui par le facteur d'indétermination qu'introduit la liberté de sa volonté, raisonnable dans son principe, mais toujours capable d'errer. C'est pour surmonter cette fragilité, affirmer la nature dans sa finalité immanente qu'intervient la *paideia*, qui a pour fonction d'aider la nature humaine à devenir ce qu'elle est, c'est-à-dire une nature raisonnable et bonne. C'est dans ce cadre que s'inscrit la conception la plus authentiquement grecque de la *paideia,* déjà implicite chez Homère, Pindare, et Hésiode, plus tard théorétisée par Aristote. C'est cette conception-là, plus que celle de Platon, qui s'oppose le plus clairement a l'idéal moderne d'un dépassement ou d'une domination de la nature. Dans cette perspective, l'idéal de l'éducation, comme d'ailleurs celui de la technique, reste la nature; il ne s'agit pas de créer une surnature, ni même d'humaniser la nature, mais de naturaliser la nature, de l'aider à réaliser sa propre essence. L'esprit de mesure qui est inhérent à cette conception est bien illustré par l'exemple de la "vigne," que nous devons à Théophraste: la vigne est certes en tant que plante (*phyton*) un être naturel, mais elle ne peut produire ses virtualités naturelles, qui sont en même temps ses fruits les plus parfaits, qu'à la condition d'être cultivée par l'homme. Cicéron commentera ce texte aujourd'hui perdu en disant que l'homme est une nature recommandée ou confiée à elle-même; elle est "comme une vigne qui se cultiverait elle-même."[11]

Je termine donc mon propos par ce qui paraît être une métaphore botanique. Mais ce n'est peut-être pas une métaphore. Théophraste, qui a écrit aussi bien un *Peri Paideias* qu'un *Peri Phyton* (Sur les Plantes), est sans doute responsable à travers Cicéron du fait que le même mot *culture* désigne à la fois la culture des plantes et la culture humaine: il s'agit dans les deux cas du souci, *cura*, du soin donné à la maturation optimale d'un bien d'autant plus précieux qu'il est plus fragile. Il faudrait évidemment ajouter ici—mais ce serait le sujet d'une autre conference—que l'instrum ent proprement humain de cette culture, qui est une culture de soi, est le *logos*, c'est-'a-dire la capacité qu'a l'homme de produire des sons articulés et signifiants et de s'élever par là à la communication réciproque et au débat raisonnable.

III

Je suggérerai pour conclure ce que cetter derniére conception peut nous enseigner encore—ou de nouveau—aujourd'hui.

Enraciner l'éducation dans la nature, c'est évidemment aider la spontanéity plutôt que la contraindre et, par là, par là, préférer à des procédés autoritaires des procédures douces de persuasion.

D'autre part et surtout, la conception exposée autorise et justifie une pratique diversifiée et pluraliste de l'éducation. La nature que l'éducation a pour fonction de parachever n'est pas une table rase, la même pour tous, malléable à merci, prête à se laisser modeler par un ordre universellement valable, comme l'était celui des Idées platoniciennes ou celui qu'implique pour les Modernes l'Idée d'un règne universel des droits. Ce que l'éducation doit réaliser en l'homme, ce n'est pas une idée abstraite de l'Humanité, mais l'humanité elle-même dans la pluralité de ses manifestations. Le droit naturel n'est pas partout le même, ce qui ne l'empêche pas d'être à chaque fois conforme à la norme naturelle, tendanciellement unique, mais diversifiée par son enracinement dans des communautés concrètes et finies.[12] Cette conception pourrait fournir un correctif "post-moderne" à l'universalisme abstrait de la philosophie des Lumières. Elle redonnerait ainsi à l'idée téléologique d'humanité, débarrassée désormais de toute idéologie, y compris "humaniste," sa vraie fonction d'intégration des légitimes différences culturelles.

Pierre Aubenque, UER de Philosophie, Université de Paris-Sorbonne, 1 rue Victor Cousin, Paris, F-75230 France

Notes

1. Sur l'exclusion des aveugles, cf. *Rép.*, VI, 484e.

2. Platon, *Sophiste*, 265 c; Aristote, *Métaph.*, 4, 1014b16; *Phys.* II, 1, 193b12 sq.

3. Pindare, *Pythigues*, II, 72. Pindare précise: "Deviens ce que tu es en apprenant (*mathon*)."

4. Aristote, *Phys.*, II, 1, 193b12–13.

5. Cf. l'opposition qu' établit le sophiste *Antiphon* entre ce qui fait l'objet d'une convention (*homologethenta*) et ce qui est le fruit d'un développement naturel (*phynta*, "gewachsen" comme traduit Diels (fragm. 44 Diels, col. 1, 29–33).

6. *Phys.* II, 8, 199a15–17.

7. *Pol.*, VII, 17, 1337a2.

8. *Eth. Nic.*, II, 1, 1103a24 sq.

9. *Métaph.*, 0, 2, 1046b4–5.

10. M. Nussbaum, *The Fragility of Goodness* (Cambridge: Cambridge University Press, 1986).

11. Cicéron, *De finibus*, VI, 14.

12. Aristote, *Eth. Nic.*, V. 10. Cf. P. Aubenque, "The Twofold Natural Foundation of Justice According to Aristotle," *Aristotle and Moral Realism*, ed. R. Heinamann, The Keeling Colloquia I (London: University College, London, 1995), 35–47.

ABOUT THE
CONTRIBUTORS

KARL-OTTO APEL was born in Düsseldorf in 1922. He has served as a professor of philosophy at the University of Kiel (1962–69), the University of Saarbrücken (1969–72) and the Goethe-Universität of Frankfurt (1972–90), where he is professor *emeritus*. He is the recipient of numerous awards, including the International Galileo Galilei Prize of the Italian Rotary Club (1988) and the International Frederick Nietzsche Philosophy Prize (1989). Among his most recent works are *Understanding and Explanation: A Transcendental-Pragmatic Perspective* (1988), *Charles S. Peirce: From Pragmatism to Pragmaticism* (1995), and *From a Transcendental-Semiotic Point of View* (1999).

PIERRE AUBENQUE was born in 1929. He has taught at numerous European universities including Montpellier (1955–60), Besançon (1960–64), Aix-Marseille (1964–66), and Hamburg (1966–69). Since 1969 he has been a professor of ancient philosophy and philosophy of history at the University of Paris—Sorbonne. He has served as director for the Center for Research on Ancient Thought and belongs to the International Institute of Philosophy. His works include *Le problème de l' être chez Aristote* (1962), *La prudence chez Aristote* (1963), *Concepts et catégories dans la pensée antique* (1980), and *Problèmes aristotéliciens* (1983).

WOLFGANG BALZER has been professor of logic and philosophy of science in the philosophy department of the University of Munich since 1984. He has published extensively on the general philosophy of science and reconstructions of special scientific theories (in physics, genetics, economics, and political science). His two main fields of research (besides the philosophy of science) are social institutions and simulations of social phenomena and systems.

DANIEL O. DAHLSTROM is professor of philosophy and director of graduate studies in the department of philosophy at Boston University. He has taught at Santa Clara University, The Catholic University of America, and Katholieke Universiteit Leuven (Belgium). His published works include *Schiller's Aesthetic Writings* (1993), *Das logische Vorurteil* (1994), *Moses Mendelssohn's Philosophical Writings* (1997), and *Heidegger's Concept of Truth* (2001).

PETER A. FRENCH is the director of The Ethics Center and chair of the department of philosophy at the University of South Florida. He has also served at Trinity University in San Antonio, Texas, the University of Northern Arizona, the University of Minnesota, Dalhousie University, Nova Scotia, and the University of Delaware. He is the author of sixteen books including *Cowboy Metaphysics: Ethics and Death in Westerns*, *Corporate Ethics*, *Responsibility Matters*, *The Scope of Morality*, and *The Virtues of Vengeance*. Dr. French is also a senior editor of *Midwest Studies in Philosophy*, editor of the *Journal of Social Philosophy*, and was general editor of the *Issues in Contemporary Ethics* series.

NEWTON GARVER is Distinguished Service Professor in the philosophy faculty at the University at Buffalo, State University of New York. He is author of *This Complicated Form of Life: Essays on Wittgenstein* (1994) and *Derrida and Wittgenstein* (with Seung-Chong Lee, 1994), and editor of *Naturalism and Rationality* (with P. H. Hare, 1986), and *Justice, Law, and Violence* (with J. B. Brady, 1991).

MARGARET GILBERT is professor of philosophy at the University of Connecticut, Storrs. She is the author of *On Social Facts* (1989), *Living Together* (1996), and *Sociality and Responsibility* (2000), as well as numerous articles in philosophical social theory and related fields.

JONATHAN L. GORMAN is professor of moral philosophy and Head of the School of Philosophical Studies at the Queen's University of Belfast. He received his M.A. from Edinburgh and Ph.D. from Cambridge, and has held visiting positions at Princeton and Queen's University, Ontario. He is the author of *Understanding History* (1992) and *The Expression of Historical Knowledge* (1982), as well as many articles on moral and political philosophy.

JORGE J. E. GRACIA is Samuel P. Capen Chair and Distinguished Professor of Philosophy at the State University of New York at Buffalo. He is the author of a dozen books, including *Individuality* (1988), *Philosophy and Its History* (1992), *A Theory of Textuality* (1995), *Texts* (1996), *Metaphysics and Its Tasks* (1999), and *Hispanic/Latino Identity* (2000).

MICHAEL HALBERSTAM is author of *Totalitarianism and the Modern Conception of Politics* (2000). He is currently Mellon Fellow at Wesleyan University's Center for the Humanities, where he is on leave from the philosophy department at the University of South Carolina.

SIRKKU KRISTIINA HELLSTEN is a docent of practical philosophy at the University of Helsinki, Finland, and a visiting scholar and the head of the philosophy unit at the university of Dar es Salaam. She is working on the issues of political philosophy, development ethics, and bioethics. She has published numerous articles on the issues of global justice, liberal-communitarian debate, as well as on pluralism and tolerance.

ROBERT L. HOLMES is the Martin Brugler Distinguished Teaching Professor in the philosophy department at the University of Rochester. He is author of *On War and Morality* and *Basic Moral Philosophy*, and editor of *Nonviolence in Theory and Practice*. In 1983 he served as a Senior Fulbright Lecturer at Moscow State University, and from 1998 to 1999 he was the Rajiv Gandhi Professor of Peace and Disarmament, Jawaharlal Nehru University, New Delhi.

IONNA KUÇURADI has been head of the department of philosophy since 1969 and Director of the Center for Research and Application of the Philosophy of Human Rights since 1997 at Hacettepe University in Ankara, Turkey. She has served as the president of the Philosophical Society of Turkey since 1979, as Secretary General of FISP (1988–1998), and as Chair of the Turkish National Commission on the Decade for Human Rights Education since 1998 . Her main publications include *Among the Events of our Times* (1997), *Man and Values* (1998), *Art from a Philosophical Viewpoint* (1999), *Ethics* (1999), and *Nietzsche's Anthropology* (1999).

GABRIEL VARGAS LOZANO is professor of philosophy and was chair of the philosophy department at Universidad Autónomo Metropolitana, México. He teaches political philosophy and philosophy of history, and is the author of *¿Qué hacer con la filosofía en América Latina? Y Mas allá del derrumbe*, among other books. He is editor of *Dialéctica* and vice president of the Mexican Philosophical Association.

NEIL MACCORMICK is Regius Professor of Public Law and the Law of Nature & Nations, and Leverhulme Personal Research Professor at the University of Edinburgh. Among his honors, he is a Fellow of the British Academy and of the Royal Society of Edinburgh. His writing has focused on legal reasoning, the institutional theory of law, theories of law and justice, and law and the state. He is the author and editor of numerous works including *Legal Reasoning and Legal Theory* (1996), *The Relative Heteronomy of Law* (1994), and *Spontaneous Order and Rule Of Law: Some Problems* (1991).

THOMAS MAGNELL is professor of philosophy at Drew University, where he is also Chair of the department of philosophy in the College of Liberal Arts, Convener of the Medical Humanities Program in the Caspersen School of Graduate Studies, and a Fellow in Medical Ethics in the Division of Medical Ethics at the Harvard Medical School. He has been president of several philosophical societies and is currently Editor-in-Chief of the *Journal of Value Inquiry*. The author of numerous essays, many in ethics and several on education, he has also edited three books, the most recent of which, *Values and Education*, was published in 1998.

REX MARTIN holds university appointments in both the United States and the United Kingdom. His most recent books are *A System of Rights* (1997), and a revised edition, with introduction, of R. G. Collingwood's *An Essay on Metaphysics* (1998). He is currently working on two long-term projects: the nature and justification of human rights and the problem of providing a moral justification for a democratic system of rights.

WILLIAM L. MCBRIDE is professor of philosophy at Purdue University and chaired the American Philosophical Association's liaison committee with the American Organizing Committee of the Twentieth World Congress of Philosophy. His most recent book is entitled *Philosophical Reflections on the Changes in Eastern Europe* (1999), and a collection titled *From Yugoslav Praxis to Global Pathos: Anti-Hegemonic Post-Post Marxist Essays* is forthcoming.

ANTONIO PEREZ-ESTEVEZ was born in Galicia, Spain in 1933. He received his Ph.D. in philosophy at the University of Louvain, Belgium, and he has been teacher of philosophy for 30 years at the University of Zulia, Venezuela. His works include *El Individuo y la Feminidad* (1989), *Religion, Moral y Politica* (1991), and *La Materia, de Avicena a la Escuela Franciscana* (1998). He is now preparing a book on intercultural dialogue. His main interests are the manifold concepts of matter in eighteenth-century thought and the concept of dialogue.

JAMES P. STERBA teaches moral problems, ethics, and political philosophy at the University of Notre Dame. He has written more than 120 articles and published 15 books including *Morality in Practice* and, most recently, *Justice for Here and Now*. He is past president of the North American Society for Social Philosophy, past president of Concerned Philosophers for Peace, and past president of the International Society for Philosophy of Law and Social Philosophy (American section). He has lectured widely in the United States, Europe, and the Far East.

OLÚFÉMI TÁÍWÒ is associate professor of philosophy at Loyala University in Chicago, and was recently a visiting professor at the Institut für Afrikastudien, Universität Bayteuth, Bayreuth, Germany. He is currently completing work on a collection of essays on Modernity and Colonialism, and is working on a book tentatively titled *Modernity's Orphans: Law and Liberalism in Commonwealth Africa*. Additional research interests include African philosophy, philosophy of law, and Yorùbá aesthetics.

RAIMO TUOMELA is professor of philosophy in the department of philosophy at the University of Helsinki in Helsinki, Finland. His main field of research is the philosophy of social action, and he is the recipient of several grants and awards, including the von Humboldt Foundation Research Award. His recent books include *The Importance of Us: A Philosophical Study of Basic Social Notions* (1995) and *Cooperation: A Philosophical Study* (2000).

NAME INDEX

A

Aarnio, Aulis 64
Alexander the Great 133
Alexy, Robert 54, 57, 64
Amin, Samir 102
Amselek, Paul 66
Antiphon 254
Apel, Karl-Otto 1, 261
Appiah, Kwame Anthony 38, 41
Aquinas, Thomas 137, 151
Arafat, Yasser 211
Arendt, Hannah 199, 200, 204, 219–222, 225, 227–230, 232
Aristotle 17, 54, 107, 108, 114, 133, 138, 151, 221, 228, 233, 253, 255–257
Aubenque, Pierre 251, 261
Audi, Robert 117–119, 122, 124–128
Augustine of Hippo 194, 202

B

Baker, G. P. 66
Bakunin, Michael 213
Balkin, J. M. 64
Balzer, Wolfgang 162, 170, 173, 261
Barber, Benjamin 106–108, 110, 111, 115
Barnes, B. 161, 170
Barry, Brian 25, 110, 111, 115
Bartkowiak, Julia 204
Baumgarten 224